DEEP COVER

HOW I TOOK DOWN BRITAIN'S MOST DANGEROUS GANGSTERS

SHAY DOYLE
WITH SCOTT HESKETH

EBURY
SPOTLIGHT

1

Ebury Press, an imprint of Ebury Publishing
20 Vauxhall Bridge Road
London SW1V 2SA

Ebury Press is part of the Penguin Random House group of companies
whose addresses can be found at global.penguinrandomhouse.com

Penguin
Random House
UK

First published by Ebury Press in 2022
This paperback edition published in 2022

www.penguin.co.uk

A CIP catalogue record for this book is available from the British Library

ISBN 9781529109412

Printed and bound in Great Britain by Clays Ltd, Elcograf S.p.A.

The authorised representative in the EEA is Penguin Random House
Ireland, Morrison Chambers, 32 Nassau Street, Dublin D02 YH68

Penguin Random House is committed to a
sustainable future for our business, our readers
and our planet. This book is made from Forest
Stewardship Council® certified paper.

First of all, to Scott Hesketh, who believed in my story and stuck to his word of telling it with integrity, and who showed great patience in putting up with me during the long process to finish this book. Thank you for your dedication.

To all the brave soldiers and police officers I have had the privilege of working alongside on my journey and that I am lucky enough to call friends. These are people who have selflessly dedicated themselves to serving the public to keep them safe, both overseas and at home, and who truly are the best of us.

To all the cops that go to work every day with good intentions and put yourselves in harm's way so the public can be safe, not knowing what danger lurks behind every door. You are the unsung heroes. Thank you.

To Christie Vincent OBE, my closest confidant, no thanks could be enough – 'keep banging the jacks'.

Lastly, and the biggest thanks of all, to my family, who lost me through my journey but who never gave up on me and found me in my darkest hour – thank you and love always.

Shay

To my loving and selfless wife, Kate, and beautiful daughters, Dottie and Penny. I love you all.

Scott

'Shay Doyle operated in the dark underbelly of society; he associated with hardened career criminals, gained their trust, socialised with them, befriended them, and shared the life they lived, all while gathering the intelligence required to send them to prison. The physical courage it took to step into the lion's den every day, not knowing if it would be his last, is without question. The mental pressure that resulted from leading this double life, living on the edge, was another battle he had to fight. This is a phenomenal story of the life of a Level 1 undercover police officer and the crushing mental challenges he had to face. People truly do sleep peacefully in their beds at night because of men like him.'

James Deegan MC, former Special Air Service, author of *Once a Pilgrim* and *The Angry Sea*

CONTENTS

FOREWORD

My name is Christie Vincent. To be clear, this is not my real name. I can't reveal that for reasons that will become apparent. I am a former soldier and was a frontline cop for over two decades. During this time, I served in Greater Manchester Police's Covert Operations Unit (Omega). I was a full-time undercover cop deployed all across the UK and Europe, buying drugs and guns, portraying a football hooligan, then a contract killer, running sting operations and infiltrating serious organised crime groups. I inadvertently became one of the highest-decorated cops in the UK. While at Omega, I also became the head of training and development and I redesigned both the Level 1 and Level 2 Undercover Operatives Recruitment and Selection courses, turning them into one of the most challenging selection and training programmes in UK policing. I have trained and mentored dozens of Level 1 operatives and hundreds of Level 2 and been a strategic advisor on numerous covert operations both in the UK and abroad.

My first sighting of 'Shay Doyle' was when he came to a covert operations recruitment day. About 200 cops had attended, and I could see he was one of the very few that were standing on their own. Before I did my pitch to the gathered audience, I did a quick walk-through, mingling with the potential applicants, listening to what they had to say. It was laughable at times. 'When do you think we'll get a gun?' 'Do you think I'll need my passport?' 'I've been told you have to move house at night.' Although there were some good cops there, few of them would have the requisite skills to pass the course.

Being a good cop doesn't necessarily enable you to portray yourself as a believable criminal. The majority of the others that came were pretty misguided, thinking they were applying to become some type of James Bond and live the glamorous high life of a jet-setting spy. The reality was that, if they passed the course, they were more likely to be initially deployed to support a senior undercover officer as a driver or portray a low-level runner, or else sent to some tough no-go housing estate for two months to buy heroin and crack cocaine – if they were lucky.

In Omega, the high-level, high-risk criminal infiltrations were not handed out to just anyone. You had to have the right look, current and in-depth criminal knowledge and believable use of street language and be able to demonstrate the speed of thought that a successful criminal would possess. You had to have all this and more, but still work within the confines of the law. One applicant for Omega selection told me that he had a high-level degree in microbiology and chemistry and thought he would be a great asset to covert operations. Another was a fully trained helicopter pilot. Both were fantastic skills, but realistically, how often would they be deployed and in what criminal role? It was great to have people like these, with such amazing skills in their backgrounds that could be called upon if ever needed, but I had something specific in mind.

I was looking for someone that could portray an armed robber, drug dealer and professional criminal 100 per cent of the time, 24/7. Someone that could work live operations and infiltrations every day of their working life. I was looking for someone like me . . . but better.

Of the hundreds of cops that attended the open day, I clocked Shay and immediately recognised something in his appearance and demeanour that made me think 'potential'. He had the same look as many of the serious criminals that I had recently put in jail. He was standing alone, ignoring the cliques around him. I watched him for ten minutes and his expression did not change. I remember thinking that he had the look, and if he could talk the talk . . . I marked his card.

Shay flew through the pre-tests to get on the Level 1 Omega course, and I quickly recognised a potential star in the making. Before the course started, each student was to be allocated a mentor, and I had first pick. I had no doubt who I would choose – it was Shay Doyle. I had found the new contender.

From the off I had my work cut out for me. His knowledge of criminal practices, illicit commodities and pricing of drugs and guns was exact. He could break down a multi-kilo deal to a ten-pound bag price and tell you the profit margin in an instant. His interpersonal infiltration skills and memory recall were amazing. Added to this, his knowledge and application of covert law and his report writing were also impressive. He was the complete UCO (undercover officer). During the Omega course, I threw every challenge I could at him. Every dirty trick I could pull to undermine or compromise him. Every scenario I put to him was worst case. I would take him to the point of exhaustion, heavily critique his every move, put him under the microscope and get him 'special' attention from every role player that I put up against him. As I had hoped, he batted absolutely everything off, consistently delivering the goods.

He passed the course with flying colours and I could not have been prouder. During the course, some of the management misinterpreted his commitment and skill, and said that he may be difficult to manage and be trouble in the future. Already they were showing signs of nervousness of someone that was not going to be a yes-man. They seemed uncomfortable that he was naturally street-smart and criminally proficient and would obviously achieve great results. Essentially, what they did not like was the fact that he was already equipped with the 'criminal working knowledge or direction' that they thought they had. They couldn't tell him anything about the streets that he didn't already know. It obviously worried them.

Throughout Shay's subsequent undercover deployments, I remained in touch with him on more or less a daily basis, as I do to this day. He quickly became a highly successful and respected undercover operative and remains a loyal friend to me. His understanding of criminality and his ability to portray himself as a high-level criminal were unrivalled. I initially thought, *This kid is going to be better than me,* and he proved me right. He was.

At the end of his time at Omega, the treatment he received from his supervisors, and subsequently from others, was both insensitive and unfair, demonstrating no understanding – and at times no interest – in how to resettle good undercover cops back into the 'real world' of overt policing. I would really like to think that such poor treatment would not be repeated or condoned today.

Shay went from being a high-level undercover cop, one of the best in the UK, to an absolute pariah. Labelled too hard to handle, he was cast off back into the overt police service to be quietly forgotten about. A lesser man would have drowned or given up. This was never going to be the case with Shay, and he subsequently rose from the back office where he had been left, resuming frontline operational duties as a top-level detective involved in some of the most high-profile criminal cases in the UK and becoming once again a leading light in the war upon serious crime.

Fortunately, along this rise, Shay's skills were recognised and put to devastating effect by particularly well-respected and knowledgeable senior officers. They saw that he could still think like a high-level criminal, always had a lawfully audacious plan and was willing to be the first into any dangerous situation and the last one to leave. Shay Doyle got the job done.

Although names have been changed, Shay's story is 100 per cent true and not only provides a unique insight into the secretive world of covert policing and the investigation of serious crime, but also explores the mental health toll it took on Shay and other police officers that stand strong and hold the line.

Not many stood as strong as Shay Doyle.

Christie Vincent OBE

PROLOGUE

He was on his knees, head bowed, his bloodied hands cuffed behind his back. My calm facade belied the rage erupting inside. Sirens wailed; blue lights flashed. Someone needed to keep cool amid the chaos. Someone needed to keep their emotions in check. For 42 days he'd been at large, 42 days that ended in his act of unimaginable horror. I stood over him at the back of the station as two firearms officers pointed their guns. The bearded fugitive, wearing baggy blue shorts and a grey hoodie, was vacant, unmoved, his demeanour more befitting a shoplifter who'd just been caught than a multiple murderer. I can still see his face. It still haunts me. We wrapped his handcuffed hands in a plastic bag to preserve the evidence. I asked him if the BMW he had arrived in was booby-trapped. The silence was deafening.

He was still kneeling. He wasn't getting up now. Neither were the two young women he'd just lured to their deaths – the two police officers he'd cut down in a hail of 32 bullets and the fragments of a grenade.

There is no training for how you're going to react when faced with a homicidal maniac who has just slaughtered two of your colleagues in an act of unspeakable evil. My fellow officer had to walk away; it was a truth too hard to bear. I had been chasing him and was tired from the hunt, but I had to remain detached and do my job, be the professional cop I was. His heinous crime was about to shake the force and nation to its core. As I faced the killer, questions swirling in my mind, one thought dominated. *How the fuck did it come to this?*

CHAPTER 1
AN UNLIKELY COP

I'd love to say that it was some kind of moral crusade, that I was fighting the good fight and serving queen and country. That it was my vocation to be the proud enforcer of the long arm of the law.

But that would be a load of bollocks.

I never dreamed I would join the police. It was never an aspiration of mine growing up. The truth is, I was far more likely to be a criminal than a constable.

I was born in the late seventies and raised by second-generation Irish parents – my mum was one of nine – on a tough Manchester council estate. I grew up during decades dogged by poverty, social unrest and unemployment. Crime would have been an easy path to take. Especially in my family.

My mum's eldest brother was the local hard nut and, along with my grandad, ran an illegal bookmaking and loan shark racket from the estate pub in the days when they would shut at three o'clock in the afternoon. On a Sunday that would usually mean my old man and my uncles throwing as much beer down them as possible and beating seven shades of shit out of each other on the green outside.

One of my other uncles sometimes took me off my mum's hands like he was doing her a favour. 'Aren't you good, taking our Shay out and giving me a break,' me mam would say, beaming. She had no idea he was using me as a decoy for his shoplifting activities.

Some of my mates were into petty crime, riding around on stolen motorbikes, even robbing houses. Doing a stretch in juvenile jail was a badge of honour. They'd bounce out like minor celebrities, with starry-eyed girls hanging off them, and think, *I am the man.*

Drugs were everywhere. I could have quite easily got myself a nine bar of gear on tick, cut it up, and started making a few quid on the street. Who knows? Maybe I could have worked my way up to the fairy tale of the big, shiny white villa in the sun. But the cold reality of that life is you're more likely to end up in jail or in the ground.

Don't get me wrong. I can't guarantee the origins of every motorbike I ever rode as a teenager. But unlike some of my mates, I wasn't a young criminal. It didn't sit well with me.

That's not to say I'd go running to the police telling tales, though. It just wasn't the done thing. Not when the welcome messages for the local bobbies comprised the words 'pigs' and 'filth' daubed in spray paint on the dirty red-brick walls surrounding the estate. We dealt with our own shit. Whether you'd been battered or burgled, you didn't ring the dibble. And you certainly didn't grass.

'Know anything about this robbery last night?'

'What robbery?'

'Did you see the car being set on fire?'

'Not sure what you mean, Officer.'

'Have you seen this man? He's wanted over a stabbing.'

'Never seen him in my life, Officer.'

It was an unwritten rule. If a copper came asking questions, you kept shtum. You handled things your own way. When I was a kid, someone made the foolish mistake of breaking into our house – a two-up, two-down council semi – and nicking the coins from the gas meter. My dad didn't ring the police. He stormed into the local pub and battered a known burglar in front of the whole boozer while he pleaded his innocence. 'I knew it wasn't him, son,' he told me afterwards. 'It was about sending a message.'

As far back as I can remember, my dad ingrained it in me. You don't back down, you don't let anyone intimidate you and you *never* show fear. Coming home crying and telling tales wasn't a wise move for me as a kid. If I came in whinging, he'd fucking leather me himself. Fearing his wrath, I took it to extremes. When an older lad, a bit of a bully on our road, gave me shit, I wrapped a cricket bat around his head. It sparked uproar on the street. When my dad found out what happened, he battered me anyway. *I can't fucking win,* I thought.

But it toughened me up. And I had to be tough, because violence was never far away. My dad was an intelligent and hard-working man – also very funny at times – but, as I would later find out, deeply troubled. He had been raised in the care system, and it had robbed him of the ability to display any emotion. Instead, he lashed out. That was just his way. It made for a volatile relationship with my mum and an uncomfortable, often unbearable, atmosphere at home. My mum was a seamstress and I remember coming down the stairs once to see his shovel-like hands forcing her head towards the needle of the sewing machine as he pressed the foot pedal and screamed, 'I'll sew that fucking mouth up if you carry on.' I look back now, horrified at some of the shit my mum had to endure, but back then it didn't feel unusual. When I was a kid she even ended up in hospital so ill that she received the last rites. I know now that her condition was purely stress-induced, no doubt from living with him.

As I moved into my teens, explosive clashes with my dad became the norm, and they would invariably end in me taking a pasting, I don't look back with sorrow and regret, though. I'm not saying, 'Oh woe is me.' In some kind of warped way, my upbringing stood me in good stead for what was to come in my life.

It wasn't all bad, either. There were tender moments. I was sent to the local Roman Catholic primary school and told I was doing Holy Communion. I point-blank refused. Seven years old and already a headstrong little fucker. They tried to talk me round, but I wouldn't budge. The priest even came to the house to try to persuade my mother and father to make me do it. 'If he doesn't want to do it then the lad doesn't do it,' said my dad, giving me a little wink.

We used to love sitting up late watching the Tyson fights. Nigel Benn was another of our favourites. We liked the all-action brawlers. I was really into my boxing and putting the gloves on. I earned a bit of a reputation as someone who could bang a bit and did so on several occasions – not all of them in the ring.

As a teenager I was one of the boys, but secretly I was also an avid reader. My grandad amassed hundreds of books, and I used to pinch them and read them in my bedroom. I'd read Wilbur Smith novels on war and colonialism in Africa and devour encyclopaedias on natural history and geography, the Seven Wonders of the World and wildlife. I had a thirst for knowledge that I hid from people. I used to sit for hours in my own world, taking in all the facts and thinking, *I'd love to go there, I'd love to do that.* Manchester wasn't the be-all and end-all for me. I was curious as to what else was out there. I craved adventure.

At secondary school I generally pissed about with the lads. I didn't particularly enjoy any lessons that weren't sports-related. My form teacher called my mum into the school one day and told her, 'Mrs Doyle, Shay just sits there in lessons and stares out of the window.'

'OK, I'll get his dad to give him a bollocking,' she said angrily.

'Oh no, that's not what we're getting at. We think we bore him. He's really, really bright, but it's like he doesn't want anyone to know it.'

My mum tried to get me to buckle down. My response, typically bloody-minded, was to do what I wanted, and I left school with barely a GCSE to my name. One thing was for certain, I wouldn't have been allowed to lie in bed every day. There's no way my dad would have worn that.

At 16 I had no idea what I wanted to do with myself, but, after taking a job grafting as a £100-a-week labourer on a site full of bare-arsed builders, then pissing it up the wall in a boozer on the Friday, I knew that wasn't it. Some of my pals had progressed from knocking out bits of weed and were getting into heavier things. I just wasn't attracted to it.

On my dinner hour one day, I wandered past an army careers office and saw some pictures in the window of blokes in camouflage gear holding guns then on the piss in exotic places. *That's a bit of me,* I thought. And just like that, at 16 years of age, I joined the army.

I had the build for it. Slim and lean but strong. I could run for miles and hold my own in a fight or a boxing ring – both useful skills for an infantry soldier. I wasn't John Rambo by any stretch of the imagination. But I could look after myself – not that being a combat soldier is just about muscles and machine guns. You've got to be able to think on your feet in high-risk situations. You've got to be able to anticipate the threat and be tactically aware. I was one of the youngest there, and I flew the six months of training. Being away from home didn't bother me. Mum and Dad were permanently at each other's throats, and my dad would turn on me for nothing, sparking nasty physical fights between us. *Why would I want to go back to that?* I thought. Looking back now, I can see that my dad's mental health was suffering, but as a 16-year-old with no understanding of such issues, I just thought he was being a nasty bastard. Being in the army gave me an escape. I had a bed at night, food in my belly, a few quid in wages, regular hard exercise and a chance to see some of the amazing places I'd read about in all those encyclopaedias. At 16 it was all I needed.

My first posting was to sun-soaked Ayia Napa in Cyprus and I had a ball. Bars, booze and a bevy of holidaymaker beauties. It was as if I'd died and gone to heaven. I'm not sure there was that much soldiering going on, mind. Drinking, shagging and fighting, yes. But soldiering? Not really. Although I did pick up some of the best skills I ever learned evading capture from the military police just to have a night out on the town. It was raucous. Some of the lads were chucking ecstasy down their necks like it was going out of fashion, others getting so bladdered they could barely walk. I had some of the best times of my life in Ayia Napa and made some lifelong friends, but it was no more than a piss-up posting, two years of sunshine soldiering. The storm was still to come.

I was sent to Northern Ireland towards the end of the Troubles in 1997. South Armagh, known to the army as 'Bandit Country', was 200 square miles of dangerous and hostile terrain. It was there that a team of IRA snipers killed 12 members of the security forces in the 1990s and where the explosives were mixed for the Docklands, Manchester and Bishopsgate bombs. Being on patrol in South Armagh felt electric. I'd come out of the barracks armed with four magazines of rounds, adrenaline coursing through my veins, knowing that at any minute I could be taken out by snipers. Anyone who tells you they don't feel fear when embroiled in that kind of heat is lying. But this was a buzz like I'd never experienced before; it was the kind of thrill – the heart racing, the raw rush of sheer exhilaration – that made me realise why I'd joined the army. And I fucking loved it.

I was carving out a name for myself as someone who was fit, reliable and proficient at the job; I was tactically astute and adept at spotting danger, pinpointing threats and working out how to negate them. I had no idea at the time, but I was building up the skills that would later be invaluable in covert operations – and even save my life.

Being in the thick of it on deployments in high-risk areas like Northern Ireland and the Middle East – with all that excitement and danger – was what joining the army was all about for me. It wasn't about the mind-numbing regimental bullshit we had to deal with back on the mainland. When I wasn't on operations, I was a loose cannon, out on the piss all the time and getting into fights.

'When not in engaged in operations, Private Doyle is a disruptive nuisance. When on operations I'd place him at the top of the pack.'

That's what my company officer-in-command, a major who'd just returned to the battalion from a lengthy posting with the SAS, wrote on my annual appraisal. It would be the story of my career. I whipped around in a souped-up white Fiesta XR2i like a boy racer and was slapped with a six-month driving ban for speeding. But I loved living life in the fast lane – always chasing the next big thrill.

After nearly eight years in the army, having joined at such a young age, I thought I was missing something and decided to give Civvy Street a go, safe in the knowledge my regiment would have me back. At the time the lads were pulling a little scam: you get out, have a few months on the piss then sign back on, picking up an eight-grand bounty – and all without losing rank. I thought I'd do the same. I hooked back up with some of my pals from the estate and some of the Manchester squaddies I'd served with who had the same idea as me. We had a tight little crew and made a pub in the city centre gang HQ. Some of the lads I knocked about with had dads and uncles that were members and associates of Manchester's notorious Quality Street Gang. Back in the day they had been a serious firm of shadowy Manchester 'businessmen', and we'd always see them at the pub and have a chat. I found them fascinating characters. These fellas had been serious gangsters – armed robbers, safe blowers, dangerous villains – yet they were also men with charm, charisma, manners and presence. I'd sit in their company and take in their mannerisms, the old-school way they conducted themselves – not bragging about their criminal exploits yet still giving off the kind of aura that said you'd be fucked if you crossed them. I'd watch them send over half-pints of bitter to the old boy sitting in the corner, and I'd watch the way the punters treated them with deference and respect. I'd drink it all in, not knowing that the traits I was observing would become of use to me.

I was offered plenty of opportunities to get involved in scams and schemes with my pals. I was seen as someone who was bright, loyal and game as fuck. A lot of the other lads looked to me for a bit of leadership within our group. But I resisted the temptation to go down the wrong path. I had a few quid saved up from the army and was working as a hod carrier for a mate. I was also seeing a girl from a nice area of Manchester who came from a straight-going family. Besides, I was missing the army. I was missing the camaraderie, the action. And I felt I still had unfulfilled potential in the military. Iraq was now fully kicking off, and I was looking forward to going back and getting stuck in with the mates I'd left behind.

And then everything changed. My dad hanged himself aged 47.

I didn't grieve. I didn't show emotion. To show emotion was weakness. He taught me that. To show emotion was to let everyone else see a chink in your armour, and you can't do that because the world is full of predators – and if they see it, you're going to be next on the menu. That was my dad's legacy. That was his gift to me as a parent, the only gift he was capable of giving me because of his own fucked-up childhood. From the moment I could walk, I was taught you back down to no one. Ever.

My dad was a tortured soul who held his demons inside. I see that now. He would never have reached out and admitted to anyone there was a problem. And that, sadly, was his problem.

It completely changed my perspective on rejoining the army. I thought, *I need to be at home for me mam and be the breadwinner. I need to be there for the family. I need to step up.* I couldn't pack my bags and jet off to the Middle East for God knows how long. I needed to be at home. It meant a rethink. *What the fuck am I going to do with myself?* One thing was for sure – whatever it was I was going to be, I was going to be the best at it. It was time to grow up. Looking back, maybe my dad's suicide was the kick up the arse I needed. I knew I was a bright and capable lad. Capable of really making something of myself. And I had an unshakable belief that if I set my mind to something, I could be the best at it – be it a bricklayer, a barrister or a criminal.

Just as I was taking stock – and perhaps by a twist of fate – days after my dad died I got a phone call from a pal I was in the army with who had joined the police. 'There's a big recruitment drive on at Greater Manchester Police,' he said. 'It's a piece of piss and the money's good. They're taking any dickhead on at the minute – even someone like you.'

'Nah, not for me, mate,' I said.

'Why the fuck not, Shay? You're one of the smartest people I know and you've got a huge set of fucking balls on you. Since when did Shay Doyle give a fuck what anyone thought of him?'

The police! I thought. *I'd never be able to show my face around here again.*

I remember lumping what must have been my thou-sandth brick onto some scaffolding on a site I was working on in torrential rain and strong winds when an old Irish brickie I used to have the craic with pulled me aside.

'What are you doin' here?' he said, his eyes squinting in the storm.

'What d'ya mean? Just trying to earn a few quid.'

'You're too fuckin' bright to be 'ere, you, Shay. You'll end up like me and that tree over there – all bent and withered. That's how you'll end up if you carry on in this fuckin' game. You're a bright lad. Get yourself out of 'ere.'

I thought back to that phone call. *The police. Could I really join the police? Why not? It'd be a bit of a challenge. Something different. Besides, I'm my own man. I can do what the fuck I want. And why shouldn't I have a respectable job?*

I'm a working-class lad, not some silver spoon dickhead. I've got respect for people. So why shouldn't I do it? If only it were that straightforward.

As the rain drove down, I stood on the flimsy wooden platform, thoughts whirling in my head like the wind around me. *My dad's just killed himself. I'm not gonna fuck my life up. I need to step up.*

Then I made my decision.

Fuck it. I'm gonna do it. Who knows? It might even be a laugh.

You can imagine the shock on some of my closest friends' faces when I told them I was applying to join Her Majesty's constabulary. Yes, me, a capable lad from good stock, who had connections in certain circles, shall we say. Me, an ex-squaddie who'd grown up on an estate where anti-police graffiti was smeared on the walls.

The truth was that despite my background and who I might have known, I was never into crime. I wasn't motivated by money or power. I didn't like bullies, I couldn't stand burglars and I resented the way vulnerable people – even smack- and crackheads – were manipulated and exploited. I had honesty and integrity, and I certainly wasn't going to join the police to be a bent cop. But if I was going to take the plunge, a decision that would cost me friendships, then I was going to be the best cop I could be.

I never actually thought I'd get in. Throughout the application process, I kept expecting a tap on my shoulder and someone to say, 'What do you think you're playing at?' The application was a three-to-six-month process designed to eliminate the dreamers, the idiots and the *Police Academy* Tackleberrys of this world who want to go out and put a hole in everybody. During the recruitment, I had to role-play and debate with other candidates, many of whom had degrees. One even had a PhD in physics. On paper she looked the business, and I'll admit at times I felt out of place. But I can tell you now, you can have all the degrees in the world and be as intelligent on paper as you want, but it doesn't matter one bit on the streets of Manchester. It doesn't make you street-smart and it doesn't make you a good cop.

Throughout the process, we were being observed by Greater Manchester Police chief inspectors. By the end, I thought I'd done OK but wasn't sure if I'd get through. Then I got invited in for the final interview.

'How do you think you've done?' a chief inspector asked me at the end of a tense exchange.

'I'd like to think I've applied myself well and given a good account of myself,' I said, without any great expectations.

'Well, you certainly did that,' she said. 'You've scored in the top 3 per cent in the country for the recruitment process.'

I opened my mouth but nothing came out. Just stunned silence.

'Not only would we like to offer you the job, we'd like you to strongly consider coming on the High Potential Development Scheme.'

For many, the HPDS is a fantastic opportunity. This is a fast-track promotion designed to produce future leaders in the police. 'You're the cream of the crop,' recruits are told. 'The decision makers. You can change the face of policing and how the public see crime.'

The chief inspector went on. 'We know you've not got a degree and this would normally be reserved for graduates, but you've scored that highly that we will put it to the force to pay for you to do a degree and then fast-track you through the ranks. We'll guide your career. If you pass the exams and hurdles, you could be an inspector in four years, and you'll probably be superintendent within ten years, in charge of your own policing division. You can be the future of command in the police.'

There I was, straight out of the army, lugging bricks for a living, not a qualification to my name and zero career prospects, being told I could become a big cheese in the police. I played it cool.

'Well, send us the stuff and I'll have a look at it and have a think about it.'

'What's there to think about?' she said. 'It's a fantastic opportunity and people would give their right arm for this. You're somebody we see as a future leader and we'd like to help make that happen.'

Most people would jump at the opportunity. I wasn't quite so sure. I pictured tedious meetings with pompous people talking shite. I pictured reams of bullshit paperwork.

'Um, I'm not sure if it's for me if I'm honest,' I said. 'But send me all the stuff and I'll read it.'

So I did. And I thought it through. I was 24 years old, had just come out of the infantry as a soldier. I hadn't joined the police to do a degree. I had joined for a bit of the action, to get my hands dirty, not to sit in a stuffy office. I turned it down. *Fuck that,* I thought. I wanted to join to be on the ground, doing the job, and getting involved in chases and the high-adrenaline stuff. That's what I lived for. They thought I was mad.

'You'd be the future of policing.' Not for me. 'You're going to lead tomorrow's police officers.' Not interested. 'You'll change how people see crime.' No, thanks.

It was unprecedented that I'd been offered this kind of opportunity, the chief inspector said. But I just wasn't that bothered. My thinking was *How could anybody in the police respect somebody who has bypassed doing the job? If you're a leader, you're a leader. I don't need a fucking leg-up. I don't need no bullshit course.*

It was a leg-up for the privileged, in my mind. Truth be told, most of the moulded HPDS 'leaders' never see a drug dealer, let alone know what to do with one.

Maybe it was a mistake. Maybe I'd be a chief superintendent now on nearly a hundred grand a year, not telling you the story of how I came to be medically discharged at 41. But I stuck to my guns and my working-class roots. I did what every other new recruit did. I put on my uniform and I went out on the beat.

CHAPTER 2
TAMESIDE

S at between the edge of Manchester and the foothills of the picturesque Pennines, Tameside is one of Greater Manchester's forgotten backwaters. People think there's not much going on there, that it's a fairly unremarkable place. I can safely say it's not. Among the overspill estates built to cater for a post-war population boom, you'll find some of the region's most poverty-stricken areas. And you'll find a history littered with notorious crimes. You've got Hattersley, where Moors murderers Ian Brady and Myra Hindley were rehoused as part of the inner-city slum clearances. Then there's Hyde, the hunting ground of Harold Shipman. Then you've got the likes of Denton, Ashton-under-Lyne and Stalybridge, all with their fair share of petty and organised criminals. Yet amid the deprivation, there are also some quite affluent areas. It makes for a melting pot of criminal activity.

Drug dealers, drug users, armed robbers, gangsters, fraudsters, burglars – you name them, you could find them in Tameside. If that wasn't enough, at the time I joined the police it was the murder capital of Manchester. Gang wars were spilling over from other areas. It was here that Stephen Amos was shot dead outside a bar in Ashton-under-Lyne. Stephen was the brother of Lee Amos, a leading light in one of the most violent and notorious gangs ever to come out of Moss Side, a place that would later play a major role in my career. Needless to say, I'd have my hands full. Tameside was where my life in the police began. I had no idea at the time it would also see an event unfold that would signal the beginning of the end.

First there was the small matter of three months' residential training. Bruche Police Training Centre in Warrington had seen better days. Tired accommodation blocks housed a dining, bar and social area, and there was a gym and swimming pool. There were classrooms, a parade square at the centre of the complex, and barbed-wire fencing around the outside, giving it the army barracks feel, so I initially felt at home.

The first night, I pressed my police uniform and polished my boots – just like I did in military training. I was quite excited – it almost felt like I was joining the army again. The next morning I woke early and showered before putting on my brand-spanking-new uniform, with its freshly ironed shirt and spotless boots, for the first time. I stood up straight and looked in the mirror. This was the moment I was supposed to burst with pride.

What the fuck am I wearing and what the fuck am I doing here? I thought to myself. I hated wearing that uniform, and that feeling would never leave me. For many new recruits the police is a vocation, the realisation of a lifetime goal. Many were following in the footsteps of family members. It was nothing like that for me. Don't get me wrong, I'm not knocking newbie officers who feel a sense of pride and accomplishment. I just didn't feel it. And almost to the end of my service, I harboured that gnawing feeling that someone would tap me on the shoulder and say, 'There's been a mistake, son. You shouldn't be here.' Fighting the urge to rip the uniform off, jump in my car and drive out of the gates, I walked to my allocated classroom to meet my fellow recruits.

There were a lot of fresh-faced graduates there and I found it hard to relate to them. There I was, 24, the Manchester council estate kid straight out of the army. I felt the odd one out. I kept saying to myself, *Grin and bear it, get the first month's wages in the bank and then fuck it off.*

I soon found that, compared to the military, police training was a doddle: an 8.30am start, bit of a lesson on the law, followed by a little bit of role play or a guest speaker, always with plenty of breaks and early finishes. Some of the recruits thought it was tough going. They had obviously never cut Mummy's apron strings. I'd been used to carrying out patrols, armed arrest operations and observation posts in Northern Ireland. I'd been injected with anti-nerve agent before a deployment to the Middle East. I'm not making out I was some kind of TV army tough guy, but I had experienced extreme discipline and this wasn't it. In truth, I found it all a bit of a joke.

However, as that first month rolled by, I found some like-minded souls, mainly ex-military lads who, like me, were not there because of a lifelong calling to be cops but who saw it as a decent fit at the time and were giving it a go. One of the tutors, an experienced cop who was ex-military himself, pulled me to the side and said, 'Listen, stick it out. It isn't like this bullshit when you get out on the street. You'll enjoy it and I think you'll be good at it.'

The lessons on law and role plays of nicking people came easy to me. I was in the gym for four o'clock every day and in the bar with my new mates for seven almost every night. I actually started to enjoy it. So I decided to stick around and give it a bash.

I passed police training, and the day of the big parade arrived. It was, as expected, a ceremonial affair – all trumpets and fanfare. The brass band played, and our perfectly polished boots crunched the gravel in unison as we marched onto the square. This was a day where families and friends would gush with pride at seeing their loved ones mark their graduations. It wasn't quite like that for me. None of mine turned up. As my fellow graduates all hugged and congratulated one another, I threw my shit in the car and drove home, ready to start work the following week.

I was posted to the police HQ in Ashton-under-Lyne. At the time Ashton was a lively place. Every weekend, DJs banged out the latest house and dance tunes in sweat-hole pubs packed with pissed-up punters. They would bounce from one boozer to the next, knocking back pints of Stella, then finish the night off with a greasy doner kebab and probably a fight. I'd be regularly dealing with brainless loudmouths who couldn't walk past the police without spitting vile abuse, then they'd end up in a cell and wonder why. Ashton was known as the 'land of the flying piss pots' and neighbouring Stalybridge was 'Stalyvegas'. Scraps were a sure bet. Then you had your underbelly of gangsters trying to muscle in on the doors. There was every kind of social problem, crime and deprivation in Ashton, and it would be a great place to learn how to be a street cop.

The first few months were not without their difficulties. I got on well with the old-timers who had nothing to prove, but I just couldn't gel with some of the less experienced colleagues on shift. They just weren't my cup of tea; they had two or three years in the cops and thought they were fucking veterans. They would look down on me as the new boy – or 'sprog' as I was known. I used to look at them and think, *I was leading armed teams at the Portadown riots and high-risk operations while you were doing a shit degree in some nonsense subject.*

Nevertheless, I got my head down and did my first ten weeks with my tutor constable. Mine was a guy called Frank, an experienced cop, long in the tooth and close to retirement, having spent his full career in uniform. He was a nice enough bloke and he knew the job inside out. His speciality was getting rid of jobs by writing as little about them as possible, and he was content on seeing out his time without any major conflict. He just wanted to pick up his wages and get out of Dodge. I, on the other hand, was no stranger to conflict and was champing at the bit. I was Frank's idea of a nightmare trainee constable.

My first arrest came three days after I started in uniform. We were on nights and driving through Hyde around three in the morning, and I spotted a lad walking down the road. He was small and skinny with a pale, gaunt face. I could tell instantly he was a smackhead. He was wearing a shiny tracksuit and a pair of Nikes with the bubble in the sole. On his back was a gleaming £1,000 set of Ping Eye golf clubs. Now, there wasn't a 24-hour floodlit golf course locally that gave night-time discounts to heroin-addicted golf enthusiasts, so it didn't take Sherlock Holmes to work out that he wasn't going for a leisurely 18 holes. They had clearly been nicked. Frank didn't want to deal with it, so I got out and fronted him up myself.

'Off for a round of golf, are we, sir?'

He didn't reply, just turned on his heels and ran. But the hapless thief didn't get very far. I grabbed him, seized the clubs and radioed through to see if a set had been reported stolen. Nothing came back. I knew they were nicked, though, so I locked him up on suspicion of theft while I checked him out. Johnny Prince, a career criminal with a history of burglary, was what came back. The next day a job came in for a garage break-in, and what do you know! The golf clubs were missing. I went to see the owner. He was built like a brick shithouse and had a chiselled but beaten-up face, the kind you'd see on a prize fighter. It turned out he was a major drug dealer just out of prison for slashing a rival's face. 'Big Mick', we'll call him, wasn't the kind of guy to go to the police if someone had wronged him, and it quickly emerged he'd only reported the theft to get a crime number and claim the insurance. I told him an arrest had been made over his stolen clubs. 'Who was it, then?' he said, menacingly looking down at me on his doorstep.

'I can't give you a name,' I replied. 'It's breaching data protection.'

We both knew what would happen if I did divulge those details, and it wouldn't have ended well for Johnny the tea leaf. I went back to see Johnny. If he was pale before, he was Casper the ghost once he found out whose clubs he'd nicked.

'I take it you've heard whose garage you've done over, Johnny.'

'I'm a dead man, aren't I?' he blubbered. He wasn't, but it did put him off raiding houses for a while. Meanwhile, Big Mick got his clubs back and probably another set on the insurance. As first arrests go, catching a burglar with the stolen gear in hand and charging him up the next day wasn't a bad one, and it got me wanting more.

I started to grow into the job and soon developed a repu-tation as a bit of a livewire who wouldn't take shit from anyone. Yes, I had a few town centre scraps, but I must stress I wasn't into police brutality in any shape or form. But there is, unfortunately, a section of the public that doesn't understand reason and can only communicate through violence. These kinds of idiots – usually of low intelligence, with no discernible prospects and on the periphery of petty crime – were commonplace on the night scene in Tameside, and on several occasions I had no choice but to speak back to them in their preferred language. I knew how to fight and I didn't give a fuck. If they wanted to be violent with me, then I'd meet force with force. And although my response was always proportionate to the threat, resorting to the use of force got me in trouble with my superiors on more than one occasion.

Despite the odd raised eyebrow, I was locking people up left, right and centre. I was doing my job and doing it well. My ten weeks with Frank were coming to an end – and he was glad to be rid of me, professionally speaking, even though personally we got on well enough. Frank was at that stage of his career where he just wanted to get home and put his feet up with his missus and his dog. The final straw for him came when some gobshite thinking he was a tough guy told me he'd rip my head off if I wasn't in uniform. I don't think he expected me to unzip my body armour and say, 'Well, let's have a fucking square go then!' I soon learned that you can't be doing that in the police. The thing is, it was all a big game to me at the time, and it had been drilled into me from childhood that if someone fronted you up, you didn't back down to them.

I was never interested in giving people parking or speeding tickets. I wanted to get to grips with the villains. The burglars who went after frail old couples. The drug dealers who spread misery, peddling crack and smack, exploiting the vulnerable. The yobs who had communities living in fear. The wife beaters, the paedos. These were the scum that needed locking up, in my mind. There was a lad on my shift who used to spend his night looking for drivers with bald tyres or people doing 36 in a 30 zone. *Nah, not for me, mate,* I thought. *I'll chase the proper criminals.* Not that nicking someone with bald tyres didn't have its uses, as I later discovered when I used it as a disruption tactic to build up intelligence on some of the big hitters.

Within months of starting the job, my eyes had been opened to the fact that crime had devastating consequences. That behind a drug deal was often serious violence or exploitation. That a burglary left a victim so terrified someone might come through their door again, they couldn't sleep at night. That a sex offence could scar a child for life and shatter a family. I started to feel a deep sense of responsibility. I realised that a lot of these victims didn't have the means to do anything about the horrors that had befallen them, and that the police are in fact the line that stands between them and the baddies, the weak and the strong, the hunter and the hunted.

I'd grown up among villains both petty and serious. I knew how they acted; I knew their modus operandi. I started to use my knowledge. Not only was I hitting arrest targets, I was nicking more than anyone else on my shift. And whenever there was a dangerous job that required a robust response, I was the one they called. A nutcase threatening his wife and kids? Get Shay in. A violent psychopath going on the rampage? Get Shay in. A knife-wielding maniac in a park? Get Shay in. Looking back, it was probably a reckless way of seeing the world, but the riskier and more extreme the job, the more it switched me on.

One major incident in my early uniform days involved Salford doorman Craig King. He was a six-foot-ten, thirty-stone monster of man. Not someone you'd want to bump into in a dark alley. Police had been called to an incident at his sister's house in Ashton, and somehow King had been contacted and was making his way to the address. Two of my colleagues were dispatched and managed to get into the house with his sister, but no sooner had they got through the door than King turned up, armed with a two-foot machete and a .22 calibre rifle. He then proceeded to smash up a four-by-four parked up outside before shooting through a window while his sister was cowering inside with her partner and two sons aged eight and twelve. This giant of a man, high on a cocktail of booze and prescription pills, was indiscriminately pinging off a rifle in the street and was clearly a threat to life. I was in the area before the firearms team, and other colleagues from my shift were inside the address. I hid behind a wall to avoid being shot, trying to take up a position where I could get a view and report back, while the chaos unfolded and armed police sped to the scene. As the crack of the fired gun pierced the night sky, Steve, a great bloke and cop who was in the house, was calmness personified.

'Yeah, I've got a visual on him now,' he said, radioing through, as if describing a run-of-the-mill stakeout.

'He's pacing up and down the street. It's a rifle. He keeps reaching into his left pocket, he's reloading, he's reloading. Do we have an ETA for firearms response?'

Once they arrived, the firearms cops could take no chances when he refused to put down his gun. They opened fire there and then, hitting him three times.

'You shot me three times,' he shouted, down but not out. 'You think you're hard, go on, kill me then.' He later died of his injuries, becoming the first man to be shot dead by officers from Greater Manchester Police.

Such dramas were few and far between, and I spent much of my time poring over paperwork or dealing with everyday complaints. I just wasn't interested in that side of policing. I wanted to be out there, chasing big criminals and nicking baddies. To make matters worse, people were making complaints of assault against me. Thugs, with records as long as your arm, who would threaten to do this and that to me, then played the victim when I used force on them to protect myself. It was fine for them to act the big man and say they had weapons. Perfectly OK for them to tell me they'd rape and kill my missus or shoot another officer's kids – I heard it all – but if I ever laid my hands on them when they were threatening me with serious violence, you could bet your bottom dollar they'd very quickly play the victim and bemoan how they'd been attacked by the 'violent bully policeman'. Still, I got pulled in.

'You need to rein it in, Shay,' said the gaffer.

'Well, stop sending me on the violent jobs then,' I snapped back. 'If you're going to send me on all the violent jobs, then I'm going to get complained about. It's the nature of the beast.'

In truth, complaints are par for the course when it comes to policing. Show me a cop who's gone through their career without facing a complaint and I'll show you a shit cop who's hidden from doing the job.

I started to get disillusioned with it all. They were willing to send me on violent job after violent job, yet at the first sign of a complaint, I was the one who had to rein it in. I felt like they didn't have my back and I trusted precious few of my colleagues. There was a real backstabbing culture. The difference between the police and the military was that on the battlefield, you knew where the bullets were coming from.

In my first 18 months, I received two police commendations, neither of which were for dealing with violent maniacs, but for saving lives.

I came across a despairing woman one night on the wrong side of a motorway bridge. As the cars whizzed past, she stared down, waiting for her moment to jump. After gaining her trust, I managed to get close enough to grab her and pull her over the railings. It wasn't how the manual said you should do it, but it worked that night. She could have jumped into speeding traffic at any moment. The carnage doesn't bear thinking about.

For the second one, I'd been tasked with locating a high-risk suicidal missing person and found him in a secluded country lane after an extensive search. He was sitting at the wheel of a locked car filling with fumes from the hose pipe he'd attached to his exhaust. He was unconscious. I smashed the window with the butt of my baton, unlocked the car and dragged him out before giving him CPR, which surprisingly worked, and he lived.

Despite the fact I was actually a pretty good cop, the job came with headaches that I just didn't need, and on a personal level I'd lost lots of friendships after a good few of my pals pulled away from me. *I've had a go,* I thought. *But this just isn't for me. I'm going to leave.* I made enquiries about going back to the army. I told my sergeant of my intentions and that my mind was made up. Then, just as I was planning to hand in my notice, I got an email.

'Come and see me – 2pm before you start your shift.'

It was from Dessie Hardy, detective chief inspector and head of the CID (criminal investigation department).

An uncompromisingly ruthless character, Dessie was old school, and if he summoned you to his office, you went. So I went, slightly bricking myself. It was really unusual for the DCI to summon a uniform. *What the fuck have I done now?* I thought.

When I knocked on his office door I found he was waiting for me, his six-foot-four frame an imposing presence in his small, dusty office.

'Sit down,' he barked. 'Are you ex-army?'

'Yes, sir.'

'You like locking people up, don't you?'

'That's the job, isn't it, sir?'

'I hear you're a handy lad.'

'Just doing my job, sir,' I said.

'I hear good things about you. I hear you're thinking of going back to the army. There's a lot more to the police than uniform policing, you know. Do you want a job?'

'Sorry, sir?'

'Do you want to come and work on my Organised Crime Unit, get out of that uniform?'

The Organised Crime Unit was a small, secretive team of plain-clothed cops who carried out surveillance and acted on covert intelligence, often from police informants. I'd see them pulling up in plain cars and walking around the nick every day in jeans and T-shirts, and I'd hear of them pulling off big drug busts. There was an air of mystery about them that intrigued me.

Sounds right up my street, I thought. *I want in.*

I was barely approaching the end of my probation. It was unheard of for someone to get this kind of opportunity so soon in their police career.

'Why not?' I replied, stunned.

'Right, you start tomorrow, 8am.'

CHAPTER 3
OCG

The silver Citroën people carrier was doing 70 along the M60 near junction 21 at Chadderton at the start of a three-hour journey to Aylesbury when one of the back-seat passengers unwound the window and retched. Keen to avoid his motor reeking of vomit, the driver swiftly signalled to pull into the hard shoulder. Before he could come to a stop, however, the man removed his head from the open window, slid open the door, jumped out and bolted towards the grass verge. He didn't stop to throw up, just kept going, his grey tracksuit flapping in the wind. It was the driver left with the sick feeling in his stomach as he helplessly watched the man's bulky frame shrinking in the distance.

The guy at the wheel was a cop and the lad doing a legger was a career criminal. Let's call him Kevin B. He was out on a temporary licence release and was returning to HMP Grendon with prison officers, having served three and a half years of an eight-year stretch for possession of a firearm. This was a dangerous individual and he wasn't going back inside of his own accord.

Shortly after he absconded, there was a spate of vicious armed robberies on shops and pubs in Tameside. The attackers would wait until closing time then storm in with knives and take the till, leaving victims – often women – terrified and traumatised. They were violent raids for precious little reward. And they had Kevin B.'s modus operandi all over them.

The Organised Crime Unit had been tasked with locating Kevin and getting him back behind bars. The team devised a plan to set up covert observation posts, with one overlooking the house of an associate of Kevin's that surveillance had revealed to be a busy crack dealer. We worked systematically to generate intelligence from various sources to locate him, and our efforts paid off, the information revealing that Kevin B. was indeed behind the robberies and was driving around in a dark-coloured Ford Mondeo, also stolen. We knew that he'd been visiting his brother, but we hadn't had the opportunity to call a strike on him. This time we would be ready and waiting. The trap was set. The plan was to use the observation post at his brother's address as a trigger and take him out while he was mobile in the vehicle – when he would be at his most vulnerable. It would require a complex surveillance operation with a MAST in support. MAST stands for Mobile Armed Strike Team; it's made up of highly skilled, well-drilled covert specialist firearms officers. To warrant the use of a MAST, the target has to be deemed extremely dangerous and potentially have immediate access to firearms or serious weapons. Kevin was an escaped prisoner on a violent crime spree who had previously pointed a sawn-off shotgun at police officers. He ticked every box.

As anticipated, and in line with the intelligence, Kevin turned up at his brother's bang on cue in the stolen Ford Mondeo. He didn't go into the house, which gave us the opportunity to get behind him with a surveillance team. The key to success would be to strike quickly without posing a risk to the public. Time and place were paramount. I sat in the lead surveillance car tailing Kevin as he headed towards Ashton town centre, taking the eyeball after being given direction of travel from the guys in the static observation point. The roads were busy and lined with pedestrians, ramping up the risk of collateral damage. We needed somewhere quieter, more secluded, to take him out, but it was imperative we didn't let him go. This was a prolific robber who'd escaped from prison and who represented a significant threat to the public.

The Mondeo crawled through traffic and eventually turned towards the main high street. It was approaching 7pm on a weekday at this point, so the crowds were becoming sparse. We were getting closer to strike territory. Now wasn't the time to fuck it up. One sniff that he had a tail and he'd be off, and if we lost him he would likely go to ground. *One shot – make it count.* He turned at the junction close to a motorbike store and crept down a back street. This was our moment.

'Strike! Strike! Strike!'

At breakneck speed the firearms team overtook the unsuspecting driver and screeched to a skidding halt as our car got right up his arse, giving him no room to manoeuvre. Sandwiched but desperate to escape, Kevin slammed his foot on the accelerator – in first gear then reverse – but he was so tightly squeezed that in his attempt to ram us he succeeded only in sending into the air shrieking clouds of thick white smoke from the melting rubber. Before the fugitive had time to open his door, the covert firearms team burst out of the MAST car and swiftly surrounded the Mondeo. They simultaneously smashed the car windows with ice axes while firing a CS gas canister into the car, filling the interior with smoke to incapacitate, daze and confuse. It was a devastating display of speed, surprise and aggression. Then they grabbed Kevin through the smashed driver's window, with him kicking and screaming, before subduing and cuffing him. The MAST lads had to use any means possible – and that included reasonable force – to stop him from escaping because there is no doubt he would have seriously hurt a member of the public or a cop in his desperation to get away. By the time the arrest was made, Kevin was black and blue and had to go directly to hospital rather than custody. The next day, his balls had swelled to the size of peaches.

'Do you want to make a complaint?' he was asked a few days later in the interview room.

'What have I got to complain about?' he replied.

Kevin was a career criminal and knew the stakes. Even though he was undoubtedly dangerous, I kind of respected him for that. He dished it out, and when it was his turn, he took his medicine. That, in my experience, is the difference between a serious committed criminal who views arrest as a hazard of the trade and a Saturday-night warrior full of sniff and false bravado, happy to gob off in the street and commit random acts of violence yet who immediately defaults to a victim mentality when his comeuppance arrives.

It would not be the most complex covert job I would be involved in during my career, and Kevin B. would be far from the biggest, baddest or most dangerous criminal I would tackle, but this was my first taste of an all-action operation that really got my adrenaline pumping and opened my eyes to a different side of police work. It was the type of operation that made the Organised Crime Unit a perfect fit for me.

The OCU was run by a hard-nosed ex-National Crime Squad career detective called Brendan, a man I hugely respected and still call a friend today. Brendan had seen it all and got the T-shirt several times over. He was a great cop and demanded results, but in turn, if you grafted, he looked after you. This was a department full of committed cops who lived and breathed the job and couldn't get enough of the over-time, the overnighters and the risk that came with taking out serious villains. If you weren't of that nature, Brendan would have had no qualms in getting rid of you in an instant.

I was the youngest and least experienced in the unit, a mixture of plain-clothed cops and detectives. These lads loved getting their hands dirty with professional criminals. I'm talking decent-level drug dealers, organised burglars, organised car ringers, armed robbers. To deal with these kind of villains, you need to be robust enough to cope with physical and verbal threats and not afraid to front up dangerous offenders. There were a lot of ex-military guys in the unit with the same mentality as me. There was a real camaraderie; it was almost like we were our own gang.

At first there were some sideways looks as to how I'd been 'gifted' entry to the unit by the DCI so early in my career, but as the weeks and jobs went by, the team saw that I was 100 per cent dedicated, had a flair for creative thinking and would back down from absolutely no one. I quickly became a trusted member of the team. I felt I'd found my niche and started to really enjoy the job. And for the first time, I felt a sense of belonging in the cops. I relished the risk of going up against proper criminals and applying my brain in planning the often complex operations to tackle them.

It was in the OCU that I met a lad who to this day remains one of my best friends. Alex had a similar story to me. He grew up in a troubled, crime-ridden area of Manchester. He became a uniformed cop but had an insatiable appetite for all-action policing. He packed 18 stone of pure muscle, was built like a brick wall and I never saw anyone get the better of him – that's if they were foolish enough to try. In many ways, we were kindred spirits. They used to call us 'the catalogue kids' because we'd turn up for work in expensive Stone

Island jackets, designer jeans and the latest pair of Air Max 95s. As was the fashion at the time, we had crew cuts and mine laid bare protruding scars on the back of my head, which added to the menacing look. Many of the drug dealers and villains we nicked would often remark that we looked more like gangsters than we did cops, and I'd be lying if I said we didn't use this to our advantage from time to time. Even though you didn't have partners then, like you see in the cheesy American buddy cop films, we always went on jobs together, becoming an impenetrable double act, and were Brendan's go-to boys.

Whenever we went through any door, there was a mutual trust. We had the same drive, the same willingness to go toe to toe with anybody. We always had each other's back no matter the odds, and we quickly gained a reputation as a formidable duo. Despite his thuggish looks, Alex was and remains one of the best detectives I've ever known. He had a keen eye for detail and evidence collection, which complemented my creative thinking when drawing up strategies to target criminal gangs. I'd found my perfect foil. Even though our careers would see us go our separate ways, our reputation as a double act would later see us join forces again on some major operations where a more unconventional approach was required.

We worked around the clock. We'd be in at five in the morning and taking someone's door off by half past. We'd have two prisoners in before dinner, with a kilo of coke or smack or maybe even a gun. We'd interview the suspects before going back out to cultivate and recruit informants. Then we'd be carrying out surveillance at night. We were gathering intelligence and building evidential cases using sophisticated covert techniques for which we'd have to get special permission from senior officers under RIPA (the Regulation of Investigatory Powers Act) legislation. There was so much scope to get involved in some real tasty stuff, and we didn't have to go cap in hand for the overtime because we were often dealing with criminals who had access to firearms.

It was exhausting but exhilarating, and I loved it. This was the buzz I was after. This was *The Professionals*. This was *The Sweeney*. This was what I'd pictured when I joined the cops. None of the mundane domestic shite. None of the daily dealings with society's underclass that underpin uniformed policing. This was where I really discovered and put to use my natural ability to think like a criminal – to manipulate them, to get into their heads, to anticipate their next move. The ability to put myself in the shoes of criminals was what made me different from many other cops and would give me a vital edge throughout my career. It was something that was picked up on by my colleagues. One day, one of the lads in the office, who was older and had been around the block, pulled me aside.

'There's an internal ad about the Level 1 undercover open day. Have you seen it?'

'No, not seen it, mate.'

It was a world I knew very little about.

'I went for it a few years back, got through the initial selection and then got knocked back at the later stages,' he went on. 'But you, Shay . . . I really think you'd be great at it. It's right up your street. You're quick on your feet, you look the part, you basically are the fucking part. Have a look at the ad, you should go for it. Get yourself down there. I think they'd like you.'

I didn't think that much of it but it was food for thought. *Maybe worth a look.* But I had no reason to want to leave. For the first time in my career I was loving being a cop. I loved the sneaky beaky stuff and getting to grips with proper villains. It was non-stop, high-octane, rewarding work. We were earning decent money. I'd smash the gym every day and come to work in the casual designer gear worn by gangsters and football hooligans. It was all part of the package and helped no end when teasing information out of criminals and recruiting informants. This was where I really started to shine. The front I presented and the way in which I communicated allowed me to build a rapport with villains, and quite often they would let their guard down and open up. Whenever a substantial arrest was made, I would be the one the bosses would send in to obtain information from the target – be it on the crime we were dealing with or something completely unconnected. It was something that just came naturally to me.

When we weren't out chasing villains, we would have a right laugh: 'work hard, play hard' was the motto. There were some real characters in the unit. Like 'Crazy' Baz, our sergeant. He'd happily hide out in a rain-sodden bush all night to get his man. The guy was a fearless hunter and there'd be many a steroid-fuelled drug dealer who made the mistake of underestimating him. But he also had the sense of humour of an overgrown schoolboy and loved a good prank. When he found out that the civilian administration manager lived next to the station where we were based, the opportunity for a wind-up was too much to resist. He took pictures of the guy's underwear hanging on the washing line with a long-lens camera then sent him them in the internal post. We'd play games like getting from one side of the office to the other without touching the floor. I remember on one occasion Baz was on his hands and knees on top of a filing cabinet, I was on the windowsill and Alex was stood on a desk, when suddenly Brendan walked in the office. He opened the door, stepped out, shut it, then opened it and walked back in again, shouting, 'Oh, I fucking did just see that, didn't I? Baz, in my fucking office now.' We all just roared with laughter. Baz was meant to be in charge of us, but he was always the instigator of mischief. It got to a point where the superintendent of the division called Brendan in and gave an order that we were to stop referring to him as Crazy Baz as it was bad for public perception. So we rechristened him 'Sane' Baz. Needless to say, the superintendent didn't see the funny side.

We'd all have a pint together and even went on holidays with our other halves. They were a great bunch of lads and I loved working with them. Every time we went through a door we had the feeling that no one would get the better of us, and that was largely down to the camaraderie we enjoyed.

My commitment to the police changed overnight. I was really starting to relish the challenge. It was in the covert world I'd found my calling. Applying my mind to complicated operations – the creative planning, the execution, the risk management – was my forte; the more complex the job, the more I excelled.

Looking back now, this is where my selfish streak really kicked in, my singled-minded bullishness to see a job through at every cost. If I was onto something, my personal life would have to take a back seat. If I needed to be in overnight and my missus had a restaurant booked or wanted to go to the pictures, she'd be disappointed. Brendan would tell me to go out and get him the most dangerous fucker on his radar, and I'd be like a bloodhound. The truth is, I was more committed to the job than my home life. There's commitment and there's overcommitment. This was overcommitment. Did I know it? Deep down, probably. But I had found something I loved doing and was good at. Sometimes police work can be dangerously addictive. It's little wonder the divorce rate among cops is through the roof.

My job was to gather evidence and build up intelligence on organised crime groups – or OCGs as you'll hear them called in every episode of *Line of Duty*. There were different levels of criminals in Tameside at that time. You had young 16-year-old lads kicking doors in for car keys, or doing shitty armed robberies then clubbing together to buy a bit of gear. Then you'd have your more established organised criminals who'd be involved in drug supply, car ringing or nightclub security. We used to assess their threat by a method then very much in its infancy but one commonly used by police forces across the country now.

It's known as organised crime group mapping and works through a scoring system. Scores are determined by factors like access to firearms or financial capabilities. Intelligence teams will ask questions like, *Can they get hold of guns? If so, what kind? Are they buying 100-year-old Webley revolvers that need reactivating, or have they got access to military-grade hardware? Are they living hand to mouth dealing drugs out of a terraced house, one week living like a rock star, the next kicking a door in for a two-bit telly? Or have they got millions of pounds behind them?* And perhaps the most significant factor would be their special knowledge. They might have someone in their group, for example, who is ex-military and understands how weapons or explosives work and is adept in the use of tactics. The higher an OCG scores on the risk matrix, the more likely it is to be on the radar of law enforcement and the more resources are required to tackle it.

A typically top-scoring OCG would be a drug-importation outfit with international contacts and a structured hierarchy, with the potential to call on associates with specialist skills. One that commits serious pre-planned violence; can access high-grade weaponry; has significant financial resources, money-laundering capability and transport infrastructure; and can even corrupt officials. That kind of OCG would be scoring off the charts and would likely be dealt with by the National Crime Agency or regional Organised Crime Units, not a local force, though there are exceptions to the rule.

But all of that doesn't necessarily mean OCGs are the hardest to catch or pose the biggest threat to the public. In reality, some more chaotic groups or street gangs who use firearms over petty disputes can represent the bigger, more pressing and dangerous challenge to police. The label 'organised crime group' often makes many gangs sound much grander than they actually are. An OCG could be a gang of teenage lads nicking cars or doing burglaries for televisions. If they've got some form of structure and they're working together to commit crime, they can be tagged with the fearsome-sounding label when in fact a more fitting description would be 'disorganised crime group'.

During my time in the Organised Crime Unit, one up-and-coming OCG grabbed my attention. It was a small-time crew but I could see straight away that it had the potential to be a serious criminal gang. Most of them were in their late teens or early twenties and were violent and unpredictable.

They all had close-cropped hair, wore tracksuits and came from the east Manchester shitholes that bordered Tameside. They were on the periphery of drug dealing, but burglaries were their thing: raids for car keys, plasma tellies (all the rage then at a grand a go), jewellery, gaming consoles – whatever they could get their grubby little mitts on. They were feral and they were brazen, sometimes kicking in doors balaclava'd up in broad daylight, and ready and willing to use violence if challenged by innocent homeowners.

Alex and I were given the lead and set up a dedicated operation to tackle them. We made ourselves experts on this crew. We needed to know everything about them: which gym they went to, where their families lived, who their girlfriends were, which cars they drove, where they hung around, their associates, their rivals. We needed to understand their MO. We carried out surveillance, setting up observation posts, watching their every move. We'd stop and search them, raid their houses, nick them for not paying fines or for carrying a bit of weed. It was about disrupting their behaviour, swarming all over them and limiting their opportunities to commit crime. We wanted them to know that we were onto them. It was about saying to them, 'We are fucking looking at you.' It was about putting them in such a paranoid state that they didn't know where we had come from or why, while all the time piecing together evidence of their wider criminal conspiracy to burgle and rob. And we had some successes, arresting different members of the group and putting them

47

away. But the primary objective was proving a much more difficult task due to a lack of specialist resources and competing priorities. They were far from the only organised crime group operating on our patch. That said, they'd been left in no doubt who Alex and I were, and that we'd have no problem going toe to toe with them.

We'd dedicated months to looking at this crew, but there were other criminal groups that needed our attention, and so we started to get pulled away. But we were under no illusions as to their threat and what could potentially happen if they weren't dealt with. I'd watched them grow in confidence and capability, and I'd seen their reputation on the streets flourish. I'd seen how they'd influenced other active criminals in their age group. I was in no doubt that there was a hardcore nucleus who would go on to offend well into their adult lives and align themselves with known criminal families in the area.

'We need to tackle this crew,' I said to my boss. It wasn't the first time I'd said it. 'Because they're fucking busy. And if we don't tackle them now and put them away for all these burglaries, they will grow. They will grow and they will expand their drug dealing and they will move on to bigger things.' And that's exactly what happened.

One member of the crew stood out, someone who was at the heart of the chaos and carving out a name for himself. In many ways, he was the odd one out. He didn't come from a shithole estate but a detached house with a respectable family in the

Tameside suburbs. His criminality wasn't driven by growing up in poverty and deprivation. Far from it.

I had no idea at the time, but he and I would pursue our chosen careers on almost parallel paths, hurtling towards each other on a collision course that would end in the most devastating fashion. His name was Dale Cregan.

CHAPTER 4
THE TEST

Nothing was flash about the venue – just a big hall in the police training centre. I was running a bit late and was one of the last of a 200-strong crowd of hopefuls, all stood looking at a tough-looking man with a shaved head on the front stage and listening to him intently.

He didn't strike me as a cop – more like some of the serious villains I remembered from growing up. In fact, he looked a bit like an older version of me – powerfully built, head to toe in designer gear. He had a strong Manchester accent and was clear, confident and assured. He struck me as someone who knew his way around the streets. As his voice echoed around the hall, he had my attention straight away. He and another guy, who looked much more clean-cut and cop-like, outlined the selection procedure, making it clear that most of the room would not pass or even get near the final undercover course, before he opened the floor to questions.

One bloke sat next to a woman in the front row raised his hand. The question went something like, 'We're a married couple. Wouldn't it be great if you could have a married couple working undercover together?'

Fucking idiots, I thought to myself.

The response from the selector with the shaved head was resounding and delivered with a look of contempt: 'No. Next question.' I liked him. He was straight to the point and clearly did not suffer fools.

Back at my office the next day, I asked my pal who the fella at the front of the stage was.

'That will be Christie,' he said. 'He's a fucking legend, mate, the guru of the undercover world.' Despite the mystique that surrounded the undercover world, I still wasn't that bothered about putting myself up for the gig. Interested, yes, but bowled over? Not quite. The selection process detailed at the presentation was lengthy and laborious. The chances of making the grade were incredibly slim. In fact, roughly for every hundred people who applied, only one would become a Level 1 UC. Despite my overriding feeling that putting in an application would be a complete waste of time, I submitted one just to see how I fared. A few weeks later an email dropped in my inbox saying I had been successful and was invited to an initial assessment for Level 1 undercover selection.

Level 1 operatives perform deep, usually long-term infiltrations into top-tier organised crime gangs or terrorist groups, and deployments are often dangerous and psychologically challenging. The selection procedure is purposely designed to be stringent and ruthless to weed out the dreamers, the fantasists and those that don't have the mental agility and robustness to thrive under the pressure that comes with the job. Less than 1 per cent of all police officers will ever become a Level 1 UC, and the vast majority of those that pass the selection will never even be used – or if they are, it will typically be in a bit-part supporting role. Only a chosen few go on to be deployed as the primary operative on live operations. It's a very select club.

I'd been a cop for around three years and was barely out of my probationary period. My career was already on fast forward since I'd been drafted into the Organised Crime Unit, and here I was with a golden opportunity to land one of the most coveted, most respected, not to mention down-right dangerous, roles in the police. It was fairly unheard of for a cop to be in this position so early in his service. Throughout my life, whether it was in the army or the police, it took something extreme to switch me on. The harder the challenge, the more my brain would fire up. The 1 per cent pass rate was like a gauntlet being thrown down for me. This was now more than just a passing interest.

Sedgley Park, a former convent on a sprawling Victorian estate, was where GMP carried out their residential training. Old red-brick townhouses had been converted into digs, and there was a memorial garden to officers who'd died in the line of duty. About ten of us gathered at 5pm in a classroom in the revamped glass-paned conference centre; the pool of applicants had been divided into small groups for this next step of the selection process. Greg, a detective sergeant in Greater Manchester Police's elite Level 1 undercover unit, told each candidate they were to complete a task then leave the site immediately. I recognised him as the guy onstage with Christie. After a two-hour wait, I was the last to be called and briefed by Greg.

'The police have received information that someone has been trying to sell a high-value stolen watch via an ad in the paper. Your objective is to make contact via the phone with the seller and arrange a meet. Once you've done that you'll go to a room, which for the purposes of this exercise is the address you are given. You'll knock and if invited in you'll enter. It has a two-way mirror. People will be standing behind that mirror and observing you. Your job is simply to buy the watch.'

Simple, I thought. *I could send me nan to do that.*

I made the call and walked into the room, where I was met by two blokes sitting around a desk. One of them was Christie. A calmness washed over me. *It's only make-believe. I'm hardly gonna get my head chopped off.* Then they hit me with a barrage of questions, bang bang bang.

'Where are you from?'

'Where do you live?'

'Who do you know?'

'What car do you drive?'

'Are you Old Bill?'

I soaked it up, answering each one without actually telling them anything. I even had them laughing. They stepped up the interrogation, but their attempts to fluster me fell flat. It got to the point where I thought, *This is bollocks. Would I stand here letting two clowns interrogate me over a fucking watch in real life? Would I fuck.* I changed tack and told them straight.

'Listen, fucking sell me the watch or don't sell me the watch. It's a fucking watch, I'm not that arsed. You're asking a lot of nosey questions over a fucking watch and I'm not wasting my time here anymore.'

Forty-five minutes we were in there for. The other candidates were out in no more than ten. In the end I gave them one last chance to sell it me.

'We're not fucking selling you it,' Christie said, now firmly in the role of a slightly irate crook. 'You stink of Old Bill. Fuck off.'

Afterwards, Greg, who had watched the exchange through the two-way glass with others, debriefed me and asked me how I thought I'd done.

'Not very well,' I replied.

'What makes you say that?'

'Well, I didn't buy the fucking watch, did I? And every other fucker was in and out in ten minutes. I was in there for three-quarters of an hour. And—'

He stopped me in my tracks.

'I'm going to let you in on a secret, Shay. Nobody in the history of mankind has ever bought that watch or will ever buy that watch. I've just had a debrief with the officers in there and they both said to me the same thing: you are an absolute fucking nightmare . . . but in a good way. They've got over thirty years' undercover experience between them and they both said you were a very difficult person to read. You never showed any signs of stress, you were funny. You had an answer for everything, but you never actually told them a thing about yourself or got caught in a lie. Yet it didn't feel that you weren't being honest, and you had the balls to walk away from the deal. It's very early days and we wouldn't normally say this at such an early stage, but one of the officers said you were potentially the most naturally gifted officer he'd seen do this exercise in ten years of running it.'

After passing the role-play phase, I had to undergo a battery of tests over the coming months: intelligence, psychometric, psychiatric, psychological. If it started with 'psych' I was doing it. I think part of it was just to make sure I hadn't tortured small animals as a kid, but in the main it was to see if I was equipped for the stresses and strains of Level 1 undercover work; that I possessed the integrity, mental dexterity, resourcefulness, intelligence and judgement to go it alone against some of the most dangerous criminals out there. I passed them all with flying colours. In fact, the psychometric and intelligence tests surprisingly revealed that my IQ was off the charts for a kid who'd left school with nothing.

The test stages whittled down the 200 that had attended the initial briefing day, and that was just at GMP. This was a process also being carried out nationally – there must have been between 300 and 400 candidates battling it out to get to the final stages. Only two forces in the country were accredited to deliver the national Level 1 undercover course at the time: GMP and the Metropolitan Police, who both ran one course a year. Needless to say, competition was fierce.

Between the tests I was still enjoying work at the Organised Crime Unit, and one day I got a phone call on my job phone. It was Christie.

'I've asked to be your mentor through this process. I want to mentor you.' It was something of a privilege he had chosen to train me. I'd found out a lot more about the mysterious Christie since that first day, and he was held in high regard. Even though he was a detective constable, high-ranking officers were in awe of him and some of the operations he had pulled off. His skill as an undercover operative was legendary in the covert world. Cops would tell me they were his pal, and as I got to know him, I would say to him, 'Oh, I know such and such, your mate,' and he would reply, 'Shay, I've never fucking heard of him.'

We started to build a relationship. He'd pick me up in his fancy Jeep and take me to the boozer for a pint. Or we'd go to a smoky snooker club and shoot a few frames. All the while he'd be giving me a glimpse of the undercover world. He'd tell me how it was all mind games, about creating an aura and a credible persona, and he'd stress the importance of thinking three steps ahead.

Christie was a war veteran from the Parachute Regiment who had seen heavy-duty close-quarter combat and had been awarded an OBE for his services to undercover policing. Obviously I'd never been on the Queen's honours list, but there were clearly similarities between us. We were both former combat soldiers who'd grown up on rough Manchester council estates and had family members on the other side of the fence, so to speak. He cut an imposing figure with his shaved head and a face that reminded me of the boxer Barry McGuigan. Christie's hard-knock looks accentuated his confident and assured demeanour. He was a very funny man with a sharp wit, but beneath the surface was a razor-sharp mind. I'm not ashamed to say I was in awe of him. All those mixed emotions – that inner turmoil I'd felt deciding whether I should join the police, that feeling of not fitting in – he'd been through the same. *And look where he is now,* I thought. *Look at the respect he commands.* He was the heavyweight champion of the undercover world, and I wanted his belt.

It became all-consuming. I wasn't bowled over at first; now, I'd been knocked out of the park. The OCU suddenly started to feel a league or two below undercover operations. As soon as I'd been shown this secret world, I wanted in. After the mentoring period ended, I was informed I had passed the second selection phase and was invited to the two-week national residential undercover course.

This was the big one, the final hurdle. Only four cops from the hundreds that had stood in that hall some eight months before made it there. When I say 'course', I don't mean a training exercise. This was me being taken under the microscope and asked, 'Do you have what it takes to be an undercover cop? Are you robust enough? Are you sharp enough? Can you think creatively while manipulating everyone around you without them suspecting a thing? Can you think straight with your head up your arse, on little or no sleep? Can you think on your feet under the most intense pressure?' And not the pressure of hitting a deadline in a nine to five; I'm talking the pressure of knowing that if you fuck it up, you might end up seriously hurt, or worse. Life-or-death pressure. That's the level you are playing at as a Level 1 undercover cop.

The final course would be residential and at Sedgley Park. We were told we wouldn't be going home and we'd be working long hours. The induction was on a Sunday night and there were eight of us – four from GMP and four from other forces – sat in a semi-circle facing the stage in the large Victorian hall. Everyone was upbeat. We'd made it here from hundreds of wannabes, and that was a huge achievement in itself. *Fucking hell, I've done alright here,* I thought, proud as punch. Then Christie, the lead instructor, burst the balloon.

'This is the most intensive course in UK policing. Don't think just because you're here you're going to be undercover cops,' he snarled. 'Level 1 undercover is the most dangerous job you will do. Most of you will fail this course, and be under no illusion – if you are not up to scratch, we have absolutely no qualms in failing everybody.'

We sat silently, hanging on his every word.

'Everything you do – you are being assessed. Whether you're on a role play or whether you're in the canteen eating your cheese butties, you are being watched. You are being watched 24/7. And don't expect much sleep. One other thing . . . this is a secret course. Under no circumstances are you to tell other people what you are doing.'

I knew then this was not going to be handed to me. I would have to work for it. It switched me on. I had an inner discipline from my time in the military, and I would need every last drop of it.

The first role-play scenario saw us tasked with going to a sting shop to buy a gun. An experienced UC, posing as the seller, unwrapped a brown bag to reveal the firearm, and our job was to secure a deal for the weapon, unaware that the bag would be swapped for one containing a spanner and a piece of wood. It was designed to mess with our heads, to show that walking away from a deal was sometimes the best option. And it was to see if we could bounce back from failure, because virtually everyone handed over cash for the bag. There were other exercises, like going up to a stranger in a train station to elicit information such as their name, job and where they were going, and carrying out reconnaissance in various locations.

We needed to know the illicit-goods market inside out: the going rate for drugs from kilos to grams and all the different names for heroin and cocaine from 'Bobby' (Brown) to 'beak'.

And we learned how to burn smack, turn coke into crack and build a crack pipe. We needed to be au fait with firearms and know, for example, how much a 9mm pistol would go for on the streets of Manchester, Liverpool or London. If you pay over the odds for a gun or a ki' of coke while undercover, you are finished. You have lost your credibility on the street and the job is over – and maybe even your life. As dramatic as it sounds, these are the margins, and it was impressed upon us in no uncertain terms time and time again during the process.

The pace was relentless, the sleep deprivation designed to break down our tolerance, cognitive thinking and concentration. In the opening week to the halfway point, the numbers dwindled, some leaving because they couldn't hack it, others simply told they weren't cutting the mustard. We were doing 20-hour days, and just when we thought we could let our foot off the gas and relax, they'd spring something on us. After one particularly gruelling day, the bosses told us to stop and take a breather.

It was around 9pm and one of the instructors said, 'We've got a Domino's order in, and a load of beers. Get them down you and enjoy yourself.' It would be a 9am start in the morning, they said, which would be a luxury. A collective sigh of relief swept the room as the candidates reached for the cold cans of Carling and a steaming slice of pepperoni or ham and pineapple before proceeding to brown-nose the course directors.

As tempting as it was, I turned down the ale and opted for a Coke. I don't want to come across as some kind of goody two shoes here, but I just wasn't convinced the day was over. My mindset was *I'll get some kip – because you just never know.*

Hours later I was dead to the world in bed, probably dreaming about those cold beers I'd turned down, when a deafening thud jolted me out of my slumber. Bam bam bam bam. The door flew open, and in the orange glow of the street lights shining through the window, I could just make out three giant silhouettes moving swiftly towards me. 'Get outside now!' snapped the guy at the front, his voice muffled by the dark balaclava that covered his face. 'Don't speak. Grab some clothes and get outside. Make sure you've got no fucking money on you, no phone, no watch. Nothing.'

I was startled but I'd felt something like this was coming. *I fucking knew it!* I thought. *They're on us 24/7. There's no way they'd give us the night off.* They were always watching, never letting us out of their sights. Never in my life had I been so glad that I hadn't had a beer. One in the morning and this was the onslaught. Two brick shithouses frog-marched me down the stairs and out into the dimly lit street where a white van was parked. It felt like at any minute a hood would go over my head, the lights would go out and I'd be kidnapped and waterboarded to within an inch of my life. The lack of sleep the previous week was doing its job and my heart was pumping. Shivering, I dared to breathe, sending a misty cloud into the night sky.

By this point we'd had something like eight days straight of sleep deprivation. It would have been easy to throw the towel in. It would have been easy to have said, 'Fuck this,' climbed back into my comfy bed and withdrawn from the process the next morning. And in that moment, freezing my balls off at daft o'clock in the morning, the thought did go through my mind. But the truth is, I wouldn't have been able to look myself in the mirror. And I wouldn't have been able to look Christie in the eye. So I quickly put that doubt to the side and braced myself for the task ahead.

'Fucking listen here. Here's a pound. You'll be taken to a location and then you'll have to find a phone box to ring this number.' He handed over the note, but before I had the time to read it, the back doors of the van opened and I was unceremoniously bundled into the darkness head first. I lay in the van in silence, trying to judge time and equate it to distance, and after what I estimated to be about an hour we stopped moving and the engine fell silent. Then two doors opened and a crunching sound got louder. *Where the fuck am I?* I thought, trying to muster up the mental strength to deal with what was to come. The back doors opened and two men in balaclavas lunged in and threw me to the freezing floor before getting back into the van and speeding off. I'd been dumped on a country lane surrounded by fields blanketed by a sea of white as falling flakes peppered my face. The icy cold stung my fingers, and I reached into my pocket for the crumpled paper before trudging across the snow, looking for any sign of life. Then the whirr of an electric engine and clink-clank of bottles stopped me in my tracks. The milkman! I pulled him over.

'Where are we, mate? Been kicked out by some bird I got with last night and I need to get home.'

'You're about three miles from Prestatyn,' he said with a faint Welsh twang.

Fucking great, I thought. *Silly o'clock in the morning, I'm freezing my balls off and in fucking Wales with a quid to my name.*

'Any idea where I'll find a phone box?'

I started to run to keep warm and cover distance, and an hour or so later, as the snow started to melt in the early-morning sun, I got to Rhyl and rang the number. An annoying voice on the end of the blower barked a list of tasks at me. The order went something like: 'You need to get a quote for a flat, some drug-injecting needles, and your picture taken with a celebrity.' There was other stuff on the ridiculous checklist, but I can't remember what they were. 'Remember: surveillance officers have been deployed on this task so you may be under covert surveillance. And if you cross paths with any of the candidates, you are not to communicate with them. You are to put a call in at 2pm to this number.' And with that the phone went dead.

You are having a fucking laugh, aren't you, I thought. My muscles ached and my stomach growled for food, but I had no money to buy it. I borrowed a pen and a piece of card from a newsagent's, scribbled down a message and plonked myself on the steps outside the train station. 'Homeless ex-soldier. Please help,' it said. Safe to say the creative juices weren't flowing at their best at that point. But I did manage to get a few quid for a brekkie and started on the tasks.

As I tried to work my way through the joke of a list, I saw one of the other lads from the course going into a baker's and coming out with a bag full of goodies. I thought, *Fuck me, he must be doing well.* I used the local library toilet to splash my face with water. I'd been on my feet all day and the previous week's sleep deprivation was kicking in. As I was taking some time out, sat at one of the tables, a bloke came over and started talking to me. I instinctively went into infiltration mode and gave him an impromptu sob story, and he reached into his pocket to hand me some loose change. *Result.*

At 2pm I put the call in as requested and was told get back to Manchester or as close to it as possible. I had £11.40 in my pocket, not quite enough to get to Manchester Piccadilly, so I paid to as far as the fare would take me and hid in the train toilet the whole way. Tired and dejected, I put the call in once I hit Manchester city centre and was told intelligence had been received that a big drug deal was being discussed in Sam's Chop House. I was to get there and get descriptions for four men sat at the downstairs corner table but not approach them, then make my way to

Oldham Street, where a car whose registration I'd been given would be waiting to collect me. I did as directed and eventually made my pickup back to Sedgley Park, absolutely knackered.

Christie rounded us all up into the classroom and told us not to speak. He was raging. 'We told you undercover work is about integrity,' he fumed, slapping the palm of his hand with the back of his fingers. 'We fucking told you surveillance was watching you. If you fucking lie to us, you are gone. This is your last chance. If you've cheated on this exercise, put your hands up now and tell us. We know what you've all done. Now is the time to fess up if you've cheated on the task.'

The lad I spotted skipping out of the baker's stood up. 'I had £60 up me arse,' he said sheepishly. The cheek of it! Christie verbally annihilated him on the spot before taking apart one by one some of the others who confessed to minor misdemeanours. It turned out only two of us made it back to Manchester city centre – me and 60-quid-up-the-arse boy. I sincerely hoped it wasn't in pound coins.

You silly cunt, I thought. *Why tell them that? They don't know. They're playing with your mind.* He would pass the course but they never used him, and I can't help but think that was a pivotal moment; the confession was tantamount to admitting that he couldn't be trusted. He wasn't a bad lad to be fair. If I'd have thought to hide £60 up my arse, I would have.

More excruciating tests followed, more role plays. I had to meet an experienced MI5 undercover agent, who played the part of a major drug dealer looking to move some product. After the meeting I sat in the classroom awaiting my time to be unceremoniously ripped apart like the others before me. By now I was operating on instinct. The agent opened by saying that I had the gift of being confident without being arrogant, that I was convincing in the role and exuded a confidence that made him believe I could shift weight, as in move significant amounts of drugs. He said I was right where I needed to be. All the instructors looked at each other and Christie said, 'You've fucking paid him to say that.'

The final exercise lasted two days with no sleep. They threw everything at me, including hiding police documents in my car and ringing my UC phone the night that I was communicating with a target, saying it was a chief police officer and I was to confirm my name because my family were at risk. Every dirty trick they could throw, they threw. But I batted them all back. I was one step ahead every time. It was all clicking into place for me. I just got it. It was like I was born to do it.

'Endex', a military command short for 'end exercise', was called on the final task and the five of us left were summoned to the classroom and called into the office one by one. Facing me were Christie, Greg and two senior bosses.

'How do you think you did, Shay?' one of them said.

'I think I did enough to pass,' I said confidently.

'You did indeed,' said Greg. 'In fact, we had to make it harder on you because you were making the others look bad. The more we chucked at you, the better you got. Well done. You're now a Level 1 UC.'

Christie just gave me a nod and I went back to the classroom. Out of the hundreds that had turned up from different forces at the initial briefings, just three of us were left standing. Along with myself, the others to pass were a young female cop and 60-pound-up-the-bum guy.

Our success didn't guarantee us a Level 1 undercover deployment. Plenty of UCs pass the course but never even see a Level 1 job, they said. I was told to report back to my normal unit on the Monday, and if the call came then it came.

I was elated at passing the course. It was a massive achievement, but it was tainted by the prospect of never being called on. All I could think about was this exciting new world, the undercover world. I thought I'd found my calling in the Organised Crime Unit. Suddenly it seemed second rate.

A few days later I returned to the OCU to start a fresh week and the lads congratulated me on passing selection. I remember being in the office, thinking, *How long am I going to be here for? Will I ever get the call?* That afternoon Brendan called me into his office.

'Don't make yourself comfy, Shay,' he said as I sat down. 'Pack your shit up. The assistant chief constable has authorised your posting to covert operations, with immediate effect.'

Euphoria rushed through me. *Fucking yes!* And just like that, I was a Level 1 undercover operative. A member of Greater Manchester Police's elite covert operations unit – Omega.

CHAPTER 5
OMEGA

In the early nineties, Greater Manchester Police pioneered the use of undercover officers to infiltrate Manchester City's ultra-violent hooligan firm known as the Guvnors.

These cops were volunteers from tough frontline detective units, like the drugs squad, with little or no training, and the undercover tactic was very much in its infancy. The operation to take the Guvnors down was code-named Omega. It was a hugely successful infiltration and a shining example of how covert tactics and meticulous planning could be used to tackle organised criminal activity.

A senior DCI – a charismatic character called Henri Exton – saw it as a blueprint to combat not just football hooliganism but serious and organised crime. Due to the success of the operation, the Omega tag was adopted as the name of GMP's Level 1 undercover unit.

Omega's focus quickly shifted to fighting serious and organised crime, and the unit fast developed a reputation as a leading light in undercover policing. Its groundbreaking tactics were shared with forces not just regionally but on a national and global scale.

Christie was at the heart of the revolutionised thinking. Like me, he had been identified early in his career as someone with the raw ability to conduct UC operations. He then had the foresight to professionalise and redesign the selection and training procedures for the national Level 1 course. He recognised that the best people to talk about criminals and crime weren't always the police, who had taken the lead in training in the past, but the crooks themselves. He sourced knowledge of crime trends from convicted dealers and robbers and police informants, as well as scientists, shrinks and soldiers. He gleaned information and insight and applied it to the training.

He also demanded that all students attending UC selection have an encyclopaedic knowledge of the law relating to covert operations, and a grasp of criminal commodities better than that of any drug dealer or thief. And most importantly, he demanded that every student had the ability to talk like and portray themselves as authentic criminals.

Murderers, drug dealers, paedophiles, gangsters, terrorists and other assorted criminals have been sent to jail for hundreds of years thanks to the lawfully audacious and courageous actions of the UCs that have passed through Manchester's Covert Operations department.

Many tried to get through Christie's demanding UC selection process, and the majority failed. There was no disgrace in that. Failing did not mean that you were a bad cop; it just meant that you did not have the required skills, abilities and demeanour to portray yourself as a serious villain or the ability to exist safely in a criminal environment 24/7.

I was one of the few who made the grade. On my very first morning back at my day job, once I was told I was being posted to Omega, Dessie, the DCI who had placed me in the Organised Crime Unit, summoned me to his office one last time. He wished me good luck and told me exciting times lay ahead. It felt like a symbolic moment, like he was saying, 'I knew you had it in you.'

On day one at Omega, I wasn't told to report to their covert base but to meet Christie outside the Apollo Theatre in Ardwick, a run-down inner-city part of south Manchester, at 10am sharp. Arriving purposely early and still in selection mode, I took a spot where I could see Christie approaching but one from where he could not see me. But who was I kidding? Knowing Christie, he was probably there half an hour before, watching me. Then, to my surprise, the female cop who had passed selection at the same time as me turned up. She had also been given the green light to be posted to Covert Operations. We had developed a good rapport on the course and she was a very capable operator. I was glad she had been posted at the same time because it meant I would immediately have an ally in the unit.

Christie arrived and took us for a brew, and we quietly chatted about the course and what lay ahead for us. He dropped the lead instructor act and was humorous and in

71

good form, answering all our questions about who and what to expect at the unit.

Aside from the supervisory structure, there were a couple of highly vetted admin ladies, a team of cover officers and, at the time, four full-time undercovers, who were deployed on operations all over the UK and in some cases in Europe.

As the day drew to a close, we were told to report to the unit's HQ the following day, and as my fellow new recruit walked away, Christie called me back for a quick word.

'Listen, Shay, training isn't over. We've just opened the door. You pissed the course. I threw everything at you and you saw it coming. When you came to that very first initial selection role play, I knew then you had what it took. I felt like Cus D'Amato seeing a young Mike Tyson for the first time, or the football scout that first saw Wayne Rooney kick a ball. So I'm going to give you everything I know and at times I'm going to be fucking hard on you, but only because I think you can be the fucking best at this – better than me.'

Just a few years earlier, I was at a crossroads, feeling lost after leaving the military and my dad's suicide. The script written for me said I should have been stuck in a dead-end job or doing time, and here I was being told by the number-one undercover cop in the country that I could be better than him and that he wanted to invest his knowledge and experience in me. I'm not given to strong bouts of emotion, but inside it was a proud moment. And I'm not going to lie, it made me feel important.

Over the coming months I spent every day with Christie, and we developed a close bond that remains to this day. He is the man that spotted my potential, took it, nurtured it and invested his time in me. He saw past the street-kid thuggish looks and Manc accent. He saw that my brain was agile and sharp, that I was shrewd and measured in the way I went about my business, and that this – disguised by the front I let the rest of the world see – would be my biggest asset. And he knew this because it was like looking in a mirror at his younger self. He saw in me the same spark that had set him apart from others.

My inauguration was like my very own version of *Training Day*, the Denzel Washington movie where he plays the veteran street cop taking the rookie under his wing. Denzel's quote in the movie to his protégé – 'It takes a wolf to catch a wolf' – resonated strongly through what Christie was showing me.

In the first few months, we travelled the UK and paired up on my first undercover job, with him playing my uncle to snare a bent cop. He challenged me every day, sometimes delivering brutal feedback, no doubt designed to make me try harder and bounce back. Nothing this man did or said was without purpose, and that is exactly what he was instilling in me.

He opened my eyes to the undercover world and made me see that everyone represented a potential opportunity; that any situation, no matter how dire it may seem, could be flipped on its head and turned to my advantage; that every word that spilled out of my mouth needed to have meaning; that my brain needed to be like a supercomputer, quickly processing information and retaining it for use whenever needed – like some kind of ace card. And he taught me to always be at least one step ahead of absolutely everyone, and that plan A never survives contact with the enemy, so always be ready to improvise, adapt and overcome.

It was a steep learning curve; the man was a master of the art. I got to know the others in the unit and felt like I fitted in, but due to the nature of the work, the operatives were hardly ever together. Still, I was getting involved in some live operations and was thoroughly enjoying being part of this secret world.

Being a Level 1 undercover cop is so far removed from being a normal police officer. It was like being in another world at Omega. It was alluring and exciting. But early on I spotted there was also a dark side to the unit. There were massive egos at play, there were cliques, and supervisors, covers and UCs who didn't get along through personal and operational issues. It was hard to know who to trust. The office politics were divisive. I soon realised that the more serious a police unit's remit in tackling crime, the bigger the egos and agendas. I tried not to involve myself. I was the new boy – none of it was my fight.

I would later find myself well and truly on the receiving end of the egos and politics that surrounded this world. But all I wanted at that moment was to be challenged operationally and kept busy. Keeping my mind engaged and put to good use was vital. The phrase 'The devil makes work for idle hands' could well have been coined for me.

CHAPTER 6
THE MOSS

The high-rise flats towered into the Salford sky. Beneath them, an empty patch of wasteland, its surrounding walls daubed with gang graffiti. In the daytime, it was an unofficial car park. On a misty November night, it was the perfect setting for an underworld meet. The rolling tyres of a black Range Rover crunched the loose stone as it crawled towards a parked white Ford Transit, barely working floodlights reflecting off its Irish plates. A police surveillance team sat in the shadows, ready to strike.

'Do I need anything?' asked the passenger in the Transit van as he shot another glance in his mirror.

'No, trust me. It'll be right,' the driver snapped back. 'Don't make a move unless I make a move. If it goes off, pile in, but until then don't make a fucking move, just watch my back.'

The driver reached for the side-door pocket for a screwdriver and quickly shoved it down the back of his jeans, making sure the passenger had clocked it. The door of the Range Rover opened and out climbed a middle-aged man with a thick neck and a bullet head, his huge shoulders hugging a crisp white shirt. The guy in the van stepped out and the pair walked towards each other. There were no pleasant-ries, just a handshake. Then the man in the white shirt handed over a brown envelope. The deal was done – but the threat hadn't gone away. There was still every chance it could go horribly wrong. The man at the wheel of the van put his keys in the ignition and calmly drove away. That was the cue for the covert police radio in the surveillance car to burst into life.

'That's tango one complete – back into the Transit with tango two in the passenger seat and off, off, off towards the bypass at normal road speed.'

Tango two was one of Manchester's most dangerous and active gang members. Tango one was me.

Why was I there? What was in the brown envelope? Let me take you back a year to where it all started, a place that had been hitting the headlines for all the wrong reasons.

There's a vibrancy about Moss Side. You can find it in the smell of barbecued jerk chicken wafting from Caribbean cafes on summer nights. Or in the beat of hip-hop, reggae and R 'n' B tunes from parked cars at impromptu street gatherings. You can find it in the deafening din of steel drums at the annual carnival at Alexandra Park. Or in the many decent, hard-working people who care deeply about the community. There is, however, also a dark side, which brings at times a palpable tension that can make the place feel almost electric.

In the late nineties and early noughties, this inner-city neighbourhood in south Manchester was home to some of the most terrifying gang violence this country has ever seen. Drug-dealing gangsters with ready access to firearms who would not have looked out of place in *The Wire*. Tit-for-tat shootings. Young men being murdered in the street. That's what the police had been up against for over two decades.

Trouble first flared in the eighties between the notorious Gooch and Doddington gangs – made up of a mixture of second-generation West Indian and white lads that had grown up on the mean streets of Moss Side, or 'the Moss' as it was known. By the nineties what had started off as fights on the street had escalated into full-blown gang warfare – not just over the lucrative drug market but also matters of respect and reputation. It was a wave of bloodshed that would rob the families of 14-year-old Benji Stanley and 15-year-old Jessie James of their sons – who were not linked to any gangs – as well as countless others.

Leading the onslaught were two of Britain's most dangerous gangland bosses. Colin 'Piggy' Joyce and Lee 'Cabo' Amos were childhood pals who became self-styled 'blood brothers' and generals of the formidable Gooch Gang. They'd earned their reputations as enforcers and killers before taking the reins. Joyce and Amos were among the most feared gangsters in the country, and their crime empire was behind a string of murders, scores of shootings and continuous turf wars in Manchester. This was a mob so self-confident, so brazen, that its trigger-happy thugs raided a sports hall with a sub-machine gun when community police officers were giving a talk in the room next door. They thought they were untouchable. And for a while they were.

But in April 2009, Amos and Joyce's reign of terror ended when they were jailed for life at one of Britain's biggest-ever gang trials. After a long-running battle with rivals from the Doddington clan, the pair and nine of their crew were found guilty of the 2007 drive-by murder of a mourner at the funeral of a man Joyce had executed weeks earlier. 'You were all involved in activity reminiscent of Al Capone and Chicago in the era of Prohibition,' the judge declared as he handed down almost 200 years for the kingpins and their gang. 'Manchester is not the Wild West, but many of you treated its streets as if it were.'

Joyce, Amos and their crew were huge scalps. Manchester's most wanted were behind bars, and the number of shootings quickly dropped after their convictions. But Moss Side's gang culture was changing.

The area had seen an influx of immigrants who had fled war-torn countries like Somalia and Libya to seek pastures new. Many of them formed gangs that aligned themselves with the established Gooch and Doddington outfits. The gang scene was evolving, and the police had to evolve with it. This meant deploying innovative tactics to get on the front foot with an intelligence-led approach. Reliable intel is hard to come by in tough areas blighted by gang crime – no one wants to be labelled a grass – so detectives had to be every bit as daring as the criminals themselves while making sure they didn't cross the line. They had to be lawfully audacious.

The community had suffered enough. There could be no repeat of the catalogue of gun violence that had brought Manchester to its knees. After discussions at the highest level, it was decided there was only one option left: to go in undercover.

That meant a Level 1 infiltration, something that had never been done in Moss Side before. Omega needed an operative smart, cunning and brave enough to go deep cover in an area where any given day could end in murder. Finding one was another story. The Moss was the hot potato of the country's Level 1 undercover network, the job that no one wanted. When police are operating covertly or undercover in a particular area, then that area is known as 'the plot'; Moss Side was seen as one of the toughest in the UK.

Police in undercover operations sometimes have the option to use covert human intelligence sources – commonly known as informants – to vouch for UCs to criminal contacts because it can give them instant credibility. There could be no such luxury for the undercover agent going into Moss Side. If a gang member or serious criminal had any inkling they were being set up by a registered police informant, then the consequences could be catastrophic – for both the informant and the undercover agent. The fact is, the best informants are usually well connected in the criminal world – they are not your average community-spirited member of the public – and so by their very nature can be duplicitous and driven by their own agenda. This presents real operational difficulties; the identities of Level 1 undercover officers and the operations they undertake are the police's most closely guarded secrets.

It therefore had to be a cold infiltration, a complex and painstaking task. The UC selected for the job would have to make any criminal contacts from scratch using only their wits and guile. Not only that, any relations would have to be forged in a way that didn't put the public at risk.

For example, Janet and John – two normal, hard-working, decent people who have nothing to do with criminality – take a shine to the undercover operative in his role as a criminal in the local pub. That operative must do his utmost to keep his distance. If he doesn't, then there's every chance that further down the line, their safety would be compromised. It's what's known as collateral intrusion, and it represents a major challenge to Level 1 infiltrations. Dealing with 'straight-goers', as they are known in Manchester's criminal parlance, and keeping them out of the firing line for their own good, can often be more difficult for the UC than dealing with the villains themselves.

Then there's a raft of legislation and guidelines – like RIPA, the Regulation of Investigatory Powers Act, and PACE, the Police and Criminal Evidence Act – that all undercover officers must adhere to. It isn't just a case of looking, sounding and acting like a serious villain. It is much more complex than that.

Unbeknown to me, Omega had been looking to fill the position for some time and had been quietly approaching specialist units in the tight-knit undercover network that exists across the country. The response was emphatic: 'Fuck that – too dangerous.' 'Not a chance.' 'Risk too high.' No UCs or senior police officers worth their salt or who valued their pension wanted anything to do with it. It was seen as a poisoned chalice.

There was also conflict as to what the profile of the undercover operative had to be. Senior management within Omega thought it had to be the job of a Black operative because the majority of active gang members in the area were historically of West Indian descent. They met a couple of Black operators, but it was felt they didn't have the presence or right demeanour. Then they looked to other forces in the country, to places like Newcastle. But a Geordie going undercover in Moss Side – the villains would see right through it.

One day, the management and Christie called me into the Omega HQ. We didn't operate out of police stations when undercover. Instead the office was a nondescript unit in an industrial park in the north-west of England. It was presented as a bland and uninteresting business. In reality, it was where top-secret, covert operations were being drawn up.

I walked in and the boss, Christie and a detective sergeant were sat around a desk drinking tea and eating digestive biscuits. The mood was relaxed – it was one of the things I liked about the undercover world: no bullshit police formalities and unnecessary paperwork. No UC would ever be called into the office just for a tea or coffee and a chinwag. I knew there was going to be a deployment on the table. I remember thinking, *Where's it going be? Am I even going to be in the UK?* As a Level 1 UC, I was now a national asset and could be deployed domestically or internationally for any partner law enforcement agency. I needed to be on a live operation, using my skills. If you're a top-flight footballer or professional boxer, you need game time or fights in the ring or you go rusty. Being a UC was no different.

'Sit down, Shay. What do you know about Moss Side?' said the boss, a seasoned detective inspector built like a brick shithouse and hardened to the ways of the street, having spent the bulk of his career taking down major drugs gangs. I gave it a professional appraisal.

'I know that for years it's been plagued by serious gang and gun violence. I know there's numerous unsolved murders. I know that there are some very dangerous criminals operating there with access to firearms who aren't afraid to use them.'

What I was really thinking was *This isn't a conversation about Moss Side over tea and biscuits. There's a fuckin' job on here.*

'Are you compromised down there?'

I paused for a moment and thought about it. *Moss Side. Infiltrating Moss Side. This is a fucking serious job. I've not been in the unit that long.* But there was a sobering reality to my situation. *I've grown up just across the city from Moss Side. I've been on the fuckin' beat less than six miles away in Tameside. I live with my girlfriend less than nine miles away. And you fuckers all know this!*

Clearly I was compromised. I was also extremely driven, single-minded and, if truth be told, incredibly selfish. My response was decisive.

'No, I wouldn't say I'm compromised.'

'Good. Because we've been looking up and down the country and we don't feel we can identify anyone that fits the bill. We just haven't been able to find anyone we think could pull it off. But we've been speaking and we think there's an answer much closer to home. You've impressed a lot of people. And we feel that if anyone can do this job, it's you. So how would you feel about that? Would you be up for it?'

Clearly it was fucking madness. I was astonished they thought it was a good idea. Thankfully the rules have since been changed to stop this from happening to other undercover operatives. But my thinking at the time was *Fuck it, no one achieves anything without taking a risk.* It was drawing me in – the magnitude of the challenge that this operation would involve. This would be a chance to show just what I could do. I lived for these opportunities.

I sat there thinking, *I'm in my twenties. I'm in the best shape of my life. I've just flown the selection process.* Call it arrogant, call it driven. Call it what you want. But the truth is I had an unshakable belief in my own abilities and I genuinely felt there wasn't a situation I couldn't handle or didn't know how to walk out of at any given moment. *The opportunity to infiltrate the gangsters in Moss Side. This is exactly the type of challenge I crave. As far as I'm concerned, give me the fucking hardest jobs you've got.*

Of course there were pitfalls. Of course I was fucking compromised. And I knew deep down that there would be huge consequences for the people in my life. Yet the selfish part of me said, *Fuck the consequences.* That was my mentality at the time. I was a selfish bastard but I was driven and I craved the challenge. I was also arrogant enough to think I could go undercover on one of the most dangerous plots in the UK – despite my compromising position – and pull it off. I had supreme confidence I could do it. I wanted to be the best UC in the country, and to achieve that you had to take on these high-level operations. That was my motivation, that was my drive.

I didn't even ask for more time to consider it. My mind was made up.

'Yeah, I'm up for it. I'll do it.'

They knew I'd say yes. I knew I'd say yes. I should have listened to my head. Because Moss Side would prove to be one of the biggest mistakes of my life.

CHAPTER 7
THE LEGEND OF MIKEY O'BRIEN

Sleet peppered the grey sky and a stinging chill tore through me. I glanced at my watch and sighed, my breath hanging like a cloud in the icy air. *Not long now. Stay focused.* Embedded in a body-shaped hole on an embankment enveloped in snow, I peered over the telescopic sight of my SA80 assault rifle and covered my arcs of fire. Eighteen hours through treacherous terrain deterring the activities of known Provisional IRA members. Eighteen hours on winter patrol in South Armagh. I was fucked. I was done in. But this was no time to switch off. Not when Lance Bombardier Stephen Restorick had been shot dead by an IRA sniper as he manned a checkpoint in Bessbrook weeks earlier, aged just 23. I might have only been a teenager, but I had a job to do, a team to lead.

We'd secured the landing zone and were waiting in tactical formation for the pick-up. As the blizzard whistled past my frozen ears, I yearned for the unmistakable sound of the Chinook's spinning rotary blades that signalled our path to relative safety. Then it came – wokka wokka, wokka wokka – like sweet music to my ears. Thoughts of home comforts massaged my aching joints as I watched the helicopter descend before the load master gave the go-ahead to peel off and board the chopper. I heaved myself up and dashed across the open ground – the crushing weight of my military gear sending each step deeper into the snow. Exhausted, I clambered aboard. The chopper took off and as its blades sliced through the sleet, I looked down at the beauty belying the danger that lurked among the picture-postcard landscape, dreaming of the warmth and a dripping egg banjo.

Peering out of the stained-glass window at a sea of white glistening in the winter sun had me reminiscing about those days in South Armagh that made me a man. Here I was, eight years later, back in Northern Ireland, in a pub adorned with loyalist flags on the Lower Ormeau Road, anticipating troubles of a different kind. I wiped the froth of Guinness from my mouth and thought of the new threats and challenges that lay ahead. I'd need to show that same mettle again. I'd need to be brave in battle. This time I wouldn't be part of an armed patrol alongside friends who would happily kill to protect me. This time I'd be going alone. Not as a soldier – but a spy.

The bosses had decided they were taking no chances. Moss Side would be a deep infiltration carried out by a Level 1 UC. There are two levels in undercover policing. Level 2 operatives are what are known as test purchasers and typically portray the role of a hardened drug addict. A classic scenario would see them get an introduction to a street dealer from a 'fellow' junkie and score a £10 bag of heroin or rock of crack. They would stick the gear in an evidence bag, go home at night to wash away the stench then do the same the next day until they'd gathered enough evidence for the police to strike. It's a stressful job that is certainly not without its risks, and the officers rightly deserve all the professional plaudits they get.

Level 1 is a different beast.

If Level 2s are the prey, Level 1s are the predators. They must have supreme confidence and conviction to convince the most dangerous criminals that they are the real deal. Level 1 UCs are on plot 24/7. They live and breathe the job and can never stray from their criminal alter ego. Not if they value their life. Their objective is to gather as much intelligence and evidence as they can, and the operations they undertake require considerable financial backing and meticulous planning.

I was going in cold, without the luxury of an informant. I would have to make every criminal connection using my own skills and initiative. It would be for my own good and for the good of the people I was trying to protect. But there still had to be a strategy. It would be amateurish to enter an operation like Moss Side by bouncing in, pretending to know a few people and making it up as I went along. Any wrong move and the consequences could be deadly. And I mean deadly. I'm not talking about a slap on the wrist from the boss. I'm talking about the kind of trouble you're in when you've got a gun lodged firmly against your head. This was not a game of chance. This was the kind of operation that required someone with the mental fortitude and presence of mind to mitigate the risks.

There was a huge amount of planning for the job and a significant investment made in developing my criminal persona. I needed a whole new identity – a character with history and presence, someone who stood up to any test or background check. It's what's known in the trade as 'backstopping'. My DNA and fingerprints were removed from the national database, and any trace of Shay Doyle was erased. It was like I'd vanished. I was given a new passport, birth certificate and driving licence. I was given bank cards, credit cards, all the essential supporting documents, under a new identity.

The next thing I needed was a cover story, or what's known in the trade as a 'legend'. This is where my tough Manchester upbringing would come into play. All those years living on an overspill estate, learning the ways of the street: how to talk, what to say and what not to say; how to conduct myself in the company of criminals; how to show respect but not fear; how to deal with bullies. I didn't know it then, but I was picking up habits, traits and skills that would serve me well. I had not been in the force long and

I didn't present or project like a police officer. I was still raw, still very much a kid off a Manchester council estate. All I had to do was put to use all the attributes I'd been unconsciously collecting all my life.

Some UCs will play the part of a bent businessman, or a dodgy antiques dealer, or a white-collar fraudster. I was never going to be any of those. They could afford to show frailty, show fear. I couldn't. I had to be an apex predator. I was only going to ever play one part: a professional criminal, an out-and-out villain. A 24-hour gangster.

I had to be the sort of criminal you would find at the sharp end – ready to involve themselves in anything, no matter the risk. They're what's known in criminal circles as 'grafters' or 'money getters'. They're athletically built, adept at armed robbery and capable of extreme violence – with access to firearms. My criminal persona had to be cunning, calculated and ruthless. The mantra had to be 'never show fear', because they'll smell it a mile off. It came naturally to me to play this role.

There was another dimension to my new persona. We decided that I'd have Irish connections. In real life, that was true because my mum's side of the family was from Ireland, and one of the main driving forces behind every successful Level 1 is that the character they portray is never far removed from who they really are.

My legend was forming. I was a grafter born in Northern Ireland but had spent a nomadic childhood and teenage years in some of the biggest shitholes in Manchester with my mum after fleeing the Troubles. I'd then moved back to Belfast to be raised by my uncle John, a career criminal who'd taken me under his wing and acted as my mentor through my rise from petty crook to professional criminal. I even had my own criminal record, logged on the Police National Computer. It evidenced my progression through my criminal apprenticeship and read something like: car theft; couple of arrests for armed robberies – no further action; arrest in Holland for firearms offences; arrest for section 18 assault – no further action. There were also warnings for firearms and violence on police systems.

The Northern Ireland connection had many advantages. I would never have outright said it, but it allowed people to assume that maybe I had links to paramilitary groups. There are some serious players in Northern Ireland and the Republic, and that is known throughout the criminal world. It's an attribute displayed by the best undercover operators: let them think it, never tell them. Give them clues, get them to draw their own conclusions. The best UCs plant seeds; only a gobshite blurts out their life story. It also helped that I'd served in the army and knew how to handle firearms and explosives and how to execute a plan with military precision.

I had all the physical and mental attributes of a hardened career criminal. I trained twice a day, whether it be running, weights or combat sports, and had the athletic physique of a cage fighter. If you're going to profess to be someone whose staple income comes from armed robbery, then you're not going to be a fat pudding. You're going to be disciplined and recognise that physical prowess is a key part of your armoury. The fact is, I had to be able to handle myself. If it suddenly went wrong for me on the plot, there would be no cavalry waiting around the corner. I would have to deal with the situation myself.

I had a good grasp of criminal language. Gangsters and grafters speak in a certain way; they use certain terms, and it's important you do the same or they'll see right through you. Most cops speak in cop language, even when they are off duty. Even now, I can tell when someone's an off-duty cop just by listening to their conversation in a cafe, for example. If I were to drop one of these 'police-isms', as I christened them, then any decent criminal would spot it a mile off. I just didn't speak like that.

I trained myself to become an expert on criminal commodities. I knew the going rate for anything from a kilo of coke to a MAC-10 machine gun – not the inflated prices you often hear on the news when the police have taken out a consignment of drugs, but what they were actually worth, on the wholesale and street-level criminal market.

I didn't have to stray too far from what I already was. All I had to do was be me, but instead of playing a cop I was playing a villain. Whatever the situation called for, I could call on the necessary expertise. It didn't matter whether it involved drugs, guns, stolen property, or hurting someone, my criminal alter ego could either do it or would know someone who could sort it. This is where Mikey O'Brien was born.

I was sent to Belfast to perfect my cover story, which is how I came to find myself in the pub on the Lower Ormeau Road. If south Belfast was to be where Mikey had spent a significant part of his life then I needed to make it my specialist subject. I spent several months going back and forth there, getting to know the people, the pubs, the bars, the restaurants, the schools. I knew where the prisons and police stations were, shielded by high brick walls and barbed wire, and I knew the geography of the city. I had to be a sponge. I may never have needed to call on any of the information I had memorised from my time there, but that didn't mean I didn't need to have it in my locker. A flimsy cover story can very quickly unravel.

I was sent to the secret Special Branch facility in Lisburn, where I received further training in handling firearms and improvised explosives because part of my backstory was that I was a professional robber. I learned how to make cutting charges to blow a hole in a wall and how to breach the skin of an armoured cash van with a shape charge. I was even sent to a diamond centre to learn about clarity and cut. No stone was left unturned. Back in London, MI5 spooks gave me a crash course in lock picking and breaking into cars. I also became adept at anti- and counter-surveillance techniques. It was a steep learning curve; I was effectively having to acquire and retain a lifetime's worth of information.

Everything was taking shape, but Christie pointed out that a man operating alone on a long-term infiltration like this could look unusual. It was decided I would need a girlfriend, someone I could be seen with, because even if you have a face like a robber's dog, if you are a successful criminal with the cash and the car and are in the gym daily, then women will inevitably be interested in you. And not to show interest back – well, that could be perceived as strange.

Enter Nikki, the typical gangster's moll, dripping head to toe in Gucci and D&G with a five-grand Louis Vuitton handbag and the air of a WAG wannabe. She would be portrayed by the female cop who'd passed the selection course with me. She was the right age to be Mikey's girlfriend, and we had built up a good rapport. She was intelligent, quick-witted, had a good sense of humour and knew how to look the part. We both firmly believed we could make it work.

We came up with a story of how we met and how long we had been together. We'd say that Nikki came from a well-heeled family in a leafy part of Cheshire, a world away from Mikey's tough Manchester-Irish upbringing. But Nikki had a wild side. She was a bit of a hedonist and loved the sun-drenched Ibiza party scene – and she liked a naughty boy even more. Ibiza was somewhere we both knew, so it was decided that's where we had met. Nikki knew how Mikey made his living and turned something of a blind eye to it in the hope that she would turn him into a legitimate businessman, and a caring husband and father. At the same time there'd have to be enough money in the pot to keep her in the party lifestyle she had become accustomed to. But above all else she was Mikey's conscience, the woman who grounded him and the one person who held any kind of influence over him. This was a useful ploy because it allowed Mikey to have someone in his life who he refused to upset, and that could be manipulated to my advantage in any number of situations on plot.

With the cover story in place, we were ready to hit the Moss and start mixing with the bad boys, right? Well, not quite. You see, Moss Side is not an area you just rock up to and give it billy big bollocks. It's a tight community – and whether you're gang-affiliated or not, you can't just appear from outer space. You need to look real. Nikki and I got a flat together – nothing special, just a two-bed on top of a newsagent's – a few miles up the Princess Parkway, a dual carriageway that cuts through Moss Side. We started going out together as a couple, hitting local bars and restaurants. We worked out in the local gym, meeting each other for food and drinks afterwards. We got to know the barmen and bouncers and a few of the punters. We'd dress in expensive gear. I'd wear designer jeans – Diesel or Armani – a Boss or Ralph Lauren polo and Members Only-style jacket with a five-grand kettle, usually a Rolex. Nikki would be dressed to the nines in Jimmy Choo heels with a Gucci or Vuitton handbag. We'd stand out and people would notice us. I'd walk out of the flat and ask Nikki, 'Do I look right?' She would say, 'You look like a villain who's made a few quid,' and I'd think, *That's good enough for me*. If you stroll into a packed pub and the barmaid asks, 'What are you having, Mikey, the usual?' it makes you look like a real person who's part of the woodwork. That's what I was trying to achieve. I wanted to be able to go back there with criminal acquaintances and let them see regulars high-fiving me and giving me the gangster hugs.

I was always trying to think three steps ahead. Laying the groundwork and getting my face known was about creating situations and building relationships I could later use to my advantage. I was like Ronnie O'Sullivan on the snooker table – always thinking two or three shots ahead while eyeing up the big break.

And so, after a few months' making 'appearances' and putting in the hard yards, it was time for the big entrance. And boy did I do that – with a 50-grand Mercedes, a tidy bird by my side, pockets fat with cash and the menace of a big-league villain.

The residents in the red-brick terraces of Claremont Road must have been tearing their hair out when they saw me roaring down the street in a black Merc convertible with private plates – roof down, Prada shades on and Heartless

Crew's latest garage hit blaring out of the speakers. Not when it happened virtually every night when the kids were probably being put to bed. It was brash. It was testosterone turned up to the max. It was fucking infuriating at times. It had to be. You know those annoying pricks with no regard for the well-being of others, the kind who park in disabled bays then leap out of their motors thinking they're a Premier League footballer? That was me. It had to be. That's who Mikey O'Brien had to be. He had to give off that 'I'm someone to be reckoned with, I don't give a fuck' vibe. Working undercover is totally different to working surveillance. Surveillance is the art of seeing and not being seen; undercover work – especially cold, long-term infiltration – is the art of being seen and using it to your advantage.

Claremont Road was where it was at. It was lively and dangerous, full of kids trying to make a name for themselves. You'd have your hoodie-wearing gangbangers on mountain bikes and BMXs delivering wraps of brown for local bagheads. Then you'd have your Somalis who you'd find in the khat cafes. They were always having it with each other. At night Claremont would come alive, and you'd be able to smell the latest pungent strain of super-strength skunk from teenage lads trying to impress wannabe gangster girls. Reggae and R 'n' B tunes would blast out of the stereos of parked cars, and the music would occasionally be drowned out by the sound of police sirens and sometimes the crack of gunfire.

The infiltration was named Operation Anchor. There were no time restraints and no specific individual targets. It wasn't about collecting evidence against street-level drug dealers. My objective was to infiltrate live gang members with a view to gathering intelligence on their criminal activities to aid the police in protecting lives.

It was also to spot 'tension indicators'– that meant identifying potential gang wars or serious threats to anyone's life – and, where possible, build up a picture of the changing criminal landscape. There was also the not insignificant matter of a string of unsolved historic murders. Only if you're part of the underbelly that exists in the community can you gather that kind of intelligence.

As an undercover officer, it's vital you get your criminal profile just right. If you go in with one that's too low, you're not going to be of interest to the serious players. Go in too high and you could find yourself the target. I needed to be seen to be a little above street level but not top of the tree. You've got to be able to choreograph the dance but not let anyone know that's what you're doing. That's the skill – and the risk. From the off, my bullishness, and what to the casual observer may have appeared to be little regard for my own safety, made my bosses nervous.

I had been assigned a cover officer. They're there to ensure your welfare and are at the end of the phone 24/7. They are your pathway to the police should you need any action to be instigated. At least that's the theory. Mine was a grizzled career detective called Jack. He had the weathered face of someone who had spent his entire working life taking down some of Manchester's most hardened gangsters. Nothing shocked or fazed him. I respected him for his experience and cool head, though at times I think it was fair to say I took a few months off his lifespan with my antics. Jack was the best cover I ever worked with; some of the others didn't have a clue.

After one early briefing, I was told that the operational team had informed Jack that a dive boozer called the Junction in Hulme, a gang-infested area that bordered Moss Side, was real bandit territory – specifically Gooch Gang territory. The intel was that drug operations were being run from there and that weapons had been stashed. It was deemed an obvious place of interest but that I should treat it with extreme caution and only go in with someone who would vouch for me. So what did I do? I jumped straight into the Merc and plonked it directly on the pavement outside before bouncing through the saloon-style doors and ordering a pint.

If you've ever lived in Hulme or even passed through on the bus, you'll know the Junction. It's a traditional one-room pub that stands on the corner of Old Birley Street and Rolls Crescent like a giant wedge of cheese. The flooring was a mix between cracked diamond-shaped tiles and faded patterned carpet that matched the dingy, dirty-coloured seating. It's closed now, but in its heyday it was booming, especially on weekly reggae open mic and jam nights when the bar room was packed with punters. One band used to bring a sound system and a beanie-wearing snare drummer with a bead necklace and a spliff-smoking Bob Marley emblazoned on his T-shirt. They'd bring the house down with classics like 'Three Little Birds'. It was daytime and not as raucous when I went in – but with enough drinkers to notice me. Management may have had grave reservations about me going in solo, but in my head I didn't see the issue. Maybe if I was an off-duty cop I'd be bang in trouble, but I wasn't; I was Mikey O'Brien, armed robber. Mikey would not care about walking into any boozer. He would stroll in with confidence, conviction and charisma. Wearing a white Stone Island T-shirt covering most of an 18-carat yellow-gold curb chain, with Armani tracksuit bottoms and a pair of gunmetal 110s, I bounced in. Bold as brass. Within ten minutes I was sat down having the craic with a few likely lads in there, then I put a call in to Jack – a well-rehearsed routine we had of me letting him know my location.

'I'm just in the Junction in Hulme, mate, it's booming,' I said loudly, over the blaring jukebox. 'Fancy a pint?'

'No, I don't,' he replied, sharply. 'What have you just been told? You're a fucking nightmare, aren't you. Give me a bell later.'

I found it amusing and walked out of there with a couple of phone numbers, some interesting intelligence and associations with naughty boys that would last until the job ended. The bosses may not have seen it like I did, but for me it was a good day's work, and putting myself out there was what it was about.

To be honest, I found dealing with the villains easy. It was the straight-goers that I had more difficulty with, the nosey ones. They didn't mean anything by it – they were just being friendly. But some people ask too many questions, which can derail jobs like this one.

Criminals and gang members don't have a daily schedule like your average Joe. They're not up at seven getting the kids ready and going to work for a nine-to-five. It goes something more like: up late, smash the gym, food in the early afternoon, then let the graft start. Socialising starts late and finishes in the early hours. I started to keep the same hours. I'd go for a jog in the morning – around the plot so people could see me – then I would hit the same bookies on Claremont Road every afternoon. I'd bounce in in my shorts and a Stone Island hoodie and a pair of 110s, and I'd blow money on fruit machine roulette and the horses like it wasn't an object. One lad used to hang around outside the bookies. He was always on the gear and a heavy drinker. I would chuck him a few quid every other day, and he'd be over the moon. He'd go out of his way to act like I was his mate, and I'd make a point of leaning on my car outside the bookies to have the craic with him.

It was a good move because it turned out that back in the day before his slide into addiction, he had been a bit of a player connected to the Doddington gang. He'd run around telling anyone who would listen that I was his younger cousin and an Irish Thai boxing champion. I'd never told him anything of the sort, but it did me no harm in the long run.

There were loads of pubs around Moss Side, but there was no point in spreading myself too thinly and bouncing around them all. I needed to pick one, make it my local and become part of the furniture there. I chose the Nest – a two-roomed estate boozer right at the heart of the action on Claremont Road.

It was an ale house that attracted all kinds of people. You had straight-goers, gang kids, grafters, builders and labourers still in their work gear knocking back pints of Carling till last orders. It had a big screen for the footie and it was rammed with Man City fans on match day or during stay-behinds for the boxing. There was a beer-stained pool table but hardly ever any chalk and often only one cue because the others had either been nicked or used as weapons. It was a real hive of activity, a den of iniquity even, but a perfect place to meet a few boys.

By now I'd moved to a swanky apartment just a stone's throw away from Moss Side in Whalley Range with a balcony, 24-hour security and underground parking so I could come and go when I pleased. It was easy for me to park the car away from prying eyes and walk to the boozer day or night. I was in there most days. I'd sometimes pop in for a Coke in the daytime after I'd been to the bookies and before my daily Thai boxing session. But mainly I'd go in at night, when I'd sit at the bar and drink bottles of Stella.

I got in with loads of characters. One was a Black lad called Tyrone, a grafter who had a daytime job as a joiner. He was on the periphery of the gangs but liked to dabble. You'd see a lot of his kind, playing it like they were a bit of a naughty boy and saying they could get hold of all kinds. So I thought I'd put him to the test. It was time to dip my toe in and make my first credibility buy.

'A pal of mine's been mithering me to get hold of an oz of sniff and his usual kid's gone off the grid,' I told him. 'If you can put your hands on it you'd be doing me a favour.'

'Yeah, I can sort you an oz, no bother,' he said cockily.

'I've got the money there, but make sure it's not shite because it will give me a fuckin' earache,' I said, regaining control of the exchange.

He fixed it up for me to meet his brother the next day at a Tesco car park. Now, to someone like Mikey, getting an ounce of cocaine would be water off a duck's back. He wouldn't make a big deal of it. So I told his brother I'd be nipping to Tesco for some bread and milk at 11am and he could meet me there. 'Listen, I'm not fuckin' about,' I said. 'I'm not meeting you here there and everywhere, mate, you can come to me.' I was walking around with three grand in my sky rocket every day for my float, so that would easily cover it. The next morning, I strolled out of my flat and into Tesco, which was two minutes down the road. I bought a loaf and two pints of semi-skimmed milk and rang him just before 11.

'I'm just on my way, bro,' he said hurriedly.

'Listen, I'm here. I've done my shopping. If you're not here in five minutes, ram it, kid.'

'I'm coming now, I'm coming now, I'm on me bike.'

Minutes later he rode up to me, slightly out of breath. He can't have been older than 18 and was wearing a black North Face coat zipped right up to conceal the bottom half of his face. He was wearing two sets of tracksuit bottoms, one ready to pull off and ditch to take police off the scent if something went down. His left hand was on the handlebar, his right down by his side and covered with a black Nike golf glove. The big thing at the time was for these kids to wear a golf glove as it was meant to signify to rivals that they were carrying a gun. It looked ridiculous.

I took the coke – wrapped in cling film and shaped like a golf ball – and gave the package a cursory smell; I was hit from six inches away with the unmistakable chemical whiff of cocaine.

'Listen, this isn't even for me but I hope it's not shit,' I said, looking him in the eye. 'I'm only whacking a twoer on it and giving it to a kid I know, so I hope it's decent shit. It's not worth the earache off the cunt if it's not. So how much do you want for it?'

'Sixteen fifty had been agreed,' he said.

I pulled out a wad of crumpled twenties from my pocket. They were in stacks of five, each stack comprising four twenties with another twenty folded across. That's how villains carried their dough. 'Sixteen or fuck all, our kid.' I held out the cash.

He shook his head and crumbled. 'Go on then.' He accepted my offer, took the money and rode away, and I walked away with a Tesco bag filled with a loaf of brown bread, two pints of milk and an ounce of coke. Within 24 hours of meeting Tyrone, I'd been introduced to a gang kid on the street and bought an ounce of cocaine from him. Buying drugs was as simple as that.

I placed the drugs in an exhibit bag and handed it to Jack, who gave it to the operational team for forensic testing. It came back as pretty fucking average gear, which left me with a situation I had to deal with.

Omega thought it was a big deal. 'Brilliant work, Shay,' they said. I sat there thinking, *Is it brilliant? Is it really brilliant? It's like taking candy off a baby.*

Buying drugs was as easy as buying bread and milk to a lad like Mikey, yet Omega thought it was a major breakthrough. It started to dawn on me that the management and I may not have been pitching this operation at the same level, and it was the first indication of the conflict to come.

When I entered the pub that night, Tyrone shouted across the room: 'Was that fucking oz alright?' I slowly walked up to him and said softly: 'To be honest with you, mate, it was a bit shit. I won't be buying from the kid again. It's not worth my fucking hassle.' He apologised and said he'd told his brother to give me the best gear. 'No drama,' I told him. 'I'll still make a couple of hundred on it.'

The fact that it wasn't dynamite gear actually did me a favour, because it meant I didn't have to keep going back to buy drugs off him. Besides, I had bigger fish to fry.

Sundays at the Nest were like something from an episode of *Shameless*. You'd have the footie on in the background competing with the music on the jukebox. Women who'd been on the Lambrini all day would get into fights, and their partners would either be peeling them away or joining in – mainly pissed-up handbags at dawn. You'd have locals who'd come in for a drink and a laugh, and scally kids with man bags smoking weed in the doorway. The smell in there was a mixture of skunk, spilled beer, and the meat and potato pies they'd stick in the microwave and serve over the counter.

You could do a week's shopping in the Nest with the shit people brought in. You'd have smackheads coming in selling razor blades and legs of meat, and Chinese blokes would go round the tables selling badly dubbed pornos. I'd like to say I didn't buy one.

Then in the night, a DJ would turn up with strobe lights and a sound system, playing a mix of reggae, R 'n' B and rap. You'd have all sorts in there – pissheads, meatheads wiping their noses after their twentieth key of coke in the toilet cubicle, which of course would always have a broken lock on it. Sundays at the Nest were wild. And I have to say I loved them. When I was in the army my dad had a pub on a sprawling council estate. This was a throwback to Sunday nights at his boozer. It was home from home for me, and I didn't feel uncomfortable in the slightest.

I'd been going to the Nest for a few months now. I was becoming an accepted regular. I walked in one Sunday night and the DJ shouted on the mic to me for everyone to hear, 'Belfast in the house!' and I thought to myself, *That's it. I've fuckin' got this place now.* I was wearing a gaudy Ed Hardy T-shirt that was scally chic and all the rage. This one had a diamante-stoned skull plastered over the front, but sometimes I'd wear one bearing the face of a roaring lion. And just to complete the head-turning look I'd have a three-and-a-half grand in-your-face gold gangster chain I hung purposely outside.

George, one of the regulars, who was quite well connected with some of the gang lads, had taken his nephew under his wing after his dad was put in the nick. He was a young white lad, about 16, and saw me as bit of a role model for some reason. In his eyes, I suppose, I was this white fella in a boozer full of Black lads who had a bit of respect and kudos. I think he liked the way I'd turn up bold as brass in my Merc and the way people greeted me, slapping my back and bumping my fist. I think he was taken in by the rumours going around about me being a bit of a criminal. Maybe he was a bit in awe of me. There's a skewed reality in tough areas like Moss Side, where men like Mikey become role models for impressionable youngsters. They see these kind of characters as exciting and dangerous because they don't live by society's norms. It isn't right but it is the reality.

One night I was at the bar and George came over. 'Mikey, where do you get those T-shirts from?' he said, handing over an ice-cold bottle of Stella. 'My nephew loves them. They're dear, though, aren't they?'

I'd heard the kid's story and that he'd had a bit of a rough time. I took a big swig from the bottle and wiped my mouth. 'Leave it with me.' A few days later I came back with a brand-new small-sized Ed Hardy T-shirt and handed it to his nephew, and his face lit up. I didn't make a big show of it. It had zero operational value for me to do it. But do you know what? I liked the kid, and he'd been through a lot, so I bought him a T-shirt. It turned out later that word of my good deed had got back to the landlord, and while it wasn't my aim, I rarely paid for a drink in there again.

Don't get me wrong. Mikey couldn't be Mr Nice Guy all the time. I was portraying a serious criminal knocking about in an inner-city pub in one of the country's most dangerous places; it was inevitable there'd be situations that called for a different approach.

One night I was minding my own business in my usual spot leaning across the bar talking to the barman when I caught someone staring at me across the room. He was a big lad, with short-cropped hair and a dark polo, and was sitting at a table near the toilet with a few fellas. I could feel him staring at me. I had no idea who he was. I'd not seen him before. I tried to make out I'd not clocked him and carried on minding my own business, but there was obviously something bothering him about me. And I would have to deal with it. All the time I was thinking to myself, *I'm not Mikey the criminal. I'm Shay the cop. And Shay the cop can't start fighting in a boozer.*

In reality, if a serious criminal like Mikey was faced with this situation, he would have bounced over and ironed the lad out where he sat without saying a word. I couldn't cross the line – I was a cop. But I did have to deal with it to retain some credibility. I looked across and his eyes hadn't moved. It was clear I had to act. I stepped off my stool and headed towards the toilet before stopping at his table. It caught him by surprise.

'You OK?' I asked, not taking my eyes away from his but maintaining a quiet and calm manner.

'Yeah, why?' he snapped back, sitting up a bit as if to give me the come-on.

'Are you nervous or something?' I said in a flat tone.

'Nah.'

'Should I know you?' I said, taking control.

'Don't think so,' he said. I could sense a shift in his demeanour. He thought he was Johnny Concrete when he was 25 feet across the room from me. He wasn't quite so bold when I was stood in front of him.

'Have I done something to upset you?' I said.

'No, nothing.'

'OK, then.' I paused. 'Let's leave it here then, shall we.'

He looked defeated, his head slightly bowed. He started fidgeting with a beer mat.

'Shall we?' I asked again, a tad louder.

'Yeah.'

'OK, then.' It was a tactic that could be perceived as high-risk, but I made a point of taking a measured approach, deliberate but not aggressive. I simply couldn't be seen to take no action.

I walked into the toilet, half expecting to be followed in and ambushed. Nothing came. I washed my hands then made my way back over to the bar where a few lads I knew had been watching.

'Who's that cunt in the corner?' I asked them, in a faux show of irritation. 'Should I know him?'

'He's a nobody, Mikey. A straight-goer. He plays footie for the Sunday league team and has a few drinks in here after the game. Think he's a gasman or something. He must have been on the sniff.'

'Fucking straight member,' I said with a snarl. 'I fuckin' hate straight-goers. OK, fair enough, seeing as he's a straight member he's getting a fuckin' pass, isn't he.'

Every time he saw me after that he'd offer me a drink. Every time I'd flatly refuse with a firm 'No.' Not 'No, mate,' just a simple 'No.' And in my head I'd think, *You fucking shithouse.*

Confrontations like this could and did develop from nowhere at any time. I always had to be one or two steps ahead in how I dealt with them. It wasn't enough to merely rely on my physical presence as an undercover cop. I had to think on my feet and adopt the appropriate psychological strategy. Operating in this way – always having to think ahead, sometimes 15, 16 hours a day on the plot – was mentally exhausting. And it would inevitably take its toll.

Nikki helped massively. Having her there gave me the perfect excuse not to get involved with women who made advances towards me on the plot – believe it or not, it did happen! She was adept at strategically dropping into conversations bits about Mikey and his criminality when I wasn't there, always hurriedly ending a revelation by pleading, 'Don't tell him I told you that,' safe in the knowledge that the information would get out because people like to talk. It was a clever ploy and gave the local villains mental cues that Mikey was a full-time grafter with some serious connections. She was a great sounding board as well, and having her on the plot gave me confidence. She did her job well.

One weekday afternoon we were sitting at a table in the Nest, enjoying a quiet drink, when the doors flew open. In stumbled a young-looking man, his long, thin face almost as pale as the white shirt he was wearing. A red pool on the top of his arm was rapidly expanding.

'I've been stabbed. I've been stabbed. Help me!' he cried, the dark red puddle seeping through his fingers as he tried to clutch his wounded arm. 'Help me, Mikey! I need a hospital now.'

It was Paddy, an Irish regular in the pub. He was a compulsive gambler and prolific coke-head who was always off his tits. I liked Paddy; he was a decent enough lad and fun to talk to. And he'd taken a real shine to Mikey. It turned out Paddy ended up paying the price for failing to pay off a drugs debt and had been jumped on Claremont Road by a blade-wielding dealer.

My immediate thought was to help him. I was after all a policeman, and a policeman's primary duty is to preserve life. But would Mikey the gangster help him? Would Mikey the gangster really want some bloke bleeding all over his freshly valeted cream leather or landing him in a situation that might bring the police to his door? Of course he wouldn't. I turned to Nikki and whispered in her ear, 'You've got to take the lead on this. You're the only person who has influence over Mikey. You've got to take the lead.'

We quickly arranged the plan. She knew exactly what to do. Leaping off her seat to Paddy, who was now slumped on the floor – what little colour he had in his chiselled face fading fast – she shouted, 'Gets some towels now, get some towels.' She pressed down on the gaping wound. 'Mikey, get him in your car. We haven't got time for an ambulance, get him in your car.'

'Am I fuck putting him in my car,' I yelled back. 'Phone an ambulance. He's not bleeding all over my fucking leather. I've just had it cleaned.'

'Mikey, you better put him in that fucking car or that's it between me and you.'

'Get him in the fuckin' car then, but he best not ruin the seats. And you're paying the valet, Nikki.'

We sped to Manchester Royal, dumped the car outside A&E and helped him in. He was in shock but could speak. 'What's your name?' the receptionist asked.

'Patrick McDonald,' he mumbled, his shirt now soaked in claret.

You lying bastard, I thought, with a smile. He had told me his name was Patrick Smith. I couldn't really hold it against him. I was, after all, the biggest lying bastard there.

A nurse rushed him through the double doors to be stitched up, and I went outside and called my cover officer. 'Do me a favour, mate. Paddy, one of the regulars at the boozer, has been stabbed on Claremont Road. Get someone on the case, and while you're doing that, can you run a check for me? Patrick McDonald.'

It turned out he was wanted in the Irish Republic for possession of over half a kilo of coke and €60,000 of drug money. Not only had the poor lad been stabbed up, he'd now be nicked as a fugitive.

There was never a dull moment on this plot. I always had to be on my toes, always ready to respond to any sticky situation. Take the drugs scene, for example. There are very few pubs in the country where you won't find someone in the toilets having a line of coke. Nowadays people don't go out just for a pint; they go out for a pint and a line. It's ingrained in modern society. It was inevitable from the outset of the operation that at various points I would be offered cocaine, and I had numerous pre-planned excuses I could roll out on the plot at any time. One night I was in the toilets and one of the lads from the pub pulled out a bag and thrust it towards me. 'Go on, our kid,' he said, dipping his house key into a bag of white flake. 'Have a key, it's rocket fuel.'

It could have looked strange for me to turn it down, especially since I was the stereotypical villain who drove round in a Merc convertible. 'Nah, not for me, mate,' I said. 'I'm trying for a baby with the missus and we're having IVF, but don't tell anyone, will yer.' It was a perfect excuse. We knew cocaine use was rife and that we'd be getting offered it left, right and centre, so we had built into our backstory that Nikki had saved Mikey from the party lifestyle after he met her in Ibiza. He'd been constantly on the sniff, injecting steroids and popping pills at the weekend; then he met her and cleaned up his act. It was a story that worked well.

This phase of the operation was all about getting my face known and infiltrating the criminal element of the community. Yes, it was a tiring and painstaking few months, but I'd be lying if I said I didn't enjoy it. Slowly but surely Mikey started to get a bit of a name. My demeanour and criminal profile had started to get me noticed. The infiltration was working. People firmly had the impression that I was a grafter, an armed robber and someone with serious criminal connections.

It wasn't as simple as just bouncing into the bookies or the boozer and having the craic every day. There was always a methodology to what I did. I was having to take in and retain information from all my interactions in the criminal community. Just because a deployment had finished didn't mean my day was over. I would go back to my flat and would have to record all the information I'd gathered in a police-issued evidence book. Fortunately, I was blessed with a near-photographic memory and could recall events and facts in almost perfect detail. Be it a telephone number, a vehicle number plate, how someone was dressed, how they spoke, what they said. It was a useful tool to have as an undercover cop.

All the intelligence I gathered was being fed back to the operational team on a daily basis, and police were finally able to start building the picture they so desperately needed. Greater Manchester Police now had in me a reliable intelligence asset on the ground in Moss Side. It was unprecedented. But there was more work to be done. Now it was time to go after the bigger fish.

CHAPTER 8
SWIMMING WITH THE SHARKS

Operationally, at least, things were going well. I had now been on the plot for almost a year and turned Mikey into an accepted figure in Moss Side's criminal circles. I had gathered significant intelligence and built up valuable acquaintances with gang members and grafters while successfully managing the collateral intrusion and limiting my connections to straight-goers. I had created Mikey and moulded him into a multi-layered character.

The big question looming over any undercover operator is *Does anyone suspect I'm a cop?* I was continually having to assess subjects, trying to detect subtle changes in their demeanour, attitude and body language towards me, or snatch snippets of gossip. Nothing ever told me that anyone had any inkling Mikey O'Brien might not be genuine. This wasn't achieved by chance, but meticulous planning, skill and an ability to think two or three moves ahead. My success on the plot, however, was a world away from the troubles off it.

I was consumed by the job. In my mind, anything less than total dedication would have meant failure. Something had to give. I was on the plot almost 24/7, portraying a career criminal, living someone's else's life, day in, day out. There was no room for anything else, and that included my personal life. Cracks appeared. I was constantly tired, which made me impatient and snappy at home. It led to rows, and my relationship with my girlfriend began to suffer. I purposely disconnected from family and friends – the last thing I wanted was for anyone from the plot to bump into me while I was with any of them. Given how close my home at the time was to the plot, it was easier just to stay in, so any social life I had was being played out under the guise of Mikey O'Brien. The fact is, it was easier to be Mikey than it was to be me.

There were also changes happening behind the scenes at Omega. New management had come in with fresh ideas on how the infiltration should progress. You see it in a lot of organisations: new bosses taking over, instantly trying to make their mark and press their own agenda, thinking they can reinvent the wheel. It was no different in the police. In fairness, they were experienced detectives, but inexperienced in dealing with the intricacies of a Level 1 undercover operation. Managing Level 1 UCs is a totally different prospect to running a team of detectives in the CID. And it was apparent from day one that they didn't have a clue how to deal with me.

There was conflict after a fallout from a separate operation. Christie left in support of one of the cover officers at the centre of a dispute with management. It created bad blood and divisions in the camp, an us-versus-them culture between the UCs and the bosses. It wasn't my fight and I tried my utmost not to get involved, but I was disappointed at Christie's sudden departure. He was probably the most experienced UC in the country, and he really understood the challenges and difficulties I faced on the plot because it was all stuff he'd seen and done himself. He was my mentor and biggest supporter. By challenging management, Christie had put a lot of noses out of joint, and because we were so close the bosses knew exactly where my allegiances lay.

The new management didn't take to me. They'd been unfairly briefed that I was a bit of a loose cannon and needed my leash tightening. Their assessment couldn't have been further from the truth. All they saw was the kid from the Manchester council estate pretending to be the villain. They couldn't see what Christie saw in me. They couldn't see the highly functioning mind. They couldn't see the professionalism or the hard work I put in behind the scenes, or that I operated with the highest levels of skill and situational awareness. They couldn't see the grasp I had of case law and undercover legislation. They couldn't see past the heavy Manchester accent and the Stone Island T-shirt.

Their style of management was more 'You do as you're told, you're a DC and I outrank you.' And they'd expect a 'Yes, sir, no, sir, three bags full, sir' response. They may not have liked me, but because I was delivering on the plot they knew I was a necessary evil.

Under the new regime, the new DS had been tasked with overseeing the operation. I was summoned to a first meeting at an off-the-plot safe house. Knackered from the previous day's deployment, I walked into the living room with Jack and Nikki to find Trevor, the new DS, slumped on his chair with his legs sprawled across the coffee table. Trevor was a failed UC; on the one job he did, he got pissed, fucked it up and was told he'd never work undercover again. Then for some reason the powers-that-be later fetched him back as a DS. You couldn't make it up. He was the polar opposite of me: slicked-back hair and thinly built. I think he thought he was a snappy dresser – to me he exuded second-hand car salesman. He didn't acknowledge any of us. Instead he just sat there, head down, scrolling through messages on his Blackberry. Eventually, he looked up and uttered one word – 'Alright' – before burying his head back in his phone, smirking to himself. This went on for about five minutes. I turned to Nikki and mouthed, 'What's going on here? What's this about?' She just shrugged. She was as gobsmacked as I was. So was Jack.

I stood up and declared, 'I'm going.' Then Trevor spoke again, his head still in his Blackberry.

'Where do you think you're going?'

'You've obviously got better things to do, so I'll let you get on with it, shall I?' I said. Finally, he showed me the courtesy of looking up from his phone.

'You'll sit down.'

In my book, there's a fine line between confidence and arrogance. Trevor didn't just step over it. He hopped, skipped and fucking jumped it.

'Trevor, I don't know how you're used to operating, but myself and Nikki were on that plot for fifteen hours yesterday. When I come to a meeting I expect it to be conducted professionally. I don't expect to be greeted by someone with their feet up on the table and their head in their Blackberry. So, whatever it is you're doing, I'll leave you to it because it's obviously far more important than the operation.'

I might have spent my days walking, talking and acting like a gangster, but there was another side to me. Despite my criminal persona, I was the consummate professional. I walked out of the flat and my phone buzzed. It was Jack.

'Shay, come back in, come back in.'

I walked back into the room. I wouldn't have gone back for anybody else. Trevor was now sitting upright with his feet off the table.

'We've got off on the wrong foot,' he said.

'OK,' I said. 'But just so you know, as far as I'm concerned, this safe house is a police station, so we act professionally.'

I'll admit I probably wasn't the easiest person to manage. But you don't send a sheep to infiltrate a pack of fucking wolves. By the same token, if people showed me respect, I was always respectful back. Trevor had misjudged me. Before we'd even met it was clear he'd decided he was going to be the one who would take me to task, and when I reacted in the way I did, he hadn't seen it coming. From that day, he bore a grudge. I'd challenged him, and he'd never let me forget it.

Clearly, everything wasn't rosy in the garden. But I was determined to let nothing stop me – not the personal problems at home, not the rising political conflict, not the fact the managers didn't get me, nothing. I was still extremely driven. I wanted the operation to be a success and, egotistically, I wanted to be the best UC in the country. Even though I knew things were starting to fall apart around me – as I'd predicted from the outset – the truth is I was hooked. Operating undercover in Moss Side was like a drug; it was *my* drug. And I couldn't get enough of it. Was that healthy? Probably not. Did I have my priorities all wrong? In hindsight, yes. But I enjoyed the risk. I enjoyed the potential danger and I enjoyed the challenge of pitting my wits against criminals. Be under no illusion, you cannot succeed on an infiltration at that level if you haven't got absolute dedication and commitment. So I pushed all my troubles aside and cracked on.

The operation needed to evolve. Police information told us some highly active south Manchester gang members were frequenting the clubs in Manchester city centre, and to target them we had to follow that intelligence.

It was a move fraught with risk. I could have bumped into anyone from my personal life at any moment. Maybe I was overconfident, but I had absolute belief in my abilities to spot problems before they developed. Operating in a permanent state of hypervigilance had become my normal. I was always subtly checking 360 degrees around myself for any threat. I always positioned myself so I could see entrances and exits everywhere I went. I clocked vehicles, reg plates, any behaviour that was out of the ordinary. I'd assess people – their body language, their demeanour – and decide if they were a potential threat, a target or a straight-going non-combatant. It was like I saw everything around me almost in slow motion.

This hypervigilance absolutely kept me safe. It allowed me to react quickly and on the front foot to any given problem that came my way. I engaged my brain before opening my mouth, acutely aware that one wrong word could blow my cover and bring the operation tumbling down. At that time, my human senses were super-tuned. Later in my life, however, this positive hypervigilance that had served me so well would spectacularly implode.

Every move I made on the operation was pre-meditated and deliberate. All those months hitting the Thai boxing club weren't just to hone my physique – they were to meet the kind of people I needed to progress the infiltration. A lot of the lads training there worked as doormen at the weekend for extra cash, so, knowing that one day the job would bring me to the city centre, I made it my business to get to know them. I'd train and spar with them, and all the time I'd be thinking, *How might he be useful to me down the line?* It paid off. By the time we hit the clubs I was already in with quite a few bouncers. Having those connections often meant I could just walk into places without paying.

You know when you're on a night out in the winter and you're standing at the back of a queue, freezing your nuts off, then some dickhead strolls to the front with his missus, shakes the bouncer's hand, then waltzes in? I was that dickhead. But as with everything I did, there was a reason behind it. My thought process was *You never know who's watching.* You can guarantee that if someone was watching, then they'd instantly think, *Who the fuck is that?* In a big city like Manchester, there's a good chance it's going to be a gangster.

It was a slow and draining process. Gradually I was getting my face known and was making good progress. But I was on a razor's edge all the time.

One of the spots I was sent to was a dark, moody basement club called One Central that ran weekly garage nights. You'd often find a few naughty boys in there connected to the Moss Side gangs. One night, the club was reasonably busy but not packed, and the beats were banging out of the speakers in front of the darkened DJ booth. I was stood at the corner of the bar with Nikki, specifically chosen because it gave me the best view of the whole club. I certainly didn't see what was coming next, though.

'Shay . . . Shay Doyle' sounded across the club over the mic. I looked up and the DJ had stepped out of his booth and was waving at me.

I turned to Nikki. 'Oh fuck, I went to school with him.'

'Shit,' Nikki replied.

'Stay here a minute, I'll have to deal with it.'

I walked up to the booth and chatted to the old school mate I'd not seen for years, who'd reinvented himself as a garage DJ. How the fuck could I have known? Luckily he had no idea I'd joined the cops. I asked him what clubs he played, saying that I'd come down and see him, making a mental note never to go to any of them. Thankfully, there was no one in there who knew me as Mikey and I'd got away with it. But it was a timely warning that the job could go wrong at any moment.

Another club we targeted was Ampersand. It was a former backstreet private members' club that had been opened to the public and attracted criminals and gang members from across Manchester. They'd mix with football stars, socialites and dolly birds with more slap on than sense and desperate for a bit of the limelight. I'd go up the stairs to the Cristal Lounge, where the VIPs hung out. It was always full of grafters spending money like water, knocking back Cristal champagne and Grey Goose vodka, and they'd be surrounded by hangers-on. I'd position myself so I could see who was coming in. It would give me time to react to any compromising situation. And I made it my business to get in with Amir, a 20-stone-plus Chechen doorman with cauliflower ears and the flattened nose of a trained fighter. He manned the VIP entrance, and I'd sometimes bung him 20 quid and always stopped to shake his hand and have the craic. My thinking was that it would be useful to have him on my side. It would turn out to be money well spent.

One Saturday night I was in the VIP section with Nikki when a mass brawl broke out near where we were sitting between a gang affiliated with the Gooch and a rival crew. Punches were thrown, bottles hurled, tables went over and a knife ended up getting kicked across the floor. That was our cue to get out of there, ring Jack and call it a night. The following week I walked to the front of the queue with Nikki and into the foyer when a couple of doormen I knew approached me.

'Mikey, the head doorman wants a word with you in the office.'

'What about?'

'He just wants a word with you, mate.'

His office was next to the reception where a girl collected entrance fees and coats. I remember standing in the foyer and thinking, *This isn't good.*

But I had to stay calm and stand my ground. 'Well, tell him to come out here then.'

I could feel my space being invaded as a handful of brick-shithouse doormen stepped close to us. It was clear I was going nowhere. I thought to myself, *I'm going in that room, one way or another. Better to walk in and walk out than get fucking dragged in.* I didn't want to place Nikki in danger. I turned to her and said, 'Go in and have a drink and I'll see what this is about.' Looking back, it might not have been the best call, but it was obvious I wasn't leaving the club.

As the bouncers circled me, I said clearly to Nikki so they could hear, 'If I'm not out in two minutes ring our fuckin' kid and tell him to come down 'ere.' What I was really saying was 'If I'm not out in two minutes, ring Jack.'

Flanked by two bouncers, I walked into the office, and sat behind a wooden desk in a black leather chair was the head doorman. I'd been told he was a Romanian ex-paratrooper. He had hands like shovels and a hard-looking face. It was clear that he wouldn't be squeamish about the use of violence. It was like a scene from a shit gangster movie.

One of the heavies next to me was Amir.

My mind was racing. *What the fuck is this all about? The fucking odds are stacked against me here. How the fuck am I gonna get out of this? Maybe I should have tried to fight my way out in the foyer. Fuck, I hope Nikki's alright and rang Jack.* But I knew I couldn't show any physical signs of distress. I needed to stay calm. I decided to go on the front foot and open the conversation.

'Need a word?'

'Your fucking boys last week cause me trouble. All that fighting – I can't have any of that in my club.'

'Not my boys, nothing to do with me. I wasn't fighting.'

He looked me up and down with contempt. 'You're Gooch, aren't you?' It wasn't a question. It was a statement.

'What?'

'You're Gooch. It was your boys causing all that trouble.'

I laughed then smiled. 'Fucking Gooch? I'm not fuckin' Gooch, mate. Do I look like a fuckin' gangbanger? I'm not fuckin' Gooch, mate. I know who a few of them kids are but they're nothing to do with me. I get what you're saying. But I can't be accountable for them. Fuckin' don't let them in. It's fuck all to do with me, mate.'

It was an intimidating situation. But I had an ace up my sleeve. I turned to Amir, whose palm I'd been greasing.

'You know me. You know what I'm about. I'm not fuckin' Gooch. Do I ever come in here causing trouble?'

'No, no, Mikey, you know what it's like.'

'Nah, I don't know what it's fucking like. I'm not Gooch. I might be a grafter but I'm not some fuckin' gangbanger. Go on, you tell him, fuckin' tell him, Amir.' This was plan A and I was silently praying it would work. Plan B was to take my chances with the heavy glass ashtray at arm's length on the Romanian's desk if it turned violent. Plan C was to plead for my life, but it's not really a good look. Plan D was to declare I'm a cop – that would have meant operation over. It wasn't going to happen.

Amir looked at his boss. I knew at that point he thought I was in a whole world of shit. What he said next I couldn't have said better myself.

'He's a good guy. My girlfriend's family from Salford know him. He's a good guy.'

Halle-fucking-lujah, I thought.

I deflated the tension by lowering my voice. 'Listen, I come out for a good time. I don't come out for trouble. I go about my business quietly.'

He looked me in the eyes and I could see the cogs in his brain turning as he deliberated my fate. The chair squeaked as he pulled his huge frame out of it then held his hand out. 'OK, OK.' The whole interaction must have taken about two minutes. It felt like an age.

I walked back into the foyer and Nikki was there waiting. She'd been having kittens, thinking I was getting my head kicked in. 'Are you OK? I've rang Jack. I've rang Jack.'

'I'm fine, calm down. Ring him back and tell him it's fine. Let's go and sit in the VIP and have a drink.'

'Are you mad?' she said. 'What the fuck's gone on? Let's just go.'

'Calm down,' I said. 'We can't go. We've got to have a drink. I'll look weak if we don't.'

We went to the bar and within a couple of minutes Amir, who'd just bailed me out, sent over two drinks and said, 'I'm really sorry for the inconvenience, Mikey.'

It was an unnerving confrontation, and anyone who says they don't feel fear in those kind of circumstances is either a liar or has a serious personality disorder. If you're alone and surrounded by three humongous doormen, then that's a fight you're not going to win. Was I frightened? Yes. Did I show it? No. I maintained control. I had to look like the swan calmly gliding across the water, even though beneath the surface my legs were paddling like fuck. Being able to manage your reaction to fear is one of the key skills of a successful Level 1 UC. If you show fear for a moment, predators will smell it and they will pounce on it. If you can't manage your reaction to fear, then you've no business being an undercover cop.

The stressful nature of the job meant compulsory appointments with the psychiatrist at least once every three months. It was a tick-box exercise more than anything else. I'd go in, say everything was great – sleeping great, relationship's great, I'd say. But I built up a reasonable relationship with him. He was astute. He said to me, 'You UCs are all professional liars. You'll only tell me what you want me to know. I can't see inside that brain of yours.' He was always looking for tell-tale signs of fatigue or irritation.

We did have some interesting chats, though. On one occasion I went to see him, I was deploying in supporting roles on a number of operations around the country. That wasn't unusual. I walked into the room and put down four phones on the glass table – one for each job and my personal mobile. 'How do you cope?' he asked. 'How do you cope having to answer those phones as four different people, including your real self?'

'To be honest. I don't have to think about it too much. I can just do it.'

'Do you know what that is, Shay?'

'No, what is it?'

'Well, let me explain it like this. When Lewis Hamilton drives down a racetrack at 240 miles per hour, taking hairpin bends and having to avoid other drivers – and doing it lap after lap without crashing, yet still managing to win most of his races – do you know what that's called? It's called unconscious excellence. That's what you have. It's skill, reflexes, instinct and talent. And that's what you have.'

Well, whatever it was I had, it was doing me absolutely no favours at home – the few times I went home, that is – because I was so consumed with the operation. I didn't want to take my girlfriend out in case anyone spotted us. Even going to the supermarket with her was a fucking drama. One time we were walking down the aisle of my local Tesco, doing a bit of shopping like normal couples do, when I spotted someone I knew from the Nest turning into the aisle we were in. *What the fuck are they doing round here?* I thought. Luckily that good old reliable hypervigilance saved me again and I quickly turned on my heels and walked out without being seen.

There was an agreed contingency plan we had in place wherever we went. If ever I saw anyone from the plot, I'd just walk away without saying a word and we'd meet back at an agreed location. Socialising for us was just a no-go. Besides, I just didn't have the energy – I was exhausted from long late-night deployments. The pace was relentless. Because we were targeting the clubs, some days I'd go from

9 in the morning until 4am. It would leave me running on empty and I'd go home and lie on the couch for days on end watching Sky Sports, not wanting to talk to anyone or go anywhere. You can imagine what that did for our relationship. Once a friend of my girlfriend rang her to say she'd spotted me in a club in Manchester with another girl. The girl was obviously Nikki, but this friend wasn't to know that. Imagine the embarrassment for my girlfriend – her mates thinking her bloke was running around town with another woman. She couldn't exactly blurt out to her mates that I was an undercover cop infiltrating Manchester gangs; she had to keep the secret as well.

There was only so much she could take. She told me it was over. I didn't argue with her. I picked up my bag, opened the front door and as I walked up the garden path she shouted, 'Shay, the police don't give a shit about you. You're a fucking idiot.'

I climbed into my car, drove back to the plot and thought, *She's got a point*. But did it make me pause and reflect about my commitment to the operation? Not in the slightest. I had a job to do and I was hell-bent on completing it. I'd become well established on the club scene in Manchester after months of late-night deployments, and I'd fed back solid intelligence, but I still needed that major breakthrough.

One night, we were in the VIP section of a nightclub in Manchester notorious for attracting south Manchester gang lads.

I returned from the toilet to find a group of guys stood near Nikki. One was clearly chancing his arm with her – a stocky but athletic Black lad, in his mid-twenties and wearing a white Gucci T-shirt and Armani shades resting on top of his close-cropped hair. The lads he was with were all well built, in designer gear and wearing sparkling watches. I can tell the difference between a heavy crew and some tinpot weekend-warrior tough guys, and this was a heavy crew. But I didn't recognise any of them. It presented me with a dilemma – would Mikey the armed blagger take kindly to some bloke chatting his bird up? Unlikely! I didn't have to worry. I knew Nikki would have had it under control and would have immediately put him straight that she was with her boyfriend, the 'amazing' Mikey.

I walked over and he was respectful and put his hand out to shake mine. There was no 'You're a bit of a mug, I'm gonna shag your missus' attitude. We weighed each other up like the two alpha males we were, and I quickly deduced that he was a cut above your average gang-affiliated street kid. I could smell it on him straight away. And his demeanour told me he had made his mind up I was also a bit of a player.

'I'm Anton,' he said. 'It's Mikey, right? Your missus here was telling me all about you, you've got a good girl there.'

'Yeah, she's a fucking diamond, mate.'

Yet again Nikki had proved her worth and taken what could have been a flashpoint and turned it into an opportunity, knowing full well I would maximise on it. Anton invited us for a drink at the table his crew had booked.

I never took the approach of shouting my mouth off about what I'd done, acting the big-shot armed robber. Subtlety was always the order of the day for me. The best professional criminals often display a degree of caution in the company of new people, and I always played this role to perfection. Slowly he was buying the package – the expensive clothes, the Rolex watch, the fat roll of cash I'd strategically pull out and peel some notes off, the coy way I skipped around certain questions about what I did for a living. It was all part of the act. What I was really saying was 'I'm a fucking grafter, mate, and a good one at that.' He got it because he was the same.

I could sense a real opportunity, that this lad was a bit of a player. This was the level I needed to be playing at, and what hitting the clubs had been all about. I wasn't walking out of the club without swapping numbers.

We both sat cautiously chatting, like two boxers slowly feeling each other out with their jabs. I made strategic toilet visits to leave Nikki to feed him bits about Mikey, things that a villain would never disclose about themselves to someone they had just met but if revealed by the chatty girlfriend after too much champagne – well, that would be acceptable.

The champagne and Grey Goose flowed and Anton loosened up. He started to ask more about me: what I was into, where I was from. I gave vague details about living in Spain and how I'd grown up bouncing between Ireland and Manchester. I said I was back in Manchester looking for some properties for my uncle and doing bits for him. I cautiously threw acceptable questions at him to show interest back, being careful not to sound like a nosey copper.

I was enjoying the interaction. It was a good test and I could see he was more and more comfortable opening himself up and mirroring the level of information I was giving him. It's a subtle trick but a basic psychological technique: people feel inclined to share with you if you share with them. It's human nature and I was a master at it.

I thought, *I've got to leave here tonight with this fucker's number and create an opportunity to take this association further.* Phone numbers can be an intelligence gold mine for the police. I'd normally have waited longer, but I threw a little caution to the wind.

'I do some bits of graft, collecting for me uncle – he has lots of business shit going on all over. To be honest I could do with some tasty boys, either to do a bit of that for me or to ride shotgun now and then. Normally it's no mither, but some cunts can get lairy, you know what it's like. You look like you might know some – maybe I can shove a bit of the graft your way?'

'Yeah, yeah.' He nodded.

'I've got some lads and I've put loads of graft their way,' I said. 'But a couple of the fuckers have let me down – like the powder too fucking much. Pissed me off.'

'Yeah, man, I hear you,' he replied. 'I can do that no problem. I know some good reliable kids.'

'Here, take my number,' I said, reaching for my phone. 'Might be something in it for you. I don't like to talk bits of work over a drink, but maybe give me a bell and we'll have a chat.'

'Yeah, we can do that,' he said, punching my number into his phone.

'Just do us a favour, our kid,' I said, further laying down my credentials. 'Text me your number before you ring, I don't answer unknown callers.'

I didn't want to over-egg the pudding and outstay my welcome at the table, so I made my excuses, shook hands with Anton and went to a quiet bar with Nikki to debrief. About an hour later my phone buzzed. It was a text. 'Yo, yo, Mikey, it's Anton. Here's my number.' I held it up to Nikki and gave her a little wink. It was a good night's work.

The next morning, I phoned Jack to get the operational team to run checks on the number, but there was nothing on GMP's intelligence systems. I had no identification for Anton and no confirmation he was a viable target. I couldn't just start asking him his full name as that would have been on top. I needed to find another way. I left it a few days and called him.

'Anton, it's Mikey.'

'Yo, Mikey, man, what's happenin'?'

We swapped pleasantries then got down to business.

'Listen, I've got a bit of graft on. Need to collect something from some Irish kids. I've not met 'em before. It'll probably be sweet but just want someone to have me back. Know anyone who can handle themselves who's not a cunt? Only an hour's work, if that. Couple of hundred quid in it, so if you've got anyone who's handy and up for it there's a job there.'

'Right, OK. Where you meeting them?'

'I don't like talking over the phone, mate. You about later? Let's meet up an' have a chat.'

'Yeah,' he replied. 'I got some running-about to do, but how about three? You know the second-hand car gaff on the petrol station in Hulme? I'll meet you there.'

I went to the flat to grab my coat then jumped in the motor just before three in the afternoon. He was parked up at the garage in a souped-up black Golf R with another lad. I turned in and they both stepped out into the forecourt. It was cold and one of them was breathing into his hands by his face. Anton looked handy. He had wide shoulders and a thick neck and eyes like a hammerhead shark's. He was wearing a black puffa jacket, jeans and black trainers with white soles. His pal looked a tasty lad as well. He had the look of a snarling bulldog, and his nose had been spread across his face like he'd boxed a bit. He clearly trained daily. But so did I. I was in the best nick of my life. We instantly had common ground.

'You look like you fuckin' train, you,' said his pal.

'Yeah, I do the Thai boxing in town, mate.'

'Do you, yeah? I do a bit of Thai boxing myself.'

All the preparation and foundations I'd put in that to others didn't make sense were all now coming into play for me on the job. They played the name game with me. Most of the names fired at me I didn't know, but I recognised a few of them from the Thai boxing and people I knew off the plot. It seemed to settle them down immediately. I turned to Anton.

'So this job then, what you sayin'? Got anyone in mind?'

'Yeah – me. I'll come with ya,' he said.

'Listen, there's only a twoer in it, though. It's a nothing bit of graft. I'm picking up something for me uncle. Shouldn't be any mither. Just not met 'em before and pays to be cautious – you get me?'

'Yeah, course, it's sweet. I'll come myself when you need me.'

'Waiting for me uncle to let me know,' I said. 'Give me a couple of days an' I'll get hold of you, yeah?'

'Sweet.' We bumped fists and they got back into the car and sped off into the early rush-hour traffic.

I drove to the flat, walked through the door and unzipped my padded three-quarter-length C.P. Company coat. It had a pair of goggles in the hood and was popular at the time with gang lads and football hooligans. I removed from the coat the tiny pinhead camera I'd been carrying. Then I unlocked a safe hidden in the wall, moved aside my evidence book and pulled out my work laptop, before downloading the covert footage and feeding it back to Jack. He didn't know who they were but said he'd send it on to the ops team to have a look.

The next morning he called me back. 'You've hit the fucking jackpot,' he said. 'These two are hot as fuck. The ops team have identified them as two of the most dangerous lads in Manchester and the two top south Manchester targets. They're live, mate.' They were leading lights in an ultra-violent offshoot of one of the main Moss Side gangs suspected of carrying out a number of shootings, kidnappings, taxings and drug deals.

'I don't know how you do what you do, lad, but you're fucking good at it, I'll give you that.'

It was high praise coming from Jack, who got excited about fuck all.

The police now had Anton's dirty number, his graft phone. It presented the operational team with a significant piece of the intelligence jigsaw in the investigation into one of the most dangerous gangland players in south Manchester.

The revelation as to who Anton and his associates were significantly ramped up the risk for the operational management. The idea I'd sold to Anton of backing me up on a little jaunt to collect a bit of something for my uncle had now taken a dangerous turn. They were concerned. Police intelligence said that Anton and his associates were involved in a number of gangland disputes where firearms had been discharged, and it was believed that Anton was almost always carrying a gun.

Omega now had an A1 intelligence source in direct communication with one of the most active gang members in
Manchester and, it's fair to say, were shitting themselves
about the risks – of which there were many. How were they
going to manage it? What if Anton was carrying a loaded
gun? What if he was setting me up for a robbery because he
thought I was collecting a large amount of cash and I'd end
up with a loaded gun pressed to my temple – or worse? The
bosses frantically discussed how to proceed. It was a big call
to make putting an undercover policeman in a vehicle with
a man known to routinely carry a gun. Jack told me they
were erring towards telling me to make my excuses and pull
out. When I heard that, I was fuming. I remember thinking,
*What's the point in doing this undercover operation if we're
not going to go after the big boys?* I put my point across and
Jack agreed before speaking to the operational leaders.

'Trust him,' he urged. 'He's good – and he'll know if it's not
right.'

They relented. They knew it was too good an opportunity.
This was a chance to have valuable alone time to ingratiate
myself with one of Manchester's most dangerous gang
members, and do some graft with him to evidence my trust-
worthiness. This was a chance to infiltrate a gang believed to
be heavily involved in gun crime. It was exactly what the operation was designed to do. There were some provisos, however.
They insisted that a surveillance team accompany me on the
meet. I had no say in the matter. It was agree – or no deal.

On the face of it, it was a simple meet and collect, but in reality, it was a manoeuvre fraught with danger to myself, my fellow officers and the general public, and I had to meticulously plan it. I got hold of Anton and arranged to pick him up the next day.

I chose the pick-up time of 5.30pm to coincide with rush hour so the surveillance team could blend in with the traffic and keep up with me, but also to give me more time alone in the van with him. Anton was a stone-cold gangster. He was in his mid-twenties and built like a bull. I'd asked a few gang-affiliated lads from the plot if they had heard of him, and it was clear he had a formidable reputation on the street. There was even talk that he was behind a murder, possibly two. I picked him up in a Transit van I had access to. No one takes much notice of the white van man, so it was the right motor for the job. Many a grafter uses a 'blender', as they are known. As Anton opened the door and stepped in the van, I assessed his demeanour and body language while looking for any unusual gun-shaped lumps around his waist. Obviously, I couldn't search him. The van was wired for sound and vison, so every word and action was recorded. He seemed relaxed and I immediately put him at ease, saying that my uncle had said the guys we were meeting would be no trouble at all. I told him they were connected to a good family in southern Ireland we had done lots of work with over the years and came highly recommended. The last thing I wanted was him on edge, hyped up that it was going to kick off with the guys we were meeting. I said it was me being overly cautious, but he was cool with it.

The tension rose as we inched through traffic on the Mancunian Way heading towards Salford Precinct. I had set it up so that an Irish UC I knew would call me and pretend to be my uncle John, and I would take the call on loudspeaker. I wanted an Irishman because that confirmed my Irish connections. It had all been scripted by me and was well rehearsed.

A sharp Northern Irish accent boomed out of the speaker. 'These guys are fine – there'll be no problems, Mikey. When you get the USB stick, get a flight tonight if you can to Belfast and give it to Martin. He has all the passwords for it and the boys can get to work.'

'Yeah, no worries, John. I'll see you tomorrow,' I replied, and the line went dead.

Anton turned to me, looking surprised. 'We are collecting a fucking USB stick?'

I laughed. 'Yeah, mate. But in the right hands it's worth a lot of money. There's stolen credit card details on it and there's a 48-hour window to smash it for two hundred thousand pounds' worth of goods, mate. I collect 'em and the lads have the passwords over in Ireland for the stick. Fucking worthless to anyone but them. They're doing one a fortnight, mate, and selling the goods off.'

'Fuck me, that's good money, man,' he said.

It may have seemed strange taking a gang member to collect a USB stick, but when I was planning this ruse – a tried-and-tested tactic I'd used against a number of subjects – I couldn't present him with an opportunity to stick a gun in my face and rob me. It couldn't be cash or diamonds. It had to be worthless but valuable. For all I knew he was sitting in the van with a 9mm handgun down his pants.

We chatted freely and I distracted him by making him laugh, but he was very wary that we could have had a tail and was constantly checking the wing mirrors for cars. He possessed the paranoia of someone in the crime game. All the time I was thinking, *I hope the surveillance team are good and not showing out*. The whole thing had the potential to go horribly wrong if he pinged them.

We arrived at the meet location and I pulled into the car park. I let him see me grab a screwdriver from the side-door pocket of the van and shove it down the back of my jeans. The meet spot on wasteland was shrouded in darkness but for a flickering floodlight. It was out of the way of prying eyes and a good spot for the surveillance team to stay hidden in the shadows yet still be able to have the eyeball on me in case it went awry. The other UCs playing the Irish villains there were bang on cue, looking every inch the part in a matte-black Range Rover with Irish number plates.

I exited the van and was met by my UC pal, a big bullet-headed guy who was an experienced operator and knew the drill. The handover went smoothly, as rehearsed. I got back in the van clutching the envelope and drove away, knowing that the surveillance team would be around me somewhere. This was potentially the riskiest part. Anton could have pulled a gun and put it to my head and said, 'Give me that – get them cunts on the phone and give me the fucking code.' But, again, I was confident that because it wasn't cash or jewels, he'd see it as worthless. The USB stick ruse is old hat now, but back then it was a useful tool. It would still be a few years before cyberfraud found its way into mainstream criminality, so at the time it was an unusual commodity to be trading in.

This theatre, as we call it in the trade, was all about showing Anton I was a player, an active criminal, not just another bullshitter in a bar. I'd said I had graft on the go, and I'd delivered on my word in quick time. It may not have been a groundbreaking deal, but it added to the package I was showing him. He'd seen me in a 50-grand motor, designer clothes and a Rolex, and he'd seen me bring out a blender van for a job. It might have been just a USB stick, but it represented big numbers.

On the way back to the plot I said to him, 'Anton, there's lads doing cash van robberies for twenty-five-grand boxes. Smashing two hundred grand on stolen credit card details is much less risk for much higher reward.' But I couldn't have him thinking Mikey was some white-collar fraudster. It didn't fit with the profile. 'We've got graft in Manchester,' I added. 'We've got graft in Spain and Ireland. This is just a bit on the side.' I pulled out £250 in notes and put it in his hand before looking him straight in the eyes and laying it down in a calm and confident voice. 'I'm the man my uncle calls when people don't pay. I'm the man who sorts it for him. But most people in our circles know that when John has sent me, then it's gone wrong for them. Listen, I'm OK on me own, I don't give a fuck. I can look after myself, but sometimes you just need that bit of backup, don't yer?'

'Yeah, Mikey. Course, man,' he said. 'I get it. Listen, I'll back yer, we will back you. I've got loads of kids there who I graft with.'

I dropped him off in Hulme and said I was off to Ireland for a few days but would be in touch. How you portray yourself to targets can be a fine line to tread. If you make out you're a highly dangerous criminal then you're potentially opening up a defence of duress for them later down the line. A clever barrister might listen to the recordings you've covertly captured and say, 'Of course my client sold him drugs, or did this or that for him. He was frightened to death of the man! Wouldn't you have done the same, ladies and gentlemen of the jury?'

I had to get the tone just right. It had to be proportionate to the level of criminal he was, and there was no doubt he was a violent and dangerous gang member. I had to show him I was game and, to a degree, also potentially dangerous. I couldn't be seen to be an easy target. He was a predator, and predators can easily spot other predators. They either

144

think, *I'm gonna take him on as an enemy,* or *I'm gonna make him an ally*. He chose to make Mikey an ally.

It was a major breakthrough. He started to ring me more often, inviting me to meet him on nights out in the city or other places further afield. I made a point of not becoming his best pal, just keeping it professional, as it were. Familiarity can breed contempt. I didn't want to be his best mate. I wanted him to think I was a busy criminal and retain an air of mystery There was also the small matter of the surveillance team that the bosses wanted around me when I was with him, which just wasn't available on a whim.

I pleaded with Jack to speak with senior management to review the need for a surveillance team. My rationale was that Anton had shown he was surveillance aware, which could present a huge issue for me if I was with him and he pinged it – nothing insurmountable but a compromise I could do without. I argued that it would severely hamper my chances of getting deeper into his crew. Jack knew I didn't have a death wish, that I didn't want to get shot in the head and that I quite liked living. If you're going to be a top-drawer undercover cop, you need a set of bollocks on you. That doesn't mean being a reckless cowboy, but someone who can identify, accept and manage high levels of risk in dynamic situations. Jack got me and he knew I had that ability; I'd demonstrated it on many occasions. He rang me the following day. 'No surveillance team required for now,

Shay. It's been reassessed, but it could change dependent on the intel, so crack on with him. Just be careful.'

I didn't jump straight on the blower to Anton. I played it cool. I didn't want to chase him; it had to be natural. Then he rang me one Wednesday afternoon for a favour.

'Yo, Mikey. Will you come with me somewhere?' he said.

'Where?'

'I can't say but I need you to come. Can you come and pick me up?'

'What time?' I asked.

'Six,' he replied.

'Let me check with Nikki. She will go fucking mad at me. I can't remember if I said I'd take her down her dad's – he isn't well. Get back to you shortly.'

I was feeding him the story to buy myself some time to make my decision if I was going to meet him. Believe it or not, a lot of hardened criminals I've met can be sympathetic to family issues, and I played on that. It wasn't ideal going to an unknown location with someone so potentially danger-ous, but he'd done it with me on the USB sketch. I rang Jack and ran it by him. I told him I was up for it. He reluctantly agreed.

I picked Anton up and asked what was happening and where we were going. 'I'll direct you,' he said. I peeled off, deep in thought while trying to keep my eyes on the road. I knew there was every chance he could be carrying. *Has he got something on me? Does he know who I am?* I didn't sense a change in his attitude, and he was alone, but if he did have something on me there was every chance he'd take me out. This was someone who didn't fuck about.

The car was teched up and recording. There I was, driving round one of the most dangerous men in Manchester, and I didn't know where I was going because he wouldn't tell me. I vividly remember one of my favourite tunes coming on the radio – 'Voodoo Ray', a Manchester acid house classic popular in the heyday of the Haçienda, by A Guy called Gerald, a musician from Moss Side. It felt apt. But in the darkening night, not knowing if the lad sitting next to me had a gun or not, it added to the tension.

He told me to pull up in a shadowy lane at the side of a country pub in Cheshire. Thoughts of dread swirled in my head. *This is a great place to shoot someone and leave them.* I started to regret my decision. I'm not afraid to say it was unnerving, but I'd had a choice. I could have thought, *Too dangerous, leave it,* or I could have seen it as an opportunity to make another huge step in taking a dangerous man off the streets, which was after all what I had been put on the plot to do. I chose the latter. I showed no fear. The minute you show fear is the minute you're done. In that world, they'll smell it a mile off.

We got out the car and a big white guy in a black baseball cap and grey hoodie stepped out of a VW Transporter. Introductions were made and it turned out he was one of Anton's wholesale drug suppliers. They chatted about the prices of kilos of cannabis while I acted like I wasn't interested and still wasn't entirely sure why I was there. It later transpired that the drug dealer, who we identified from the reg of his van – which I'd memorised along with his description – was on the police's radar over an investigation into a gun-running operation. It looked like my gamble had paid off.

After the meet we drove away and Anton asked me if I wanted a drink. He said he had a proposition for me. We stopped at a quiet bar in Manchester.

'Listen, I've been thinking,' he said, sipping on a bottle of beer. 'Why don't we graft with you. You've seen how much weed my guy can get, and you're obviously earning, Mikey, so put your money to use. We can shift it: weed, coke, rock, brown, whatever. So if you can get decent coke, my boys will knock it out for yer. What I'm saying is you finance us, then we'll be your distribution network. We'll shift it all. My boys will graft with you.'

He basically wanted me to fund and enter the hierarchy of his crew, which was one of the most, if not the most, dangerous in south Manchester at the time.

I laughed inside and thought, *This is fucking mad. Here I am, a cop, being asked to align myself with one of Manchester's heaviest crews.*

He said that the guy we had just met only sold a minimum of five kilos of skunk at a time but that it was top drawer. 'Why don't we start with that. Take five ki' off him and we'll knock it out. Quick money, what d'yer think?'

I didn't say no because a good UC would never immediately say no unless he had a good reason, but it clearly wasn't possible to buy the gear and supply it back to him. At the same time, I'd have to come up with some good reasons that didn't end the relationship I was developing. I had to manipulate the opportunity into something that worked to further the operation.

'I'm not buying five ki' straight away,' I said. 'I know my own guys who sell as well. I'd need to sample it first. I might take a bit but depends on the price.'

'Right, OK,' he said, now firmly in business mode.

'Another thing, Mikey – can you get your hands on any shooters?'

Now it was getting interesting. I spotted another opening to play up to the Irish connection. 'Kid I know in London got some coming over from Ireland, but they're spoken for. Glocks, clean and brand-new. But they fly out every time, so they'll be gone. Let me have a chat with him. I might be able to put my hands on something down the line off him – leave it with me.'

Of course I was never going to be supplying him with a gun. *But why close off an avenue?* I thought. I was confident I could spin it on its head and turn the situation to my advantage. Not only that, Anton talking about wanting to source firearms could potentially be damming evidence against him down the line. Jack set up a meeting for me with the Omega management, and I gave an overview of the situation I was in with Anton and the offer to take five kilos of skunk.

'Look, of course we're not going to buy five kilos and supply it back to him, but how about I say I've got a mate in
Liverpool who'll take a kilo of it off me and let me know if it's
any good? If it is we can talk again about upping the amount
and myself and Anton putting some graft together.'

I explained that it would increase my credibility with the
supplier, who we all knew was on the radar of an investigation
into supplying firearms. I said I would get straight into him,
and I argued that a kilo wasn't going to break the bank but the
credibility it would buy with the supplier would be potentially
worth much more. I might as well not have bothered.

'No. We are not going to authorise you the funds for that.'

I was bemused. 'I'm knocking on the door of one of the
most dangerous crews in Manchester here, and you're saying you won't sanction that buy?'

'That's exactly what we're saying.'

I couldn't get my head around it. It seemed a no-brainer
to me. What was the point of me going out day after day, pla-
cing myself at risk and creating these opportunities to take
out serious players, if I wasn't going to get supported to buy
a poxy kilo of weed? A kilo of weed that would buy me huge
credibility with a firearms supplier – the type of firearms
that could be used on the streets of Manchester and further
afield to maim and kill. In short, the very reason the operation had been initiated.

It was apparent to me after that meeting that the rejection
was based on animosity towards me and that the job would

ultimately be unworkable. It was a massive opportunity missed. The management just didn't share my foresight or vision. By now, communication between us had virtually broken down. I couldn't stand Trevor and it was clear to me that the feeling was mutual. I thought this operation was doomed. I just didn't do mediocrity. I remember thinking for the first time on the job, *Fuck this, I've had enough on this plot now. It's ruining my life and I just cannot work for this shower of cunts.*

I made my excuses with Anton but kept up my association with him, while continuing to feed back all the intelligence I could: cars his gang had access to, places they went, valuable bits about their lifestyles. It helped the operational team fill in the jigsaw around him and his crew. But the golden nuggets were the dirty phone numbers I was able to provide.

Early one morning I got a phone call from Jack, urgently telling me to stay off plot and not answer the phone to Anton. They were running on him, he said. That meant something big was going down. Not long after the call, a surveillance team with an armed covert firearms team struck on Anton and three of his crew in a stolen car. They hit hard and fast, subduing the targets with highly rehearsed, controlled violence. In the car was a fully loaded MAC-10-style machine gun and a couple of kilos of skunk in the boot.

We'll never know who those bullets were meant for, but this crew didn't carry guns for show. Not only did my intelligence put a team of dangerous gang members behind bars, it very possibly stopped someone being killed. The men in the car were all convicted and landed substantial prison sentences.

Christie was in the serious crime unit at the time of the strike. He had been told by the head of the unit that Omega bosses didn't want him communicating with me and that any contact was to stop – just further evidence of their spite towards us both. To be fair, he didn't give a fuck and nor did I, so after the strike on Anton's crew he rang me to say one of the bosses from the operational team had asked him, 'This Mikey lad – he your mate? Tell him from me he has got balls of steel, that kid, absolute balls of steel.'

On the face of it I'd established myself as the undercover cop on the plot that no one wanted. I'd brought down some of Moss Side's most dangerous gangsters and thwarted serious threats. Everyone should have been happy. But what about me and the sacrifices I'd made? The secret life just a short drive away from where I lived; the relationship that had gone up the wall; the family and friends that I'd alienated myself from, thinking I was doing the right thing to protect them. I was an undercover cop infiltrating serious criminals, people who could easily source a firearm, come at me and kill me. That's what I had to manage daily; those were the stakes. I knew when I started the job it was madness, and that's exactly what it turned out to be – absolute fucking madness.

My relationship with the management deteriorated; we barely spoke. I don't think they had a clue about undercover work. Maybe they should have pulled me out. Maybe they should have saved me from myself. What it came down to was that the intelligence and information I was gathering was just too good. GMP had their very own Manchester gangster, and it was just too good to let go.

Yet, despite the chaos and the conflict, despite the turmoil and personal strife, I wanted to continue infiltrating Moss Side and taking dangerous criminals off the street. I may have had days when I was at my wits' end, but I was still very much all about the operation. Deep down, however, I knew the writing was on the wall. I didn't have the backing of the bosses and I would go to bed at night with a sense of dread grabbing at my chest. *Surely it's only a matter of time before my cover is blown?*

CHAPTER 9
PANTOMIME

With Anton and some of his crew arrested and now on remand, we had to ensure there was no compromise to Mikey. They might have been behind bars, but they still had reach on the street. It was expected that there would be finger-pointing from the gang, but we had to be sure that they weren't levelling accusations at Mikey. My continued involvement on the plot had to be risk-assessed, but ultimately Omega were satisfied that there was enough distance between the strike on Anton's crew and the information I had supplied for me to carry on undercover in Moss Side.

What it did mean, however, was that I had lost direct access to the most dangerous criminal outfit in south Manchester and would have to start rebuilding. Anton was my bridge to the rest of his crew, and it would have looked suspicious to suddenly start chasing the rest of them without good reason after his arrest. By not sanctioning the drugs buy from his wholesale supplier, who was believed to be connected to a gun-running operation, Omega bosses had missed a chance to take the infiltration to the next level. To say I was frustrated was an understatement.

Don't get me wrong, I still had the hunger to keep going. I had other criminal contacts in Moss Side and on Claremont Road to keep that potentially life-saving intelligence coming in. Creating angles from nothing was what I was good at. *I can do it all again,* I thought. But this time it felt different. My personal life was all over the place, and the distinct lack of support from Omega served only to widen the gap between us. If that wasn't enough to contend with, the compromises on plot were coming thick and fast.

I was in the Nest with Tony, one of the gang-affiliated regulars, who was always in there coked up. We'd decided to hit the Orange Grove in Fallowfield. It was a Wednesday night, which meant it would be rowdy and full of students. I remember it was pissing down when we got to the pub and the doormen were sheltering in the foyer. It meant I wasn't able to get a close look at them – something I would always do before I went into a club as Mikey just in case I knew them away from the plot. I went to bounce in with the usual Mikey swagger, and as we got to the entrance, the bouncers emerged from the shadows and I felt a pit form in my stomach. It was the last of the three doormen – I knew him. He was an Asian lad I'd taken a six-page witness statement from regarding an affray in Tameside a few years before. He was a bouncer at a bar in Ashton and had to give his account of a 20-man brawl in there. *For fuck's sake!* I thought.

His eyes seemed to narrow as he looked me up and down. I couldn't turn away and walk out. I was past the point of no return and was virtually through the door; it would have looked on top. Pretending not to see him, I quickly looked away and headed straight for the bar. 'I'm going to the toilets for a line,' Tony said, his mind only on one thing. 'Get me a bottle.'

My mind whirred. *Did he recognise me? It was a few years ago and I was in uniform then. Nah, he can't have, can he?*

Playing out the different scenarios in my head and how I'd get myself out of them, I carved through the crowd to the bar, stood half-facing the entrance so I could see the whole club, then ordered two bottles of Stella. Tony was still in the toilet, sniffing his brains out. A minute passed, nothing. I gulped my beer, my eyes not moving from the entrance. Then another minute, and another. I started to breathe easier. I looked at my watch. *Thank fuck for that,* I thought. *I've got to be in the clear now.* I looked at the packed dance floor at the students dancing, cheesy pop hits drowning out their screeches. Then I saw him. Striding towards me. *Fuck. I'm gonna have to front this out.*

'Alright, Officer, how are you doing?' I don't know if it was by luck or design that he approached me while Tony was in the toilets, but I just glared at him.

'Eh? I don't know what you're talking about, mate.' There was no chance I was going to cough to being a cop.

'You're a police officer, aren't you? I've seen you before.'

'Don't know what you're on about, mate. I think you've got the wrong guy. Police officer? Are you taking the piss?'

'Nah, I'm sure I've seen you before. Didn't you interview me once? A while back?' Of course he knew who I was. I'd spent an hour with him taking a lengthy statement a few years earlier.

'Listen, I don't know what the fuck you're talking about, pal, but I'm here to have a drink with me mate. Do I look like fucking Five-O to you?'

'Right, OK. I must be mistaken then,' he said, a look of confusion etched on his face.

'Yeah, you are,' I replied, a look of 'Fuck right off if you know what's good for you' etched on mine.

My hostility was designed to make it uncomfortable for him to approach me again. I'd have been fucked if that had happened in front of Tony. It would have been operation over immediately, and more than likely ended up with me rolling around the floor of the bar, scrapping with him. I had to create an excuse to get out of there. And fast. I went out the back into a smoking area and rang Jack.

'Jack, don't say anything, just stay on the line and go with it.'

I walked back to the bar and waited until Tony came out from the toilets and was within earshot. Then I spat it all out.

'What d'ya fuckin' mean? He's there now? He's there now? Right, don't fuckin' tell him I'm on me way. He owes me a bag of sand, that cunt. Cheeky cunt on the piss when he owes me a grand. Right, I'm on . . . What? Listen, I'm on . . .

Listen, I'm on me way, don't fuckin' tell him. Keep him there, I'm coming now.'

I put the phone down.

'What's going on?' said Tony, coked up to the eyeballs.

'Listen, we're going to have to go. Some cheeky cunt has been ducking me, owes me money, and he's in the Whalley now. Come on, we're going to the Whalley. Quick. I'll give you fifty to stop his pals jumping on me while I knock the fuck out of him.'

'Come on then, let's get the cunt,' replied Tony, going into fight mode, as I knew he would.

We walked out of there and I could feel the bouncer's eyes bearing down on me. I flashed past him so he didn't have the chance to say anything, and we flagged a taxi and jumped in it before I dialled Jack again.

'Is he still there? What do you mean he's fucking gone? . . . What do you mean? . . . I'm on me way now. Where's he going? . . . Did he say? . . . No? . . . Cheeky bastard. I'm gonna knock the fuck out of that cunt when I get him. If you find out where he is give me a buzz, yeah? In a bit.'

I put the phone in my pocket and turned to Tony. 'He's gone. Giving me the fuckin' run-around. I'll get him next time. Right, we might as well go back to the Nest. Clare-mont Road please, mate.'

I sat back into the leather and breathed a huge sigh of relief. *How much longer can I ride my luck down here?*

A few weeks later I walked into a Caribbean food shop and saw a girl I went to school with. The two lads who owned it were naughty boys and knew Mikey. Luckily they didn't cotton on but it was another close shave.

Then, another time I was standing outside a shop one lunch-time with a gang kid when my mate's dad, who knew I was in the police, spotted me off the scaffolding he was working on.

'Oi, oi! What are you doing round here?' he shouted.

'Just out and about, mate, you know how it is.' Luckily, he had to get off quickly and a catastrophe was averted. But it was getting silly.

My relationship with Omega management was now beyond repair, and I knew deep down that my days in Moss Side were numbered. Without consulting either myself or Nikki, Trevor and others came up with a new strategy to open up a shop on the plot selling protein powder. The plan was to make it look like a money-laundering pit for Mikey's criminal enterprise. They told me they also wanted me to introduce other UCs who they'd identified without asking our advice on whether they were the right profile for the job. Given we had survived, even thrived, on the plot, you'd have thought our insight might have been operationally valuable. Clearly, they had other ideas.

Opening a protein shop seemed such an obvious move to me. I told them I thought it was lazy and unimaginative. 'If you're going to open a shop,' I said, 'then at least offer something more original than protein powder, for fuck's sake. Turn it into something like an MMA-themed shop or something.' At the time, UFC was taking off as a mainstream sport. But the whole shop idea had been done many times before and I didn't feel it would be a progressive move. I suggested an MMA shop because I got that it could potentially attract local gangs. But any criminal worth his salt would see right through it. A load of white boys setting up an MMA shop in Moss Side – it stinks of police. In fact, I saw it as a disaster waiting to happen and I didn't want any part of it. I thought, *That's it – I'll set this shop up, introduce these UCs and then I'm asking to get off this plot.*

I secured an empty unit on a row of shops on Princess Parkway. We called it Combat MMA and had the name plastered in big letters to the shop window. We decked it out with tracksuits, boxing gloves, protein powder, all the training gear. There was a red leather sofa and we put in a PlayStation and a big screen so customers could come and play *FIFA*. It was designed to be a honeypot for the street gang members running around the Moss and was wired up for vision and sound.

They brought in a newly qualified UC to run it, and I had to mentor and introduce him to my criminal contacts. His name was Ricky and he was Trevor's golden boy. His backstory was that he had Irish connections but was coming to run the shop for me as one of Mikey's boys. He was a decent enough lad, but I didn't think he looked the part for that particular job. You'd expect someone running an MMA shop to be in prime condition, yet he'd be smoking outside the shop. It just didn't look right to me.

I showed Ricky around the plot, took him to the Nest and introduced him to some of the associates I'd made. I didn't wish him any ill will and wanted him to make a success of it. My rift with management wasn't his fault. He was just keen to get on plot and do a job, as I was when I started in the undercover game.

I started to mentally pull away from the job. I felt uneasy with the new strategy that had been imposed by management without any consultation with me and Nikki, and their dismissiveness of my input – with the exception of the MMA shop, which I still thought was a bad idea – pissed me right off. Trevor and I could barely stand to be in the same room. I can accept I'm probably not the easiest person in the world to manage. Will I stand my ground if I think I'm right? Yes, I will. Can I be forceful in my delivery if required? Yes, I can. Do police management like that? No, they don't. But here's the thing. Who do you send into a dangerous world like that? Some submissive snowflake yes-man? They wouldn't last five minutes. Omega just didn't get that.

Ted, the new boss of the unit, pulled me in. 'We need to start pulling you back from this job now, Shay,' he said. 'You've been on it long enough. We want you to bring in the other UCs that will be taking over, and we'll look at what happens with you next.'

Ted was a detective inspector and had no background in undercover policing. Yet here he was managing a top-level undercover unit. I thought, *Who the fuck recruits these people?* He always struck me as a rabbit in the headlights. Ted taking over the unit felt like the Accrington Stanley manager taking the hot seat at Manchester United. I nodded in agreement. 'Fair enough. I don't want anything else to do with it, to be honest. I'm done with it.'

I got on the phone to Jack and asked him to find me another job. I don't care where it is, I said. Just anywhere out of Manchester. I was tired of fighting it. I was physically and mentally exhausted. I'd had enough, I felt I'd been used, and I'd go to bed at night with my girlfriend's words echoing in my ears. 'The police don't give a shit about you, Shay.' She was right.

Members of a low-level street gang called the Moss Side Bloods started hanging around the shop. I had got to know a few from being around the plot, and they'd been in a gang fight on Alexandra Park with a Somali crew. They were only young but they were dangerous little fuckers and would carry knives. One of the key lads from the gang, already well versed in gang culture and approaching his twenties, regularly came into the shop, and I thought it would be good for Ricky to get in with him. I said to Ricky, 'Say you've got an errand to run in Birmingham, that you need to see someone for me, and ask him to back you up.' I figured Ricky would have a captive audience with him for a few hours and could build his relationship with the lad while eliciting information about the tensions with the Somali lads. It didn't take much for these low-level disputes to escalate into bigger feuds involving guns, and I was well aware that people in Moss Side had been shot for much less over the years. To be fair to him, he did the job, but when he came back I listened to the recording in the safe house. When I heard it I thought to myself, *For fuck's sake.* In part of the recording Ricky was bragging about Mikey's gangland prowess.

'Mikey is a badman ... Mikey will slash you across the face if you cross him.'

I turned to him and said, 'Mate, do you not understand?'

'What do you mean, Shay?'

'You've just opened up a potential defence of duress there. Say later down the line you buy something from him – drugs, guns, whatever – and he gets charged. That recording is potentially disclosable as evidence, and you've handed him a potential defence.'

'I'm not with you, mate,' he said, looking puzzled.

'All he would have to say is "Of course I sold him a kilo of coke, of course I sold him a gun – because I was terrified of Mikey."'

I never once gratuitously told anyone during my time undercover that I was some kind of violent maniac. It was all about subtlety and suggestion that was proportionate to the target. That's the skill.

Management brought in another UC from the home counties called Gaz, and he was meant to be my replacement, slipping in as Ricky's boss and a criminal associate of

Mikey's. He had no physical presence and for some reason I can't for the life of me fathom, he came onto the job sporting a mockney accent. As soon as I saw him, I thought, *You ain't gonna last five minutes here, mate.* He had no presence or gravitas.

I did as I was told and tried to integrate him into the criminal community. I took him to the Cavendish pub in Hulme to introduce him to a few criminal contacts and give him a bit of a leg-up. We were standing outside in the smoking area and he said to some lad I knew, in the kind of mockney voice you'd see in a Guy Ritchie film, 'Alwight, you cunt?' He thought he was being funny and clever. The lad didn't see it that way.

'Eh? What did you say?'

I had to smooth it over and vouch for him. 'He's from London, mate, you know what I mean? That's what they fuckin' say to each other. He's alright, our kid.'

'Alright, Mikey. If you say so.'

That was it for me. I wanted no more of this pantomime. Because that's what the job was turning into – a pantomime, and one with a growing cast list. A few days later I was sitting in my apartment mulling over my next move and Jack called.

'Mikey, there's not much knocking about. There might be an operation kicking off down south, but it's not for you. It's a low-level infiltration, living on some shithole estate with a burglary problem. It's not for you, mate, I think you want to be aiming higher.'

'Jack, I don't care,' I said, thoroughly fed up now. 'Just get me off this plot. I don't care what it is.'

I'd given my all to the job, dedicated my life to the operation. I'd lived and breathed Moss Side gangs. Along the way, I'd lost my girlfriend, friends, any semblance of a social life. And for *what*? They didn't include me on the planning, they didn't ask for my advice. They just edged me out; they took what they needed and effectively said, 'Thanks very much – now you can fuck off.' I felt like I'd had the piss taken out of me. I felt angry, used and undervalued – isolated even – and pushed out because I challenged them. Other than Jack, there was no one at Omega who got what I was about and understood my way of working.

This operation was probably one of the last, if not the last, major undercover operations where UK police would use a hometown boy to infiltrate the underworld. It simply would not pass a risk assessment now and, in all honesty, probably shouldn't have then. To this day, I have to look over my shoulder if I'm visiting Manchester. To this day, I carry the burden of this operation. To this day, I bear the mental scars. This was the job I thought would allow me to achieve my goal of being one of the best UCs in the country. It turned out to be one of my biggest regrets.

I needed to get out of the city. It was closing in on me. My personal life had turned to shit and I felt like I couldn't breathe. Maybe I should have walked away from undercover work, but I knew going back into mainstream policing just wouldn't cut it for me or provide me with the challenge I needed. I still harboured the hunger and desire to be the best I could be – just not on that plot.

I took a road trip south to the new plot with Greg, the longstanding Omega DS who'd got me the gig and set up a meet with the bosses of the new police force I'd be working under on my next undercover mission. Greg was stumpy and balding, with a heavy northern twang. He was experienced and understood undercover work, having been both a cover officer and manager for a number of years. Like Trevor, he had his own agenda and we had had our disagreements. Unlike Trevor, I had a flicker of respect for him.

'Look, this is going to be a level below what you've been doing, but I tell you what,' he said as we crawled through a grotty, crack-riddled council estate. 'You're gonna be a rock star down here.'

CHAPTER 10
SMACK, CRACK AND TWO STOLEN TELLIES

D reary flat-roof buildings stood among a maze of ginnels, mugger's-dream walkways and greens so neglected they should have been renamed browns. It was a shoddy arrangement of drab 1970s council houses designed to replicate a pollution-busting model popular in the Netherlands for putting people before cars. Instead, it spewed up a different kind of traffic.

The Arbury, a sprawling council estate spanning 100 acres, was nothing more than a crack den shithole you might expect to find in the poorest inner cities around the country. It was actually in Cambridge. Yes, Cambridge, the land of punting and spectacular architecture; the esteemed city that gave us one of the world's finest universities and the great minds of Stephen Hawking and Charles Darwin. Well, I'll tell you now, just a short bicycle ride from the impeccably manicured lawns lurked a different kind of species. No scholars here – and certainly no saints. This was the school of skulduggery.

Burglars, prostitutes, gang members coming from London to muscle in on the vulnerable, setting up crack-dealing bases at their homes long before the terms 'cuckooing' and 'county lines' were coined. Thieves taking bikes from students; thugs, teen-age tearaways. Scrubbers, scroungers sponging off the state. If you wanted a lesson in crime – you'd get one at the Arbury.

Cambridgeshire Police were struggling to stem a drug-fuelled crime wave. A surge of burglaries and car, motorbike and cycle thefts – what we call volume crime – had the force on the back foot. To tackle the onslaught, they wanted to set up an undercover operation.

I'll be honest – I thought the job was beneath me, but I didn't have much choice. Level 1 undercover jobs are few and far between. You can't just wait for one that you really like the sound of. Besides, it was an opportunity to get out of Manchester. So I took it on.

The Moss Side job was shut down amid acrimony six months after I left. Chaos ensued after my departure, and I was happy I had made the decision to exit stage left from that particular pantomime. The shop got burgled twice after the back door was kicked in. Gaz, the mockney UC, rang Jack – who had taken over covering him – and told him he wouldn't be deploying on the plot anymore as it was too dangerous. One month, he lasted. A month! He even refused to go back to the flat to collect his clothes.

Then they fetched in another lad to replace him – who was a good operator, to be fair, a lad called Mick. But in another calamitous management oversight, it turned out Mick had done an undercover job just a couple of miles away from Moss Side and had given evidence against some of the subjects in court. It was just fucking amateur. They even gave him the Mercedes I'd been driving. One day it blew a tyre on the border of Moss Side, and while he waited for the AA he was robbed at knifepoint and the car was swiped. So that was Mick finished after a matter of weeks.

Ricky carried on opening the Combat MMA shop, in fairness to him, and met a couple of young chancers unconnected to the gangs. He asked them if they could put their hands on any metal – street slang for guns – so they spotted an opportunity and supplied two battered 9mm pistols. Ricky brought in two other UCs to make the buys, but they ended up paying well over the odds. I mean, why fucking complicate it? How many undercovers was Omega going to expose to these low-end targets? They were hardly major firearms suppliers to the Manchester underworld, just some lads who'd spotted an opportunity to make a quick buck with guns that were viable but far from state-of-the-art hardware.

The UCs were asked if they wanted a third gun, and they duly obliged. What they didn't do, either through complacency or lack of knowledge, was bother to get the seller to pull back the slide and check if the barrel was blocked. If they had, they would have seen that the gun was deactivated and therefore no more than an ornamental fucking paperweight – useless and worthless. They handed over thousands for it. Then they tried to rectify the situation and put a call in to the supplier. 'You've sold us a dud and we've paid over the odds,' they moaned.

While he may not have pinged them as undercover cops, his reply spelled out exactly what credibility he thought they had as criminals. 'If I see you around here again, I will fucking light you up.' And with that, Operation Anchor was dead.

Many young men from crime-ridden council estates in cities like Manchester or Liverpool can make a couple of phone calls and be in contact with someone who would probably be able to put their hands on a gun of some description, and that's what happened here. These lads weren't top-end villains, importing and regularly supplying guns to gangsters. They probably just rang their mates pissing themselves at the silly money they were getting for the first two, then clearly thought, *This lot are mugs,* so went one further and sold them a dud.

Don't get me wrong, I'm not saying taking a couple of live guns off the street isn't a good thing. It is. But when I found out that's what finished the job, it was a massive disappointment. The operation that I'd nurtured so carefully, so meticulously, was undone in a matter of months in such a clumsy and wholly avoidable manner; all that good work undone just to take two rusty old guns off the street from chancers who weren't even Moss Side gang members. I'd put so much effort into that operation and I can't help thinking that it should have amounted to so much more. It will be a long time before police have the opportunity to place a Level 1 UC into the Moss Side underworld again.

While waiting for Cambridge to start, I kept myself as busy as I could to avoid going into the Omega office. I deployed in Holland for the Dutch police, and in Belgium. Then I did a buy-bust job in London for the Metropolitan Police. It involved me setting up a deal to buy some guns. Typically in these deals, a UC establishes contact with a target and arranges purchase of a criminal commodity. During the exchange, covert cops strike and arrest everyone. Such operations are difficult to pull off, but when they succeed they are a thing of beauty.

I was still thirsty for the challenge, still laser-focused on the operation. I'd need to be, as Cambridge – or Operation Northwood, as it was christened – would prove a real handful.

It was back to being Mikey. Not Mikey O'Brien this time – but Mikey Bulger. Mikey was a thief whose speciality was hijacking lorries at night on the M62 corridor between Liverpool and Leeds. He'd been nicked and had paperwork from Leeds Crown Court that said he'd been bailed on the condition that he be at home between eleven at night and six in the morning. I had a tag on my leg, and G4S even came and fitted a tracking box in my flat. The bail document gave me credentials as a heavy thief, and the curfew provided the perfect excuse not to have to stay out deploying till all hours. They were both my idea. Wearing a tag says immediately that you're a bit of a naughty boy while the curfew allowed me to go home early.

I wouldn't be the only UC on the job. Joe, my 'uncle', was a wheeler-dealer in the *Minder* mould – a dyed-in-the-wool Yorkshireman who drove round in a classic Jag just like Arthur Daley. He even wore the sheepskin coat and sported a couple of loud-as-you-like sovereigns. He'd be played by a legendary undercover, a fella knocking on for 60 and the longest-serving UC in the country. The idea was that he'd come on the plot twice a week to support me. He was brilliant, a real pro, but also great company and a very funny guy. It didn't matter whether you were a low-level street kid or a serious villain, male or female, he'd always say in a gravelly Yorkshire twang, 'Now listen, luv.' I thought it was hilarious. You'd never have pinged him as an undercover agent in a million years.

Our backstory was that my mother had begged Joe to get me out of the north because her boy Mikey was being led astray by a bad crowd. She wanted Mikey to start a new slate, and with Uncle Joe being a man of means, he could make that happen. He had worked in the Cambridge area many years before and thought it would be the perfect place to set Mikey up in a little business away from his terrible Manchester pals.

If I thought Cambridge was going to be respite from Moss Side, I was in for a shock. Sure, the chances of being shot had significantly fallen, but fuck my life, everyone was at it. The Arbury and nearby estates were littered with wannabe gangsters, prostitutes, crack and smack dealers, junkies, career burglars and car ringers; almost from day one my phone was ringing 24/7. 'Mikey, can you get me this?' 'Mikey, can you do me a favour?' 'I've got a nice Rolex there, Mikey.' This was the *Shameless* of the south and it was non-stop. If I hadn't had that self-imposed curfew to give me a breather from the hive of criminality, I never would have slept.

The brief was simple: buy stolen gear to build up a dossier of evidence against those at the centre of the crime wave and put away as many villains as possible. I'd always had a healthy dislike for burglars. Anyone who breaks into someone's house to steal from them or worse is a piece of shit in my book and deserves all they get. I'd seen many a decent person traumatised after being burgled: frail old ladies scared to answer the door, kids frightened to be in their own home. It's a scummy crime. Goods can be replaced but you can't put a price on the feeling of safety in your own home, as I quickly found out on the plot.

I moved into a ground-floor flat the cover team had identified and immediately didn't like it. Being where it was, bang in the centre of the plot, it was easy for the targets to work out where I lived. The gaff wasn't particularly secure either and had flimsy sliding patio doors that could be opened with the flick of a screwdriver. It's not somewhere I would have chosen and I was constantly on alert. I purposely chose not to operate out of the flat. Instead, I found a little lock-up next to a butcher's on the main road running through Arbury, rented that and used it as a base. I knew lots of people would be walking past, curious as to what was going on in there. We decked it out with bikes and bits and pieces from the police property store. We even had a sign made saying 'Wardy's Wheels', which we put up over the door. It was a veritable Aladdin's cave of gear and a setup aimed at enticing thieves to come in and fence bikes and other stuff they'd nicked. But it needed to be handled with care. English law offers someone accused of a crime a defence if they can show an officer acted as an agent provocateur, meaning they initiated or instigated the crime. They had to come in of their own accord. I just dangled the carrot – if they took a bite then that was their own fault.

From the get-go people would pop by the lock-up or ring my mobile, which was plastered on the Wardy's Wheels sign, offering to sell me all kinds of stolen goods. It wasn't long before I was into the local thieves and became the handler of choice in the area. I was always careful not to buy just any old shit, and I never paid over the odds. Unlike Moss Side, where I painstakingly had to craft Mikey into an accepted part of the criminal community because of the obvious potential risks of serious violence, here, the criminal community came to me. I would buy everything from diamond rings, to Rolex watches, plasma tellies, cars, motorbikes, laptops, computer consoles. You name it – I bought it.

This might have been a level down from the infiltration of Moss Side, but in many ways it was much more challenging – and riskier. Sometimes I'd do ten separate criminal transactions in a day. From morning till late my phone was ringing and I was meeting people, buying knocked-off gear. I had to be switched on all the time because I wasn't just doing business in the lock-up but all over the estate; a professional handler of stolen goods wouldn't want to bring too much attention to a single location or it wouldn't take long for local police to take interest and smash through the door. Then there was the threat of being robbed. A handler of stolen goods needs ready cash to hand, so there's always the chance that whoever you're meeting is going to be with a group or carrying a weapon and can roll you for it. One young crew of burglars I knew must have been ten strong. I used to meet them in a house to buy swag they'd lifted from raids. They could have turned on me at any moment, and there was just no way I would have been able to fight them all. My strategy was to have a laugh with them but always take control. Sometimes I'd do that by acting in an unpredictable manner; people don't like unpredictability – it unsettles them. I'd been around proper dangerous villains; these boys were puppies by comparison. Ten of them in the room or not, there was no doubt who was in control.

Within a few months of the job starting, local cops did take an interest. One day I was at the lock-up and two blokes dressed in shirts and ties walked in. I thought, *'Ello, 'ello, 'ello, these don't look like they're here to sell me some bent gear.*

'Can I help you?' I said, politely. Straight away the elder of the two flashed his police ID and took the lead.

'You Mikey?'

'Yes, I am. Can I help you, Officer?'

'Listen to me, we know you're bang at it and we're keeping an eye on you.'

'Nah, not me, Officer.'

'This is a friendly warning. There won't be another one. Any more and we'll be back with some warrants.'

I decided that being polite and listening rather than talking would be the best option. When they'd walked out I immediately rang my cover officer, and he kicked it up to Andy, who was in charge of the operation. Andy was a good guy and a good boss. He discreetly did what he had to do to make my problems with the local old bill go away without blowing the job out to them. I actually thought, *Fair play to them.* They were doing their job. As was I.

Every day was lively on this plot. I had to be on the ball 24/7 because there was so much potential for my cover to be blown. In the space of one day on a sting operation like this, where I was living on the plot, I could be faced with numerous choices, dilemmas and risks that many undercovers on other operations would only get once in a blue moon. In many ways it was far easier to be Mikey O'Brien than it was to be Mikey Bulger. The only let-up was that on Operation Northwood, I didn't have to permanently keep my eye open for someone I personally knew wandering into the operation. That really was a weight off my mind.

As I did with the Nest in Moss Side, I made a pub called the Jenny Wren my local and became part of the furniture. It was a shithole, flat-roofed pub, slap bang in the middle of the estate and full of wrong 'uns. The gear being offered up every day was hotter than the chicken curry and microwave rice they used to serve up. Even the barmaid's son and husband were at it, offering me knocked-off jewellery, watches, bikes, you name it. Her husband was the local school caretaker and even took me into the school boiler room, where he stashed nicked gear. You just couldn't make that shit up.

I wasted no time in building up a reputation. I decided the best method of self-preservation was to give off a 'fuck with me today, and I'll fuck with you tomorrow' vibe. There is a pecking order in the criminal world, and Mikey Bulger was a professional lorry hijacker from Manchester. Cross someone like that in real life and there would be serious consequences. Local criminals quickly got that message. I took control. I never paid anyone what they wanted, and I was always prepared to walk away if the deal wasn't right.

Many of my customers were heroin and crack addicts. Quite sad creatures really, shoplifting crap on a daily basis to grab a few quid for their next fix. I'd often just refuse to buy off them as they weren't the targets of the operation – well, they weren't mine anyway. I had no desire to get someone nicked over a grafted packet of razors or a couple of cans of deodorant. But there was definitely a wider drugs problem gripping the estate. Everyone seemed to be smoking crack, and let me tell you, people off their heads on crack or chasing money for a hit are unpredictable beasts; they'll stab you and not even remember they've done it.

Bobby was one of the drug-addled thieves that would pour into the lock-up to try and sell me stuff. He was a 20-stone ex-doorman who was hooked on crack. And I mean hooked. He'd come in with hollow eyes, as white as a sheep and with sweat pissing out of him – desperate for his next fix. One morning he came in with a nicked bike. Days earlier, Joe had bought something off him, but Bobby didn't have the right change to give him and owed him a tenner. It was agreed he'd drop it in next time he came to the lock-up.

'Alright, Mikey. I've got a bike here for you,' he said, getting his words out as fast as he could. I remember his eyes bulging at the thought of his next rock. The bike was a worthless piece of shit and I told him as much.

'Besides, you owe me a tenner so I'm not buying anything,' I said, shooting him down.

'Nah, I owe that to Joe.'

'Same fucking thing, Bobby.'

'You need to buy this off me, Mikey. I need to get sorted now.'

'I'm not buying anything off you.' He started to sweat profusely again, greasy liquid filling the creases in his fat forehead.

'Come on, Mikey, I'm desperate.'

I had to show I was no pushover. Mikey was a serious criminal who'd held up lorry drivers at gunpoint. He would not have been fazed by this clown.

'Sort me a tenner and don't fetch me shit here like that. Do you think I'm a mug, Bobby?'

He was clucking for crack. It made him unpredictable. He started pacing frantically.

'Listen, you're fucking buying this off me,' he said, trying to intimidate me.

He was a big unit, not in great shape but could definitely pack a punch and could have had any weapon concealed on him.

His voice was getting louder. He edged towards me in the lock-up with an air of desperation.

I was stood next to a counter and under it could see some tools, among them a hammer.

I inched towards it, thinking, *I'm gonna have to threaten this prick with it if he starts. He's fucking huge. I'm gonna have to hit him with it.* It would have been like trying to put an elephant down. I resisted and shot from the hip instead.

'Don't you fucking mouth off to me, you cheeky cunt,' I snarled, tensing my muscles like a boxer at a weigh-in. 'I don't give a fuck – no cunt tells me what I do.'

The show of rage did the trick and he thought better of what he was doing, retreated and walked out with his tail between his legs. Two days later he came back and apologised, not because he was sorry – sorry doesn't exist in a crack addict's world – but simply because I was an outlet for his stolen goods and he didn't want to ruin that.

It had been a tricky situation. I was under threat but had to stand my ground. If I'd have backed down I'd have lost complete credibility. Haggling with criminals over stolen gear becomes tiresome, and standing my ground to varying degrees was something I had to do every day.

G and his girlfriend were both hopelessly addicted crack and heroin addicts. Flesh hung off their bones and drug-ridden veins bolted through their arms. From the kick-off, I'd been buying stolen gear from G and one of his mates, who the op team had identified as one of the most prolific house burglars in Cambridgeshire.

G was a real piece of shit, always shouting at his missus, who was a timid little thing. I felt for her, stuck in this cycle of misery. G was someone you'd never tire of punching in the face, and it was a struggle to resist sometimes. They would ring me all the fucking time to meet me on the estate so they could flog me stolen gear, usually electrical goods – laptops, iPads and televisions – that had been taken from his burglaries. One Wednesday night they asked me to come to their house to buy a laptop, which was unusual as they would always meet me on the estate outside a row of shops near the Jenny Wren.

I got to the front door, which was slightly ajar, and nearly retched from the stench. It was a mixture of shit, skag and sour milk spilling out of plastic bottles in stacked-up bin bags. Holding my nose, I walked in and couldn't see the floor for dog shit and silver foil. On the coffee table in the middle of the living room were burnt spoons, needles and asthma inhalers that had been converted into crack pipes. There were scattered milk bottles that had been cut open to make bongs. Half-eaten pizza and fried chicken boxes sat on dirty workplaces. I tried to work out which had more flesh on them – the discarded KFC hot wings or the heroin addicts who lived there. Then my heart sank. Crawling around among it on the floor was a toddler. He was about 18 months old. My blood started to boil. *No child should have to live in such squalor,* I thought.

I snapped at G. 'What you selling then? C'mon, hurry up, I haven't got all fuckin' night.'

Then a deep voice boomed across the room. 'What's happenin'?' It was clearly a London accent. I looked up and there was a Black lad standing there glaring at me, with the hood of his dark Nike matching tracksuit over his head. At the time drugs gangs from London were making the 45-minute shuttle trip from King's Cross to Cambridge to deal crack and heroin. They'd muscle into a smackhead's house and use it as their drug-dealing base, what's now known as 'cuckooing'.

G had set me up. These London drug dealers had heard about me and wanted to feel me out, assess the threat. I knew how these crack-dealing cunts operated – just bullies who preyed on addicts and the weak.

'Who are you?' I said, eyeballing him back.

He sucked his teeth in contempt. 'Roy.' For some reason the London lads coming up all called themselves Roy.

'Who are you sucking your fucking teeth at?' I said with venom. I didn't know if he was carrying a knife, a gun, or any other weapon. But I had to take command and dominate like I owned the place, like he was on *my* turf. I exaggerated every move, filling every space and making sure my presence was felt. I couldn't show any sign of weakness or fear. But I was acutely aware there was a child in the house and the last thing I wanted was a violent confrontation near the toddler, so I said to G's girlfriend, 'Take the baby in there,' and pointed to a bedroom.

'Just wanted to see the competition, man, there's no problem,' he said, backing off. By this point he had firmly got the message that I was no walkover.

'Listen, mate,' I said. 'You're a fucking crack dealer. That's not my game. I've got my own thing going on. I'm not interested in you. Not one fucking bit. D'ya get me?'

'Yeah, man, safe.'

I turned to G. 'And you, you fucking rat. You can fuck right off. I'm buying nothing more off you. And don't you ever – *ever* – set me up like that again.'

I kicked the door open and walked out, saying nothing more. I'd confronted many a crack and smack dealer before. It was a dance I'd done a thousand times. But when you're on your own with no backup, it can be a bottle tester. The way I often operated throughout my police career, going on the front foot when faced with confrontation, isn't for everyone and isn't without its risks, but I knew my limitations and knew where the line was. It was a tactic that worked for me. For others I'd say, 'Don't try this at home, kids.'

The rage I felt at the encounter soon gave way to disgust, sorrow even. A feeling of helplessness for the poor baby being brought up in that shithole. I rang my cover officer immediately and told him what had happened.

'Listen, I don't give a fuck about this job or how it looks, or if it compromises me, but you need to get that kid away from that house and away from those parents. The conditions he's living in are inhumane.'

They fed the information to social services and the police safeguarding unit while not revealing the undercover source. The pair were already on social services' radar, and what I'd seen and reported back prompted them into action. I kept my word and refused to deal with G and his missus again after that. Besides, I'd already gathered enough evidence against them. G would end up getting nearly five years' jail time because of the op. I hope the time gave his missus some respite and a chance to get clean, but somehow, I doubt it.

That night I went back to the ground-floor flat I lived in on the estate and I felt empty. I didn't want to be on a shit-hole council estate, in a flimsy two-bed with shitty patio doors. Joe was there a couple of nights a week, and that was great, but when he wasn't, I was alone. Working undercover, far from being glamorous, can be lonely and anxiety-inducing. There was no let-up from the plot and I didn't feel secure in the flat. I used to wedge the front door at night for extra security and sleep with a hammer on the bedside table just in case someone tried to break in and confront me – or worse still, make a move on me because they suspected I was a cop.

I'd been live on operations every day since I walked into Omega. Every single day. It was taking its toll. I was start-ing to tire. I'm not ashamed to say there were times I felt vulnerable and isolated. Every night, I would put my head down on the pillow and fight desperately just to sleep. I thought Cambridge would give me the breather I needed from the mental entrapment of Moss Side. And at first it did. But it didn't ease my anxiety, it didn't make me any hap-pier. I had to just keep on going; no room for self-pity, no room for taking my eye off the ball. I had a job to do.

Word had got round that I'd fronted up one of the Roys from London. Some of the lads on the estate even asked me to start serving up crack and smack because I had built up a reputation, saying, 'We'll sell for you, Mikey.' Obviously I couldn't take them up on it. If I had, however, I could have run that estate, of that I have no doubt. It's the model now adopted by the big county lines drug gangs: travel from the city to the smaller towns, dominate everyone and corner the market. I've seen first-hand how easy it is to do.

Wardy's Wheels went from strength to strength and the loot continued to flood in. God knows what the butcher must have thought, seeing bedraggled smackhead burglars coming and going by the hour. The phone didn't stop ringing. A well-known local burglar I'd been dealing with came in one day clucking for smack and showed me a diamond ring and a Breitling watch. I knew instantly it was the real deal from the training I'd done at a diamond centre before the Moss job. The watch had seen better days, but everything pointed to it being the genuine article. I could see he was going cold turkey for gear, and he said he wanted 500 for them. After I stopped laughing, I told him what I thought.

'The stone is from Argos and the watch is from Turkey, but because I quite like the watch, I'll give you a hundred quid for the both of 'em.'

His protests fell on deaf ears. I knew he wasn't walking away without cash, so we settled on a ton. He asked me if I had 20p for the phone box as he needed to make a quick call, clearly to his dealer. I handed him my mobile and said, 'There, use that but be quick.' So I even got a smack and crack dealer's phone number thrown in for the price. It turned out I was right; the watch and ring had a combined value of over £20,000 and had been stolen from a doctor's house that morning.

I even bought a laptop within hours of it being stolen in a burglary committed on a plush Cambridge apartment. It was a good job I did because it turned out that it only belonged to an American CIA agent who was posted to the UK.

Within months I had amassed a treasure chest of hooky gear, ranging from electrical goods to a garage full of high-powered stolen motorbikes. I had a small army of thieves coming to me with their ill-gotten gains. The evidence was mounting. Crucially, this wasn't a crime wave I'd created. These people were actively out there stealing and making law-abiding families' lives a misery long before Joe and Mikey Bulger turned up. If they hadn't sold to us, there was a queue of unscrupulous handlers and fences ready to cash in on their swag.

Our business was putting a few noses out of joint, and I'd been warned by the ops team that a guy who lived on the estate was known to be the biggest handler of stolen goods in the east of England. He had done time and was apparently a shrewd operator in his late forties.

I'd noticed him casually walk by the lock-up a few times and nonchalantly poke his head round and walk away. It was clear he was scoping us out. He never engaged with either of us and we both distinctly got the impression his snooping wasn't as innocent as it was meant to look. One day I spotted him walking down the road towards the lock-up and it looked like he was on another of his scouting trips.

I was stood on the pavement outside next to the battered Transit van I was using and had my cover officer on the phone. 'Just go with this,' I said. The guy approached me and as he did I flew into an almost psychotic rage down the phone. I pretended to be embroiled in a ferocious domestic with a girlfriend, spitting out the most vile abuse you could imagine. 'Fucking slag', 'cunt', 'ugly bitch'. Then I slammed the flat sole of my size 9 boot into the passenger door of the van, leaving a huge dent – just as he walked past, not knowing where to look.

It may seem utter madness but I thought, *There's no way he's going to think I'm a cop.* Even an undercover one wouldn't behave in such a disgusting way. The following day he came to the lock-up and sold Joe a china tea set. From then on, he'd nervously say hello to me and look away. I could pull off a phony psychotic rage quite well when required, and it had its uses.

Day after day I was covertly capturing evidence against the villains, always mindful that everything I said was also being captured and could potentially undermine the evidence or be seen as entrapment. On operations like this you need your wits about you at all times. It kept my undercover skills sharp. With time, I realised how wrong I'd been when I'd thought this job was beneath me. Operations like Northwood should be compulsory for all UCs.

I'd been told categorically I wasn't authorised to buy drugs, or I would have had no problem wiping out all the dealers on the estate as well. I asked several times for that to be reviewed but the answer was always the same: 'No, carry on as you are.' I had no lack of ambition, though. Taking bits of stolen gear off slaves to crack and heroin gave me no thrill or satisfaction. I thought they needed help and support. The organised crews out there were a different matter. They weren't just robbing, stealing and burgling but would often have their fingers in other pies – like drug supply, weapons and violence. I had no moral quandary when it came to taking them down.

Word was getting around among the organised criminals that I was a reliable buyer of decent stolen gear, and I would get calls from people who'd been given my name. One evening I was back at the flat after a busy day and half thinking about switching the phone off, just to give me a break, when it rang from a number I didn't recognise.

'Hello?'

'Mikey, isn't it?'

'Who's asking?' I said, cautiously feeling the caller out.

'It's Kevin.' He told me he'd got my number from a contact I knew. 'Listen, I've got a car, a laptop and a telly if you're interested and can meet me now.'

'Kevin who?' I said. 'I don't know you, mate.'

'Kevin Wells,' he replied, like I should have been impressed. I wasn't.

But I did instantly recognise the name as I'd been briefed

about him and the crew he knocked around with. Wells was a nasty piece of work and a dangerous man. He was on Cambridgeshire Police's radar after being found not guilty at a gangland trial. A gunman from the back of a motorbike had fired a magazine of bullets from an AK-47 automatic assault rifle at an alleged drug dealer's family home. Wells was suspected to have been part of this hit team. So, this was a chance to take out a key player.

'Don't know you, mate, but it sounds good. What time are you thinking?'

'Eight, at the car park by the roundabout in Milton.'

Eight o'clock? I thought. *That's less than an hour away.* I had minutes to make my mind up.

'Let me ring you back in a min, Kev. Just need to rearrange something quickly.' I was buying myself time.

I rang my cover officer, who – not for the first time – didn't answer his phone, unlike the ultra-reliable Jack, who'd never once let me down. I had a decision to make. Joe wasn't around and I couldn't reach my cover officer. Absolutely no one on earth would have any idea where I was going and who I was meeting. This was a violent man with access to firearms who I knew wouldn't be on his own. I'd never met him before, and now he wanted to meet me in a darkened car park. On the other hand, he was a cut above the other criminals I'd bought off. This was a potentially significant breakthrough and I might not have had the chance again. *But if this goes wrong,* I thought, *I'm truly on my own.*

If I'd have got through to my cover officer and said Kevin Wells had rung me, he'd probably have said to give him an excuse and hold him off, given the intelligence the police had around him. I pondered again for a minute. *Fuck it.* Of course I was going to go. In my mind, after all, there wasn't a situation I couldn't walk out of.

The darkness was illuminated by the hazy glow of a few orange street lights. I turned towards a quiet corner at the back, and at the top of the car park, a few hundred metres away, were three parked police cars in a row with their lights turned off, the officers leaning out of their windows chatting.

'This is all I fucking need,' I muttered to myself, turning round and heading towards the opposite end of the car park. Wells was there with two other guys in a shadowy corner. He was with one bloke in a black Fiesta. Parked in the bay next to them was a dark-coloured Subaru Impreza they'd just stolen. It was fresh off someone's driveway and taken with the keys. Wells and the guy he'd ridden with got out, and I was struck by the bulging frog-like eyes of his pal. It looked like he could see not only what was in front of him but to the sides as well. Then I caught a glimpse of Wells, his dark, malevolent eyes glinting in the street light. There was no small talk.

'I've got the Impreza and there's a Dell laptop and a plasma in the boot,' he said, opening up the dodgy deal.

'Five hundred for the lot,' I said.

The price was agreed. I checked out the telly and laptop and told him to leave them in the Subaru. 'I'm gonna shift it now,' I added, conscious I was buying stolen gear from under the noses of three parked police patrols. Suffice to say I was keen on getting the fuck out of there as soon as possible. 'It's on top here.'

Wells and his boys drove away, and when they had disappeared, I coolly drove the car past the unsuspecting uniforms and out of the car park, hoping they wouldn't decide to give me a pull. We had a location with a large hangar about 40 minutes away from Cambridge that I had been taking all the stolen gear back to for storage. Two giant wooden doors opened and I steered the stolen Subaru into the hangar and parked it up next to the rest of the hot gear I had amassed, all stocked up like goodies at an Amazon warehouse. The value of the loot amounted to hundreds of thousands of pounds.

The operational team identified the three from the covert footage I had taken. One was confirmed as Kevin Wells, and the other two were also ID'd. All three would go on to receive substantial sentences as a result of my evidence. Yet again I'd shown that having a set of balls and going for the prize when others may have hesitated was what undercover work was all about.

After a year on the plot, the weight of evidence against scores of subjects was astounding – way beyond the expectations of the bosses. The job was coming to a close, but the operational team would have a mammoth task of putting the evidence together and planning mass arrests.

I was relieved that the end was coming and we were slowly winding down on plot. Joe said to me one night, 'I'm sick of that Jenny Wren shithole. Shall we go somewhere nice for a drink for a change? I've seen a lovely looking pub down by the university.' As a one-off treat we took ourselves down there on what turned out to be the weekly quiz night. Joe was in his usual sheepskin coat and awash with gold sovereigns and chains, me in a full Lacoste tracksuit with my electronic tag bulging underneath my trouser leg. Talk about fitting in. Not so much *University Challenge* as universally challenged, I bet the quiz boffins thought. The pub was packed with upper-middle-class types.

'Let's have a bash,' Joe said. For the next hour we jotted down our answers and laughed at the serious faces of the quiz geeks competing for the £50 jackpot around us. You could tell they lived for it every week. When the questions ended we swapped papers with the table next to us, who, it turned out, were a collection of lecturers from the university. I clocked them looking over at us suspiciously as they marked our paper. As well they might have. Because we only went and won the fucking quiz! The whole pub looked at us in disbelief: a load of academics had just been handed their arses by Arthur Daley and his tag-wearing nephew in their own backyard. We snatched the 50 quid and gleefully headed off. There's a moral tale involving a book and a cover somewhere.

We got the heads-up that the job would be wrapped up after 14 months living on the plot. So when a local prostitute asked me to come to her house as she had something to sell, I went safe in the knowledge I'd be recording everything. It turned out she had nothing to sell and was more interested in outrageously flirting with me. I politely declined her advances and made my excuses to leave – only for her to give me the location of a local dealer's drugs and cash stash in a false bottom of a fish tank. 'Why don't you rob him?' she said. I thanked her for the information and said I would have a think about it.

Then, on the very last day, I bought a stolen 1,000cc super-bike from a lad who was part of a large burglary and motorbike ring. I had bought thousands of pounds' worth of stolen gear off him and his crew the previous months. He wheeled the motorbike up the scaffold plank onto the back of my van, and as he put the stand on he said, 'Mikey, Gary has said you could be a copper.'

'Who the fuck is Gary?' I replied angrily. 'I tell you what, this is my fucking livelihood. Why don't you tell Gary to come and see me and say that to my face. Going about saying shit like that, the cheeky cunt. Now, are you selling me this bike or what?'

'Yeah, course, Mikey.'

I drove back to the hangar with the bike in the back and added it to the rest of the stolen property. That was the last time I ever set foot in that shithole.

As a result of the intelligence and evidence I gathered, Cambridgeshire Police made a string of coordinated raids, seizing stolen goods, drugs and weapons, and arresting scores of suspects. The operation obliterated the burglary and theft rings operating in the city and sent shock waves through the criminal community. Not one of them saw me coming. Over four weeks I gave evidence behind a screen against those silly enough to plead not guilty even when I had them handing me stolen goods in glorious technicolour. One by one they fell with guilty verdicts from the jury. On the last day of giving evidence against the last defendant, the barrister representing his client addressed me in his cut-glass accent.

'So, undercover law enforcement agent Mikey, would you care to read the transcript of the conversation where you allege my client sold you a pair of stolen ladies' Ted Baker prescription glasses? I'll be my client and you play the role of yourself.'

Me: 'What are them glasses?'

Barrister: 'Oh, you won't want them. They were just in the laptop bag from the car. They are prescription ones, no good to anyone.'

Me: 'No, I'll have 'em. Chuck 'em in the bag.'

Barrister: 'What the fuck do you want them for, Mikey?'

Me: 'I'll make me bird wear 'em when I shag her tonight.'

The jury erupted into laughter as the judge, Mr Hawkesworth called order while giving a wry look over his glasses before slowly shaking his head.

The barrister then turned to me and said, 'So let me get this right, Mikey. You've come down here with a made-up story about who you are and lied to absolutely everybody?'

I wondered where he was going with it and what the sucker punch would be.

'Yes, sir. That's correct.'

'Well, you must be very good at it then,' he enthused, before putting his hands together and turning to the judge. 'No further questions, Your Honour.'

In total, 52 people were convicted for 192 offences and handed nearly 100 years of prison time. 'OPERATION NORTH-WOOD ROCKS THE CAMBRIDGE UNDERWORLD' was the splash headline in the *Cambridge News*. Greg was right – I was a rock star.

The operation heralded a sharp fall in burglary figures and gave the good people of Cambridge a well-deserved rest from the predatory thieves that had for so long wrought havoc and misery. I was awarded a Crown Court judge's commendation for the work in Cambridge – one of the highest accolades a police officer can receive. I felt proud at my achievement and had shown I could turn my hand to any undercover work. I thought, *Surely I'll be welcomed back to Omega with open arms*. The reception I would get would be nothing of the sort.

CHAPTER 11
A VILLAIN'S WELCOME

My stock was high on the undercover circuit after Cambridge, Moss Side and other shorter-term operations. Joe, my oppo on the Arbury estate, was a respected figure on the circuit, being the oldest and longest-serving UC in the country at the time. He knew about my clashes with Omega bosses and that the relationship with them was thin at best, and he thought the best move for me was to get on a fresh undercover op well away from Manchester. I agreed. Fair play to Joe, he called on his contacts, including a guy who headed up one of the leading regional special operation units outside GMP and the Met.

'He's the best undercover in the country, this kid,' he told them. 'Grab him while you can.' It was high praise coming from someone with his CV, and after they called Christie – who backed up Joe's appraisal – the unit made direct contact with me about a job that was still in the planning stages. A force in one of the UK's major cities had been targeting, with little success, a dangerous, high-rolling organised gang of drug importers. They had been looking for a UC with the right profile to infiltrate the OCG. I listened to the brief with interest. No longer would I be slumming it on a crack-infested estate, but I'd be back playing the professional criminal with a plush city-centre pad and Range Rover Sport, pitting my wits against Premier League gangsters. Another exciting challenge beckoned. It's fair to say the crack den toil of Cambridge had taken its toll on me, but it would anyone – 14 months living on a scummy estate with thieves and junkies for your daily company would be enough to dampen the sunniest disposition. However, I still loved the job, and the desire for the unique challenges undercover work posed still burned strong inside me.

I was a different animal now from the young cop that had started out knowing nothing about this secretive world. I had developed at a rapid rate, having spent almost every day of my Omega tenure on live operations, going head-to-head with criminals. I'd gone from being Christie's protégé, the raw trainee, to an accomplished UC who could operate on any level, against any kind of crook. The simple fact was this: everyone who came up against me went to jail. *Who wants to be next?* That's the way I thought. I was at the peak of my powers, and I was hungry to go on and achieve more. *Fuck it,* I thought. *Back playing with the big boys.* And back in the league where I belonged.

Despite the personal troubles undercover work brought, I'd somehow managed to resurrect my home life. I got back with my girlfriend, having made a real effort to repair the relationship. The time apart in Cambridge – and the relief from the pressure of being on a live op in Manchester – certainly helped. It took patience and forgiveness on her part. But we were making inroads and I had an element of domestic stability that I hadn't felt for some time.

With this fresh opportunity in the offing and my home life as sturdy as it could be for me, I went back to Omega with the Cambridge convictions and Crown Court judge's commendation in the bag. I even returned with a fresh outlook, hoping my clashes with management over the Moss Side operation would be consigned to history, allowing us to move forward. After all, I'd just gone to another force and city as a representative of GMP and Omega and smashed it.

I couldn't have been more wrong. I wasn't expecting bunting and bugles – but recognition of a job well done would have been nice. Nothing. In fact, their attitude towards me was one of ignorance and passive aggression. *Fuck you, then,* I thought. *I'll be gone from here soon anyway.*

One of the lads from Omega was into some big heroin dealers on the other side of the country and asked me to go on the job with him, which initially kept me busy. But it wouldn't be without its mither. We ended up embroiled in a nightclub brawl after it kicked off between the targets we were with and a rival OCG. Neither I nor my colleagues were given to being anyone's punchbag, and I have to admit the CCTV didn't look good. But our actions were in self-defence and justified. We fought our way out and got away as soon as we could. Needless to say, it didn't go down well with police bosses, but if you hang around with organised criminals, your chances of involvement in a violent confrontation significantly increase.

I kept regular contact with the detective sergeant at the unit that had approached me for the drugs gang op, and preparations were being put in place for the job to commence. He did, however, tell me that the unit had made the official request to Omega, as was the protocol, and that the reception had been somewhat frosty, although he didn't think it would be a major issue. A few days later I was called to a meeting that I thought was to discuss my secondment to the new operation. In the office were the three supervisors, Trevor, Greg and Ted. It's fair to say, there was no love lost between us. I had zero respect for the professional capabilities of Ted and Trevor, and Greg always had his own agenda at heart. Ted, giving me a rabbit-in-the-headlights look he seemed to have perfected over the years, made the opening gambit.

'I'm just going to be straight with you, Shay. This undercover job – you're not doing it. You're not going to be going there. In fact, we've decided you'll be leaving the unit and going back to conventional policing.'

As he spoke, I clocked the smirk on Trevor's face and I could tell he was loving it.

'Why's that?' I said.

'For one, you're burnt in Manchester because of the Moss Side operation and you're a GMP asset,' Ted replied. 'We've seconded you out to several forces now and, well, it's time for you to go back to normal policing.'

Then came the telling line.

'Also . . . between us we've got sixty years' experience of managing in the police, and you're the most difficult person we've ever had to manage.'

They were revelling in the condemnation. I felt deflated but I wasn't going to let them see it. I maintained a poker face as I delivered my response.

'I think that says more about your collective ability than mine.'

They also accused me of bypassing protocols by speaking to the external undercover unit without going through them first.

It was grade-A nitpicking, but I knew there was no arguing. Besides, I have more self-respect than to plead. And in all honesty, I'd anticipated this was coming, judging by the cold reception I had received on my return from Cambridge and the lukewarm response the DS from the planned operation faced when he told them he wanted me.

Who knows what it boiled down to. Maybe it was professional jealousy. I could do the job with comparative ease. The statistics don't lie. I'd put more criminals away during my stint undercover than the rest of the Omega operatives put together. Not that numbers were everything, but my track record was unquestionable. I'd challenged Trevor in Moss Side; I'd crossed swords with Greg once too often as well. And as for Ted, well, his track record spoke for itself.

'What we're going to do is facilitate your resettlement back into conventional policing. We haven't thought about it yet, so while we sort that out you can go on gardening leave.'

As always, I had plan B in my pocket. I'd not lost the ability to think as many steps ahead as the situation required. I looked at the smirking Trevor with a stony face, stood up and left the room, skipping the pleasantries.

This kind of exit was not unusual at Omega. Several other cops, including a long-serving, talented and remarkably intelligent cover officer, had been forced out of the unit after highlighting failings of the management over UC ops. Then there was Christie, one of the best undercover operators of his generation – if not the best – banished because his knowledge, experience and willingness to point out failings were seen not as an asset but a threat.

I immediately rang my contact at the undercover unit where the job had been teed up and told him what had happened. We discussed the whys and wherefores of it, and he was pissed off. He said they'd started the planning for the op, anticipating I'd be the primary UC. He said he'd speak to his boss and explore the potential of me transferring to his force so they could post me straight to the undercover unit and do the job that way. 'Good idea,' I replied.

A week into my gardening leave, I met with management from my prospective employer's undercover unit at a motorway service station. At the time there was a national ban on transfers between police forces – other than for specialist skills reasons cleared by the chief con – which made any move less than straightforward. We had a good chat and I gave them my loose thoughts on the legend and other operational matters, and they all agreed they would fill out the relevant forms and approach the chief constable to make the transfer happen. A week later they called me saying they had been forced to pull the plug. 'I don't know what's gone on, mate,' the DS told me. 'But you've upset someone. There's words been had at the top level. We want you but we've been told we're not having you.'

If Omega kicking me to touch was a knock, this was a hammer blow; one born out of spite and deep-seated malice. I was fucking fuming. *Why not just let me transfer? What's it to them?* I thought. Clearly, they had it in for me.

Christie got wind of what had happened and rang me up. He said he'd heard that management at Omega were saying I had Stockholm syndrome – that I was 'Stockholmed up' – and that I didn't know what side I was on. No undercover unit worth its salt would take a risk on a UC if that were the case. Yet the slur was being bandied around with no foundation or shred of evidence to support it. It was a disgusting trick to pull.

The truth is that the bosses didn't get me at all. They were dyed-in-the wool cops; they couldn't be anything but cops. Whereas I found it natural to play a criminal. I didn't have to get into character. I didn't have to do the breathing exercises and visualisation like the method actors you see in Oscar-winning films. I just had to be me. Yet it would appear that I was so convincing a criminal, I'd fooled even those supposedly on my side. And they mistakenly saw me as some confused, potentially corrupt loose cannon. It was ludicrous. What's more, if that is what they truly believed then where was the safeguarding? Where was the duty of care and psychological support? Surely, if they thought an undercover was so enmeshed in that murky world that he couldn't distinguish between the role he was playing and who he really was, then you'd expect at the very least a professional intervention. The fact is, they never offered me any support after the psychiatrist sessions, which were meaningless to me – and were probably box-ticking to the police.

I was being punished, discredited. My integrity was in question – my career potentially ruined. The words of my girlfriend echoed through my mind once again. 'The police don't give a shit about you, Shay.' I'd been a fool. She was the smart one in our relationship – there was no doubt about that. Bitterness ripped through me. I'd had something taken from me that I was good at and loved doing, something I felt I was born to do, by people who didn't have the brains or balls to do it themselves. And there was no credible reason for it. It was now me versus them.

For weeks I stewed at home, barely sleeping. There was no contact, no word on how my transition would look or where I'd be going. They wanted me to stew. *What the fuck am I going to do now?* I thought. I'd been running around playing the gangster for the biggest part of my police career, yet just like that I was supposed to put Mikey in a box and be DC Doyle again. It may work in theory, but let me assure you, it just isn't that simple in practice. Working undercover changes you. I decided that was it – I was going to leave the police. But on my terms. And I wasn't going quietly either.

I got called back into the office where the head of the unit, the superintendent and Ted were waiting.

'Where do you want to go?' asked the superintendent. 'What do you want to do?'

'I'd like to fly the police helicopter,' I replied facetiously.

He screwed his face up at my retort. 'I'll tell you where you're going,' he said. 'You're going to be posted to the surveillance unit where you'll be the office manager.'

'Office manager?' I said. 'You're having a laugh, aren't you? What does that entail?'

'You'll copy disks of the day's surveillance footage and carry out administrative tasks as directed by your supervisor.'

I could almost smell the smug satisfaction filling the room. I felt belittled and demeaned. If you are ever in charge of reintegrating Level 1 UCs – who have spent the largest part of their police career portraying serious criminals – back into conventional duties, a fucking admin role copying disks is not the way to go. However, if you wish to use it as the catalyst for a serious decline in their mental health, it's an absolute winner.

I would never let them see me defeated in meetings and would always deploy my well-practised poker face that had stood me in good stead when up close and personal with some serious villains. And that's what I did here. I showed them a face that said, 'Do your worst – I am fucking impervious to you.'

'Right, OK. If this is how you wanna play it, let's see how it goes, shall we?'

In my final days at Omega I was called to attend an appointment with the force psychiatrist, which felt like another box-ticking exercise by management designed to document that they had discharged their duty of care to me. It was, in fact, bollocks.

I sat down and his opening line was 'You do know you'll never work undercover again, don't you, Shay?'

'Oh yeah? Why's that, then?' I replied.

'Because, Shay, how can I put it? They kick you, and you kick them back.'

In my opinion you don't send weak-willed, compliant yes-men to infiltrate criminal gangs. Yes, you need professionalism, and I'd always displayed that – you don't get jobs home in the Crown Court without it. But in the world of undercover and serious crime investigations, too much compliance breeds mediocrity. The leadership style I would adopt later in my career would be to encourage people to challenge me and think creatively. Rank does not mean you have all the answers to every problem. Give people a problem to solve and a platform to showcase what they can do, and you'll be amazed at the ideas and results they will bring. But you need strength of character as a leader to let that kind of culture flourish. Omega management were devoid of it. And that, ultimately, was Omega's downfall. The management team brought in compliant officers – most of whom simply would not have got through Christie's UC selection process – and slowly but surely the castle crumbled. Successful operations became a rarity, and the unit was besieged with staff grievances and even allegations of criminal conduct against management. To allow a unit with Omega's rich history, one that was once the envy of international undercover policing, to fall from grace in this way was akin to leaving a Formula One Ferrari in the hands of a taxi driver. Eventually, the undercover course and dedicated unit was taken away from GMP. Omega, sadly, was no more.

After a month's gardening leave, I was seething. But there was more humiliation to come. As I stared at the computer screen on my first day in the surveillance unit broom cupboard, I felt like smashing the room up and storming out. I could picture Omega management's smug faces laughing at how they got one over on me, and it was winding me right up.

It started to affect my behaviour at home. I was angry and impatient. I found it difficult to switch off. That hypervigilance, so useful to me when tackling Moss Side gangsters as Mikey O'Brien, was now rearing its head in an ugly way. Unlike some UCs who spent months of their time legend-building, I was operational every day. I didn't need complex backstopping. Give me some cash wrapped in an elastic band and I'll go on the street against anyone – that was my mindset. Some UCs wanted ten years' business accounts behind them before they would step on a plot, or wouldn't entertain going on a job without the right car. The props were inconsequential to me. I truly believe I'd have done the same job wearing a donkey jacket and a pair of steel toe-capped boots. My most powerful weapon was my mind. But when you've dedicated yourself to something so high-risk, it consumes you mentally. You can't just flick a switch and turn it off. It started to feel like my best asset was working against me. I'd wake up at night thinking of ways to get back at Omega management.

I'd been undercover for the best part of my police service in intense, high-stakes jobs, rarely departing from my role as a round-the-clock criminal. The shadow of Moss Side still hung over me; the potential risks still loomed large. Just because I was no longer in Omega didn't mean the threat subsided. It was something I would have to manage the rest of my life. Yet this was their idea of my transition. This was me being eased back into conventional policing. I didn't know then what I know now about mental health, but there was no safeguarding, no support, and no reintegration.

Instead, I was dumped in a broom cupboard. *That* is fucking criminal.

Self-loathing swept over me. I started to question my decisions. *Why did I go into Moss Side? Why did I let them have me over? They've chewed me up and spat me out. I'm a mug.* I realised that I'd got all my priorities wrong and that they didn't give a fuck about me. Letting me go undercover in my home city – virtually in my own backyard – was nothing short of negligence. I wanted out. *Fuck the police* was now my thinking. *Fuck 'em.*

Ian, the surveillance unit inspector, was baffled as to why I had been sent there to undertake a civilian admin role. He was a decent guy, to be fair, and I had no axe to grind with him. But I had to get out. On my first day in there, I pulled him aside.

'Boss, you've got a week to get me out of this unit and get me somewhere decent – or I'll do it my way. I'd rather not cause a fuss but I'll tell you now, I am not staying here doing this – it's taking the piss.'

There was still time to add a sprinkling of salt in what was now a pretty open wound. Cambridgeshire Police sent up my framed commendation issued by the Crown Court judge, with a plaque and letter of appreciation from the chief constable, to be presented to me in force. Normally it would be done over a cup of tea and a handshake with the chief. But I'd been informed in an email from Ted that mine had been plonked in a bin bag and given to a security guard at Sedgley Park for me to collect. Aside from the fact that it potentially identified me as an undercover operative to the security guys there and compromised operational security procedures, it was a pretty shitty way of dealing with someone who had gone above and beyond in the line of duty.

I contacted Brendan, my old boss at the OCU, seeing if he would have me back, but he had moved on after a promotion and no longer held sway there. As my first week at the surveillance unit drew to a close, my mood was as dark as the stuffy broom cupboard I was working in. I could see no sign of an escape. Then on the Thursday, a civilian manager swung open the door and started barking orders at me, including one to fill his personal car with de-icer.

Ignoring the look of shit-on-your-shoe disgust he gave me, I simply replied, 'I'm not a mechanic, I won't be doing that.' To which came the retort, 'You bloody well will.'

The following day I was chatting to one of the surveillance lads when the door flew open again. Standing there was the civilian manager, face contorted with anger, pointing at me.

'I fucking told you to do something, so you do it.'

I smiled inside and thought to myself, *You have just crossed the line and opened the door into my world now.* Bingo. This was my ticket out of here. I was always taught in the police to speak to people in a language they understand; this person obviously thought swearing and pointing with a

raised voice were acceptable. So I deemed it equally acceptable to bring Mikey into the room.

'Who the fuck are you pointing at, cunt?'

The manager recoiled, like a playground bully who'd met
their match, before running to Ian telling tales. Luckily the
lad from the surveillance unit corroborated what happened
and they had nowhere to go with disciplining me. Within
two hours Ian informed me that I could go home and I would
be starting at the murder squad on Monday morning.

CHAPTER 12
THE CHRONICLES OF WYTHENSHAWE

For many detectives, the murder squad, or Major Incident Team, represents the pinnacle of their police career. Christie had served there and assured me it was an interesting place to work. But after everything that had gone on, my mistrust for senior cops was at an all-time high. I had no love for the job anymore. I was consumed by bitterness over the Omega saga and was planning to quit the force. The only thing stopping me was that, like everyone else, I had bills to pay and so needed to find something first.

My new boss at MIT called me in on the first day, and I barely registered a word he was saying. He was the polar opposite of me, a career desk jockey fast-tracked through the High Potential Development Scheme I'd turned down. He did little to sway my view that police management weren't to be trusted. I just glared through him while he showered himself with praise. I was simply biding my time, waiting for the first decent opportunity to leave the cops. By the same token, I knew I needed to try and pick my mood up and put Omega behind me, for my own sanity if nothing else. Forcing their hand to get me out of the broom cupboard was a minor victory at least. But if I thought Omega bosses had finished fucking with me, I was very much mistaken.

I'd only been at MIT for a week and was internally struggling with the transition from portraying a swaggering street criminal to a tie-wearing detective. It felt alien. I was sullen and withdrawn and wasn't engaging much with the team. I turned up for work one morning and two detectives from the Professional Standards Department were waiting for me. These are the people who investigate corrupt cops or cops that commit serious disciplinary offences. They told me an allegation had been made from an anonymous source, claiming I'd been taking cocaine while working undercover in Moss Side. I burst out laughing. *They are taking the piss,* I thought, giving them an incredulous stare. *These fuckers won't just settle for kicking me out of the unit, they want my job as well.*

They interviewed me under caution for possession of cocaine and recorded it like any other criminal interview. In fairness, the DS who questioned me had a look all over his face that said he was perplexed as to why he was quizzing me over it. 'Would you consent to a drugs test?' he asked.

'Yeah, piss test me now,' I said, struggling to control my anger. 'I can't believe we're even having this conversation.'

I told him they were nothing more than malicious claims, part of an ongoing smear campaign led by management at

Omega. Anonymous and unsubstantiated allegations years after I'd done the job. When the recording was turned off the female constable accompanying the DS during the interview piped up. 'If we don't get you for this we'll get you for something else.' It was at this point I lost my shit. This now had gone beyond a personal dislike of me. This was Omega bosses misusing their position and power in an attempt to turn the force against me. It was blatant organisational bullying. I felt powerless. How could I stand up to the machine?

'Oh, will you now? Oh, fucking will you now? Sergeant, you've just witnessed that. Get me for what? I haven't done anything. Get me for what? Are you gonna fit me up? Are you gonna plant evidence on me? I think what you've just said is totally inappropriate and I'd like you to document that, Sergeant. I want to make an official complaint.' Of course, I knew they wouldn't make an official complaint from me against one of their own.

I left the interview in a state of fury. I felt completely isolated. Lesser men would have crumbled, and I'll admit, it was wearing me down. But I'd only been taught one way to go when my back was against the wall. And that was to come out fighting. All I could think of was *That's it, I'm going to fuck with each and every one of those bastards at Omega.* I started to wish I'd never stepped foot into the toxic world of undercover policing.

Within an hour of the interview ending the DS rang me and was almost apologetic in his tone. He said it was ridiculous that they had to interview me and that the allegation would not be pursued further. He asked me to drop the complaint against the female constable. I refused. 'You sent the lamb to the slaughter,' I said. 'Maybe you should choose your partners more wisely next time.' They never asked for the drug test.

I went back to the murder squad reeling from the audacity and sheer malice of it all. Not only had Omega taken away from me the undercover job I loved, blocked my transfer and humiliated me by putting me in a broom cupboard, copying disks; they had now tried to disgrace me, get me sacked and take away my livelihood. I felt under siege. It was a lonely place, and the whole thing was starting to have a huge impact on my mental health. But just when I couldn't see a way out of the dark, a chink of light came my way.

Paul, a DS at the murder squad, was a tough and seasoned detective. I'd heard of his formidable reputation when I first started at Tameside. Paul had been designated as my immediate supervisor, and he'd been quietly observing me from the day I arrived. He knew my background and could see I was deeply unhappy, but instead of bombarding me he gave me space to settle in. It was a shrewd move. Paul very quickly read the situation and grasped that playing the overbearing detective sergeant wouldn't wash and would inevitably lead to confrontation.

At this point I was thinking long and hard about going off sick – I just didn't want to be there. I felt it was me against the police and that I owed them nothing. But the words of my dad that had haunted me all my life bounced around my head again. 'Never back down to anyone.'

Fuck 'em, I thought. I wasn't going to pull a sickie; to do that would be to show weakness. To do that would be to tell them they were winning. But I still couldn't see a way through the turmoil.

Paul said, 'Let's go for a walk, Shay,' and asked me about the PSD interview. He was well connected in the force and had been doing his own due diligence.

'I've heard good things about you, Shay. You're a switched-on, brave lad by all accounts. Don't let them grind you down. So, the undercover work is no more. Doesn't mean you can't be the best detective you can be. You've some unique skills. Put them to use here. I will see you right, Shay. I don't go in for the rank-pulling bullshit. I know you've spent most of your career lying, but all I ask is you never lie to me. And, Shay, remember, the best revenge is success.'

I liked Paul. He was a top cop and, importantly, he was right. Success is indeed the best form of revenge. So, I decided to pick myself up and make that my mission.

I threw myself into the murders we were dealing with. They were mainly domestic killings. It surprised me a little, but I started to enjoy working on them. I had an inquisitive mind and a natural ability to glean information from witnesses and offenders. My friendship with Paul grew. I learned loads from him. Paul was eccentric and unorthodox in his approach to investigations. Other cops thought he was a bit off the wall. And in many ways he was. He was like Manchester's version of Columbo. But that just made me like him more. I enjoyed watching people underestimate him. The guy was a very, very shrewd detective.

Paul came to me one day and said, 'I've got one for you, Shay. You know Wythenshawe and guns, don't you?'

'Yeah, a bit,' I said.

'The boss has given me this job to review and write off, but I think it's got legs. It's a non-fatal shooting – do you fancy having a look at it?'

'Yeah, why not.'

I always found Wythenshawe a strange place. It once held the unenviable title of being the biggest council estate in Europe. It's predominantly white working class and has always had its fair share of street gangs and OCGs serving up drugs and the inevitable violence that goes with them. There's a perceived 'don't talk to the police' or 'grass' culture – though let me debunk that little myth now. There is zero honour among thieves, and in my experience most villains, no matter their reputation on the street, or the bullshit they spout, will talk if the motivation is right. And I can tell you personally, criminals love to talk. Perpetuating this myth merely puts off decent people who have to live in these communities from talking to the police if they have witnessed an incident. The last thing they want is bricks or bullets going through their window, and frankly, who can blame them?

A few weeks earlier, Mark, a Wythenshawe lad, was standing on the pavement talking to his mate when a man in a black Volvo S40 opened his passenger window and fired four rounds from a semi-automatic pistol. It was the lad he was standing with who was believed to be the intended target, but Mark took one in the leg. The spent cartridges scattered over the pavement revealed they had been fired from a Glock pistol, now a weapon of choice in gangland disputes but back then relatively unheard of. It might have just been a non-fatal firearms discharge, but the fact a semi-automatic pistol was used made it a serious enough job for the Major Incident Team, and Operation Bezant was launched.

My initial focus was on the getaway vehicle. After some covert tasking, I obtained information that gave me the reg plate of the Volvo and revealed that it had been taken to a scrapyard to be disposed of. On a hiding to nothing, I secured a warrant and turned up at the scrapyard, and after some gentle persuasion and a lesson in the law on assisting offenders and the potential prison sentence that can carry to the owner, I was pointed to a cube-shaped mesh of metal. 'I think that was a Volvo,' said the scrap man.

'Well, get your machine then and get to work. I want it unfolded, pronto.'

It was the black S40 and the registration matched. Bingo, we had the offending car. On further inspection, the key was still in the ignition and a jumper on the back seat, so I forensically recovered them and sent them to the lab. DNA on the key came back matching to a guy called Paul Taylor. He was a middle-aged man and a relative nobody in criminal terms. The only reason we got a match on the DNA database was through a conviction for drink-driving.

We obtained a firearms warrant, and the plan was to arrest him for possession of firearms and attempted murder and take him in for questioning. Even though we could put him to the car, we couldn't put him at the scene of the shooting. Besides, he didn't fit the profile. It was a speculative effort, but off we went for the early-morning knock at his house. We would end up with much more than we bargained for.

In hoodies and jeans, two of us stood on the doorstep of the two-bed red-brick semi, primed for the 6am raid. There was no need for the battering ram. A woman, still in her nightie, answered our knock swiftly. Her eyes widened at the sight of our uniform backup – two officers wearing high-vis coats in the misty October dawn. She needed to see exactly who we were. There could be no mistaking that it was the police. When you're making an arrest at a house you have reason to believe contains guns, the last thing you want is someone mistaking you for a rival because you're in plain clothes, and opening fire.

The door opened and, skipping the pleasantries, I sprinted past her up the stairs, followed by my colleague Paul. Sitting up in the double bed was the man we'd come to see, Taylor, his fingernails clawing at the covers, betraying his desperate attempt to remain calm. He knew what was coming.

'Are there any guns in this house?' I asked firmly.

'No, nothing.' His voice crackled slightly.

I'm not sure why I did it – call it instinct – but I knew he was lying and I could tell he was shitting himself. I stepped forward and pulled back the sky-blue quilt he was under. Lying proudly across the creased white sheet, pointing directly at me and within arm's reach of Taylor, was a pump-action shotgun. My military training kicked in and I closed the space between us as fast as I could, limiting his ability to grab the weapon – hoping I was quicker than him – while simultaneously shouting, 'Fucking get down now! Gun! Gun! Gun! Get fucking down now!'

I was quicker. And I smothered him, getting the cuffs on as quickly as possible as the echo of boots steaming up the stairs reverberated around the thin plastered walls. There was no fight in him. Once I had him under control I inspected the bed more closely. The firearm was a Benelli semi-automatic shotgun, a military-grade weapon used by the US Marine Corps in Afghanistan. Next to it was a crumpled shiny blue plastic bag containing a loaded Glock 9mm pistol and ammunition. *That's another one of my lives used up,* I thought to myself.

Taylor didn't know how lucky he was. If I'd have been an armed cop that day, there would have been a good chance I'd have shot him dead. He had panicked and hurriedly hid the shotgun and pistol under the quilt – there was no intent to use them against us – but in the split moment that quilt came back, one wrong move from him and his life would have been over had I been armed. Of that I have no doubt.

We took control of Taylor and his missus, who was now also under arrest, and made a cursory search of the address to ensure there was no one hiding, waiting to jump out on us with other military hardware. We followed standard operating procedure and called a halt to the search for a scenes of crime officer to come in and photograph the evidence in situ.

At this point there was a real buzz. There hadn't been many – if any – police forces in the country at the time who had recovered any Glocks. Our boss even rang the chief constable minutes after getting wind of the seizure. 'There's a job on here, Chief,' he told him excitedly.

Taylor was 46 – although the wrinkly bags under his eyes and the grey hair tinted with specks of light brown suggested otherwise – and had no form, but on closer inspection we had discovered he was connected to one of Wythenshawe's most active OCGs. I wasn't satisfied that those were the only firearms in the house, so once the guns on the bed had been secured, I searched the room for more.

I opened the wardrobe. Bingo. Forget Narnia, this was the Chronicles of Wythenshawe. Sitting there in a camouflaged aluminium case was a Škorpion sub-machine gun. Next to it was a pair of bright blue latex gloves and 1,000 rounds of hollow-point and soft-point bullets. It was a serious piece of kit.

On the top shelf of the wardrobe was another 9mm pistol and more rounds. No ordinary pistol either. It transpired that it was an Iraqi Tariq pistol, a replica of the Beretta M1951 and used by Saddam Hussein's Republican Guard in the war with Iran. On the grip was a gold medallion bearing the portrait of Islamic general and Muslim crusader Tariq ibn Ziyad. A squaddie had clearly got his hands on a war prize and brought it back from Iraq.

The total haul consisted of two 9mm pistols (the Glock and Tariq), a 12-bore pump-action shotgun and a Škorpion sub-machine gun with over 1,200 rounds of assorted ammunition – we had clearly hit the OCG's storeman. This was serious hardware capable of causing multiple murders and mayhem. Ballistics experts were able to link two of the guns to a string of gangland shootings over the previous decade.

They were able to show unequivocally that the Tariq was used in three shootings in Manchester, including one in which a bullet narrowly missed a baby.

They found that the Škorpion sub-machine gun had been used to shoot a man in a car in the chest and by gangsters who sprayed up the Sugar Lounge Bar in Manchester city centre. It was also fired inside Jalons Restaurant on Liverpool's Smithdown Road ten years previously while several stars from Liverpool FC were inside. (What we often found was that an OCG from one city had a stash of guns they'd swap with weapons belonging to an OCG from another.)

Paul Taylor was clearly storing these guns for a heavy Wythenshawe drugs gang and was by no means a major player, or even a gangster at all. He probably was paid very little – maybe even in drugs – yet took all the risk. And he paid a heavy price. Taylor was bang to rights, with nowhere to hide.

'You should have come last week,' he told me off the record. 'You'd have found all kinds.'

He was clearly having one of those moments when you know the walls are closing in, you're resigned to your fate and you can either laugh or cry.

He could have supplied intelligence or evidence to bring down entire organised crime groups in return for a lesser sentence and potentially gone on witness protection. He chose, probably wisely, to say nothing.

Taylor was found guilty of running a round-the-clock weapons safe house for criminals from the home he shared with his lover, Kimberley Bray, a teaching assistant at a Catholic school who fancied herself as a bit of a gangster's moll. She even had a bullet pendant, which was used in evidence against her.

He was dubbed 'quartermaster to the criminal underworld' in court and got 17 years after admitting possessing guns and ammunition with intent to enable others to endanger life, as well as production of cannabis. The judge threw the book at him. Bray was jailed for eight years for possessing the 9mm pistols, the shotgun and ammunition. She was cleared of possessing the machine gun and producing cannabis.

I'd uncovered the biggest single seizure of firearms that year in Manchester. You could say it was luck, but I say you make your own luck. I'd pieced together intelligence and followed up on it where others may not have bothered. And we weren't done there. I sent all the bullet packaging off to the lab, and fingerprints on a Robert Wiseman Dairies plastic bag containing shotgun cartridges came back to an HGV driver who worked there, Robbie Vincent.

It was another tenuous link, and it was wholly conceivable that an HGV driver that worked for Wiseman could have touched a carrier bag that came from his place of work. Add to that the fact that shotgun rounds aren't even illegal to possess unless you're prohibited to do so. But Vincent wasn't your average lorry driver – he was a violent, jet-setting gangster who had served a long stretch for shooting his former girlfriend in the legs with a shotgun while in their kitchen and was subsequently banned from possessing any kind of ammunition.

Despite the flimsy forensic link, I decided to nick him for possession of ammunition at work to limit the chances of him kicking off before we could execute a warrant at his house. I arrived at the dairy in Trafford Park and secured his private-plated BMW M3 in the work car park. Then I rang him.

'Robbie, it's Detective Constable Shay Doyle from Greater Manchester Police here, I'm just at Wiseman Dairies and I need to speak to you about something.'

'Oh right,' he said, thinking he could play me for a mug. 'I'm just out of the country at the minute.'

'Are you sure about that?' I said. 'Because I'm standing next to your car at work.'

'I'm going to fuck off then,' he said angrily.

'You can do that if you want,' I told him. 'But I know where you live, I know where you work, I know where your girlfriend lives, I know where your family and mates live – eventually, I will track you down. If you want me to visit all of these people, that's up to you.'

I purposely didn't tell him what I wanted to speak to him about. I didn't exactly have much on him – just his fingerprints on a plastic bag from his workplace that wouldn't have stood up in court, despite what was in the bag.

'I'm here now, so we might as well speak now,' I said.

Eventually he gave in. 'Right, I'll come out then.'

He had time to dump anything incriminating, and after five minutes or so he walked out of the warehouse and was arrested and immediately searched. He had nothing on him apart from a solitary key in the side pocket of his trousers. It was a key that would cost him 13 years in prison, and I

THE CHRONICLES OF WYTHENSHAWE

would forever scratch my head as to why he didn't dump or hide it; he had ample opportunity to do so.

The work site was vast and had numerous staff lockers. We painstakingly tried each and every one until the key eventually clicked one open. Concealed in a portable strong box was a Glock 26 handgun, two magazines and 143 bullets. He also had the obligatory cannabis grow on at his house. I interviewed Vincent and he got 13 years in prison.

Around a year later another Glock was found under a cushion in a caravan in Pendlebury, Salford, and NABIS, the National Ballistics Intelligence Service, traced it to the original shooting in Wythenshawe.

The two Glocks recovered provided invaluable evidence to international gun-running investigations. One gun-running outfit was headed by Steven Greenhoe, a former US Marine and Madonna's bodyguard, who was legally buying Glocks in America but splitting them down and shipping the parts to Europe to be rebuilt and sold on to crime groups. The second importation turned out to be connected to an investigation into an organised crime group from Bradford, who were using contacts in the US to legally buy Glock pistols before dismantling them and hiding their parts in clocks to import them to the UK. The probe was nicknamed 'the Glocks in the Clocks'. The big appeal for gun runners was that the Glock is predominantly made from polymer plastic and not metal, making it easier to evade customs checks.

Every year NABIS delivers talks to detectives around the world and cites Operation Bezant as a flagship example of what it can do. I received a Chief Constable's Commendation. Each and every one of those guns had enough bullets to start a small war and could have killed and maimed on a biblical scale. I'd like to think my actions prevented that – and even saved someone's life.

All's well that ends well, but the Taylor job could well have gone very wrong. When a firearms warrant is being conducted we have to go to a tactical firearms commander to assess the risk and clarify if the entry will be made by armed or unarmed officers. The rationale from the superintendent in this case was that this was someone with no previous convictions and that there was no intelligence he'd arm himself to thwart police entry to the house. Any weapon would be well hidden and not to hand, they decided. They played the odds, like they always do. They figured that there'd been 60 firearms warrants that year and no cops had been killed, so it didn't merit a firearms response with rapid entry. The reality is such decisions are more about resources than properly assessing the risk, and it's a gamble that I'm sure will one day lead to an officer being killed.

Taylor had enough guns on him to wreak havoc. He could have just sat there and thought, *I'm not going to fucking jail today,* pulled out the Benelli or Škorpion and started spraying it around. Of course, luckily, that didn't happen, but let's just say it did. We'd have been defenceless and unarmed, like sitting ducks.

The truth is, the bosses are more worried about sending firearms teams to jobs like this because if a firearms cop shoots somebody, it comes back to them for authorising it.

Whenever I speak to cops in other countries, they are astonished that British officers aren't armed when they're executing a firearms warrant.

The cops do get it wrong – they are only human – and I can see both sides of the argument for arming and not fully arming the British police, but I do fear it will take cops to be shot dead on a firearms search to change the risk-assessment policies.

Little did I know then that the debate about whether police officers should be armed on duty would soon be reopened in the most shocking way imaginable, and I would be slap bang in the middle of the storm.

The success of this operation helped me get my mojo back. I'd shown that I was more than a one-trick pony. That didn't mean the damaging impact of Omega didn't still play on my mind, though. My view of the police had been tainted. I'd seen that it wasn't one for all and all for one and that it was a dog-eat-dog world where many people were out for themselves and their own promotion. I decided to stay in the police. But I was determined that I'd never put myself in a position of vulnerability again, that I'd firmly take control of my career path and choose my allies carefully. I'd been stung but I'd learned valuable lessons. It was time to put all that shit behind me and move on. Because the jobs on the murder squad were coming thick and fast.

A lot of detectives may get one marquee job in their career. I would spend mine going from one to the next. I investigated the Stepping Hill saline scandal and won a judge's commendation for being part of the team that brought to justice serial-killing Filipino nurse Victorino Chua. I worked on the case of conman killer Stephen Seddon – who blasted his parents with a sawn-off shotgun after trying in vain to drive them to their deaths in a canal. I'd proven without doubt that I was more than just an undercover cop. I was a highly competent detective, with numerous high-profile murder investigations under my belt, and I was the go-to man if anybody needed bringing in over a killing.

However, my real skill in the police lay in the targeting of organised crime groups. And I was about to be thrust back deep into that dangerous world. This time, the stakes could not have been higher.

CHAPTER 13

MANHUNT

Twenty-four seconds it took. Twenty-four seconds to end a life. Twenty-four seconds to trigger a chain of events that would end in unimaginable horror. Horror that lives with me to this day.

Ten minutes before midnight on 25 May 2012, a blue Ford Focus with its hazard lights on pulled up outside the Cotton Tree pub in Droylsden. The passenger door opened and out stepped a man in a black balaclava. He calmly walked through the side entrance and took a single step before he lifted his arm and from his outstretched hand unleashed a volley of seven rounds from a self-loading pistol. Seconds earlier, amateur boxer Mark Short had been playing pool with his dad, David. By pure chance, David went to the toilet as Mark stayed around the table with his pals. A bullet through the neck sent Mark's six-foot-plus frame crashing to the floor. The gunman then fired rounds into John Collins, Ryan Pridding and Michael Belcher. They survived. Mark Short didn't. As the shooter sprinted out of the same side door into the getaway car, David emerged from the toilet to find his son lying motionless, blood gushing out of the open wound. He put his hands under his head and tried to talk him round but could only sob helplessly as he watched the life drain out of his son's face.

This was brutal, cold-blooded revenge – a ruthless gangland execution that came 12 days after a long-running family feud between the Shorts and another east Manchester crime family, the Atkinsons, was reignited during a petty row at the same pub.

Soon after the shooting, word got to me that the suspected gunman was Dale Cregan – the one-time up-and-coming criminal whose crew I had gone toe to toe with during my Tameside Organised Crime Unit days. I thought back to the time I warned that his team needed to be tackled before they grew into something bigger, more dangerous.

I had a good idea who the others in the getaway car would be – they were a tight little crew. Cregan, now 29, and his mates had progressed from kicking doors in for car keys and serving up a bit of weed. He was now a multi-kilo cocaine dealer, having worked his way up the ladder. He was by no means a top-tier gangster, but he had built up some serious gangland connections and was an active, violent and dangerous criminal. He'd lost his eye in a fight in Thailand, which only added to his menacing look. There were several rumours how he had lost it; some said he had crossed Thai gangsters, others pointed to an altercation with Thai police. Either way, it was said to have had a significant impact on him mentally. I was still on the murder squad but not on the investigation into the Cotton Tree shooting. But out of professional interest and due to my history taking on this group, I kept my ear close to the ground amid underworld talk of escalation.

Police had intelligence that indicated Cregan would be targeted in a revenge attack. The gunman had taken the life of David Short's son. David had earned a chilling reputation in the Clayton area for being seriously violent. Muscular and fearsome-looking, David had been a boxer in his youth and had maintained a strict fitness regime. He was even known on the street as a 'one-man army'. Many in east Manchester, however, also regarded him as a bully. Intelligence suggested he and his criminal associates were involved in everything from drug supply to loan sharking, with David at the head of the OCG. A child protection order was issued for Cregan's young son amid grave concerns that Short was going to target him directly.

Cregan fled to Thailand but GMP arrested him on his return to Manchester Airport on 12 June. He was questioned over the Cotton Tree murder but released on bail. Was there enough evidence to charge him? Should the CPS have been more robust? Should the police have pushed it more? Peter Fahy, the chief constable at the time, defended the decision, claiming GMP had to release him because they had insufficient evidence to charge. I can't help but think it was the first big mistake.

On 8 August, detectives charged two men in connection with Mark Short's death. Luke Livesey, from the Hattersley area, and Damian Gorman, from the Glossop area, were both charged with one count of murder and three counts of attempted murder. But they didn't charge the prime suspect.

Two days later, with talk of retribution mounting and fearing retaliation, Cregan struck again. Along with accomplice Anthony Wilkinson, he sprang from a van parked outside David Short's house in Clayton and opened fire. Short was chased through the house and back outside and shot at least nine times, including three in the head at point-blank range. Then a grenade was thrown onto his body where he lay. He died from multiple gunshot wounds and a blast injury. Another hand grenade was hurled at the house of one of Short's relatives in nearby Droylsden ten minutes later, though no one was hurt.

A double gangland shooting with high-grade military hardware. Serious weapons used to maim and kill in broad daylight on residential streets. Criminals using grenades on the British mainland – weapons normally reserved for warfare and terrorism. This was something police outside Northern Ireland had never dealt with before.

Cregan went on the run and Greater Manchester Police launched one of the biggest ever manhunts in British history. Firearms teams were drafted in from all over the country as armed cops from forces including the Met, West Midlands, and Merseyside Police swarmed the streets where Cregan and his associates were known to prowl.

I remember watching it all unfold and thinking it was like Northern Ireland in the bad old days. There was an air of excruciating tension unlike anything I'd ever experienced in the police before. A picture of Cregan showing his black onyx false eye was distributed to the media. The public was warned not to approach him. Airports and ports were put on alert. CCTV footage of a man throwing a grenade at the house in Droylsden was released, and police issued a photograph of a getaway van abandoned nearby, which was also blown up with a grenade. They offered a £25,000 reward for information leading to his capture, then quickly upped it to £50,000. The faces of Cregan and Wilkinson were beamed on screens ahead of Manchester City's game against QPR. Police were taking unprecedented measures, and GMP made him the most-wanted fugitive in the UK. From afar I couldn't help thinking they were making a huge mistake going so high-profile this early into the manhunt, elevating him to almost Bond villain proportions. It's inconceivable to think police weren't using covert tactics to bring the fugitive in. Yet despite everything they were throwing at the manhunt – the scale of which we'd never seen before – they couldn't get near him.

With potential breakthroughs continuing to lead to dead ends, one afternoon I got a phone call from my old mate and colleague Alex, who I'd worked with on the Organised Crime Unit. He said he'd been summoned by a superintendent from the Serious Organised Crime Group, who wanted to tap into his knowledge and experience from the days when we investigated Cregan and his crew in the OCU. The superintendent confided in him that covert strategies in place were going nowhere fast and that cops were coming back from making enquiries with Cregan's criminal associates with no information and their tail between their legs. The investigation needed a small, robust team who weren't scared of challenging villains but at the same time could hold a conversation with one. Cops that could get among the criminal community and gather intelligence by any means necessary. Alex told me he'd agreed to do the job along with another cop, Rob, who we had both worked with in the past and who was known for a no-nonsense approach. They told the superintendent that two men weren't enough – it would need three.

'Who do you want, then?' he asked them.

'We need someone who's targeted them before, knows who they are and how they work. And, boss, if we're going to be going through doors three-handed then we need someone who isn't going to give a fuck about doing it,' replied Alex. 'What about Shay Doyle? Shay knows them – he targeted them with me – and he won't give a fuck about going through anyone's door.'

Rob immediately backed up Alex's appraisal. The boss knew me vaguely through reputation and told Alex to get me to come and see him. He had a reputation as an old-school copper's cop; they were a dying breed. And he was someone I had a lot of respect for. I was briefed and the boss proposed that I join the team.

'You'll answer directly to me. I need some robust lads on the ground, getting information to catch this fella.'

'Look, I'm more than happy to help but I'm on the murder squad so not sure if I can do this,' I told him.

In my head I was thinking, *I need on this*. This was going into the eye of the storm, on the ground, doing what I was good at. And Rob and Alex, who both had a military background like me, were exactly the right blokes to do it with. I had not one shred of doubt we would all have one another's backs.

The superintendent said, 'Leave it with me, Shay. There's a bigger organisational need at the moment, and it's all hands on deck. Bringing Cregan in is the force's number-one priority.'

Within the hour I was pulled off the murder squad and cleared to work on the Cregan manhunt, and the three-man gang we had formed was dubbed the Proactive Intelligence Cell. It was a title that covered a multitude of sins. Our brief was to be on the ground in plain clothes, complementing the covert strategy and obtaining information on Cregan's whereabouts.

We made a covert vehicle our mobile office: blacked-out windows with hidden police lights and a siren. We loaded up the vehicle with body armour, helmets, crowbars, a sledge-hammer and an enforcer to gain rapid entry into buildings. We had batons, CS gas, a glass entry kit, handcuffs, restraints, torches, medical supplies, a search kit – equipment for every confrontation, every eventuality.

We were relentless. We secured warrants at the magistrates' and smashed through door after door. We locked up his gangster pals – they didn't intimidate or impress us; we had all been in the game long enough to know that very few so-called gangsters actually live up to their reputation. We spoke to his family, his friends, anyone with links to his crew. We worked tirelessly, building up contacts, recruiting informants, cultivating anyone willing to offer snippets of information.

It was a fast-paced, high-octane, robust response. We were getting in the faces of criminals, but equally, we could play it smart if we had to. You can't just arrest your way out of a problem like this one. When subtlety was needed, we were adept at targeting people's weaknesses and getting information or building relationships with key players. We were much more than mindless door-kickers, and that's why we were picked to do the job.

There was a double killer on the loose, a madman with the means to murder again, and this was a manhunt being played out hour by hour to the national media. The world was watching. And the pressure was mounting. For the police not to bring him in wasn't an option. Not given the scope and scale of the hunt. It was proving difficult. People either didn't know where Cregan was or they were scared of him and the comebacks from turning him in. Whichever it was, they were refusing to give us anything substantial.

I felt uneasy about the way the manhunt was progressing. I remember thinking it was going wrong, that it was potentially heading somewhere really bad. GMP had turned Cregan into public enemy number one, and that for me felt like a perilous move with potentially disastrous repercussions. Yes, he was a stone-faced killer and a dangerous fugitive that needed to be tracked down, but the plastering of his face on the screen, the £50,000 reward ... it all felt like it could backfire in a big way. I felt the force was making fatal strategic errors. And the more notoriety they gave him, the more a sense of dread would creep over me.

Cregan's family unsurprisingly closed ranks, largely in protest at what they deemed to be a witch-hunt and at some of the tactics GMP were employing. Cregan's young son was taken from his mother in the street and placed into protective custody for his own safety. Police had no choice but to act to safeguard an innocent child caught up in gang warfare through no fault of his own. That said, I can't help but think the execution could have been more sensitive.

They also sent two female hostage negotiators – a DS and a DI – to try and sweet-talk and influence Cregan's mother into making a live televised appeal for her son to hand himself in. They went round dressed to the nines with their hair done and make-up on in an attempt to build a relationship with her. If they had done their homework they'd have found that Cregan's father, who had not been with Cregan's mother for some time, was now in a relationship with a former cop. Now, I'm no forensic psychologist, but I'd suggest that that particular profile of officer, given the history, would not have been the most appealing and persuasive.

It's well documented that a listening device had been installed in Cregan's family home and that police were monitoring conversations in the hope they would reveal information that would bring the manhunt to a peaceful end. The three of us were called in by the superintendent and briefed that info had been received regarding a plan to drop off a significant amount of cash by one of Cregan's criminal associates at the family address. It was feared the money would go to Cregan to fund him while on the run. Alex and I were two of a very small number of officers that had maintained any form of reasonable dialogue with the family. We were always polite, professional and respectful to his mother; going in heavy-handed with the family would have been entirely counterproductive.

Our job was to get round to the house, come up with a reason for them to invite us in and keep them talking to stall any opportunity for the cash to be dropped off, until we got the call saying we could leave. The boss anticipated we would be in there half an hour or so. We would end up in there for hours. I had to constantly think up ways to keep the conversation flowing until we got the green light to withdraw with the objective complete. At the house was his brother, sister and mum and they were all having a drink. It's fair to say his mother was living on her nerves by this point, and we had long conversations with her. The subject of the two female detectives came up. 'Sending them two fuckin' slags to talk to me,' was her irate response. It was clear the negotiators were doing nothing more than putting her back up.

At the debrief at Serious Crime HQ the following morning, I fed back her disgruntlement to the team. 'You've got the wrong profile here,' I said.

A senior boss shot me a stern look like I was some kind of idiot. 'How do you know we haven't sent them to disrupt her?'

That's a new one on me, I thought. *Surely, you send negotiators to negotiate.* An unwillingness to own fuck-ups and take steps to rectify them was a trait I'd seen all too often in senior cops over the years.

It wasn't just the family putting up a wall of silence. There was precious little coming from Cregan's extensive criminal network. His contacts were reluctant, frightened even, to offer information. Truth be told, most of them likely didn't know where he was or what he was doing. But not all of them. There'd been talk of a few sightings but nothing substantiated. Cregan remained at large and the pressure on GMP continued to intensify. Then came a breakthrough.

I'd had a long day that had started at 6am going through a drug dealer's door. I'd been on the street all day since, gathering what information I could from both sides of the criminal divide – on the Short side and those connected to Cregan – and didn't get home until nine that night. It had been a long few weeks on the hunt, and I'd been consistently working 18-hour days. Shattered, I'd just kicked my trainers off, sat down and started to eat a late evening meal when my job mobile rang. It was a call from a well-placed and reliable source.

'Cregan's in the area,' said the voice. 'He's in Droylsden.'

A bit more information was offered as to his potential whereabouts, and I asked the source to keep in contact if they heard any more. I immediately phoned Alex and the boss to tell them what I had been told and that I'd opened up a line of communication with the source. The boss made some calls and confirmed there was other intel that corroborated Cregan was back in the area, and he told us to get back into work and be ready to react. I pushed my half-eaten tea to the side and slipped my trainers back on. While I tied my laces I told my girlfriend, who had been watching me on the phone nervously, that I needed to go back into work. I told her Cregan was back in the area. She didn't reply, but just before I walked out of the door she grabbed my arm and said something I'll never forget.

'Don't go, Shay. I've got a really bad feeling about this.'

'I have to,' I said. 'It's fine – don't worry about it.'

'Why is it always you, Shay?'

I didn't answer, instead giving her a peck on the cheek before leaving the house and heading back to HQ. It was a pertinent question and one I've since spent many hours thinking about. Just not then, not in that moment. All I could think of was *Cregan's in the area and I've got a job to do.* As I drove through the deserted, dimly lit streets, back into work, this time it felt different, like we were heading into new territory. I felt on edge.

I met Alex and Rob back at HQ and we established a plan of action of how we would react if the call came. I listened intently to the police radio while constantly scanning my mobile for any information. We took turns to snatch some sleep on the office floor to make sure we had some rest just in the case the call from the source came and we needed to get on the street. It didn't. But a job did come in in the early hours of the morning – reports of a man kicking at a door in Droylsden. *Cregan's around,* I thought. *We can't be taking chances here. We need to be mindful. This could be something sinister.* I spoke with the force duty officer and suggested sending armed cops, given what we knew. But a standard police response patrol was dispatched instead, and the disturbance turned out to be exactly what it had come in as – some pisshead trying to get into his own flat. On this occasion, it was a false alarm.

The night passed. Still, no Cregan. This wasn't good. If Cregan was in the area – and we had every reason to believe he was – then he had to be caught. There had been intelligence that he might try and shoot police. I tried to put myself in his shoes. *He knows the chances are he's going away for 40 years. What's he got to lose?*

Dawn broke and the three of us jumped in the unmarked car and sped to a house in Mottram just after 6am, where we smashed through the door with a battering ram. It belonged to a drug dealer pal of Cregan's, and we were convinced he would know where the fugitive was. So we weren't fucking about. We weren't picked to do the job because we were nice and cuddly. We were picked because we were prepared to go toe to toe with the nastiest of criminals. We were well aware of the stakes, that this was a dangerous job. That we could be targeted. But it needed cops that were unconventional, who would go the extra mile, who could accept the risks. The clock was ticking. And all we wanted to do was get that nugget of information that would end this madness once and for all. It wasn't the first time he had seen the three of us come through his door, and it was fair to say he was sick of the sight of us. We hit him with a robust, forceful and dominating raid. He was a broken man.

'Tell us where he fuckin' is and we'll stop coming round, won't we.' I was convinced if anyone would know, then it would be him. And maybe he did.

'Even if I knew, I wouldn't tell yer. I'm more scared of him than I am of yous.' I remember his response like it were yesterday. We left him in the house and headed for the next target.

A few hours later the police radio burst into life. 'Shots fired in Mottram.' The radio crackled again. Then again. A quickfire flurry of updates, one after the other. It was frenetic. The radio operators were frantically trying to raise the collar numbers of two officers. It was quickly becoming apparent that something catastrophic had happened. Uniformed cops close to the area blue-lighted it to the scene, and more information came through at breakneck speed. Amid the mayhem we grasped the key information: two female PCs shot and grenade explosion in Mottram.

As the chaos unfolded, our covert blue lights went on and we screeched towards Mottram at 100mph. Cops desperately fought to get onto the radio to give updates from the scene. Myself, Alex and Rob were in the car thinking, *What the fuck's gone on?* We knew it would be Cregan, and our initial instinct told us he would be making away from the scene and possibly heading to Droylsden, where he was from. We decided to head that way to see if we could identify him and attempt to intercept him somehow, even ram him if needed. We were prepared to do whatever it took to stop him. Lights flashed and sirens wailed around us. Breathless updates continued to bombard the radio. As difficult as it was, we had to stay calm amid the storm. Then the superintendent called.

'Cregan's just handed himself in at Hyde nick. Get there now and deal with him. Think about forensics, preserving the evidence. Someone has to remain calm. We've got to make sure we do it right and we've got to get this home.'

He was right. Yes, there was shock. Yes, there was outrage. It was the most desperate of situations. But it was one that demanded calm heads. *Stay focused. Do what you have to do and get the job done.* The manhunt had come to a crescendo now. I couldn't allow myself to be washed away with the raw emotion of it all. I had to detach myself from the terror. It was how I'd been all my life. And it was how I had to be now. There was business to take care of. *We need to deal with this bastard.*

Forty-two days he had been hunted. Forty-two days of blood, sweat and tears that ended when he casually swaggered into Hyde police station and told the clerk in a broad Manc accent, 'I'm wanted by the police and I've just done two coppers.'

CCTV showed a brave uniformed cop jumping over the police counter to arrest the killer. I knew him. His name was John and by coincidence he had been through police training at the same time as me. We arrived minutes after Cregan. By this point, he had been taken around the back of the station to a spot out of public view. He was kneeling on the floor, his hands cuffed behind his back, flanked by two firearms officers pointing guns at him.

He was wearing blue shorts and a grey hoodie and sported a beard. I stood above him and stared into his eyes. I remember thinking, *He looks like nothing.* He was vacant. There was nothing there. There was nothing in his demeanour that suggested he was bothered about anything. It was as if he'd just been caught for a bit of shoplifting. Alex personally knew one of the girls Cregan had killed and couldn't even look at him, so myself and Rob wrapped his handcuffed hands in a plastic bag to preserve any forensic evidence. They were bloodied. He moaned that the cuffs were hurting him. 'You need to loosen them,' he whined. 'They're too tight. And I'm not a mardarse.'

My calm exterior disguised the anger coursing through me. He had murdered two unarmed, defenceless young women in cold blood. He didn't have the balls for a shoot-out with armed cops. *Fucking coward,* I thought. But I had to stay professional. The blue BMW he had driven from the scene was parked at the front of the station and had been cordoned off. We had to ask him some emergency questions.

'Is the vehicle you've arrived in booby-trapped?' I asked. 'Are there any guns or grenades in the car?'

The silence was deafening.

I peered down at the top of his head. He was still kneeling, head bowed. He wasn't getting up. Nor were the two young officers we'd just lost in his savage, senseless attack. We now knew who he'd shot dead and exactly how they'd met their fates. Fiona Bone, 32, and Nicola Hughes, 23, were called to reports of a burglary at Abbey Gardens in Mottram. They were unarmed but for a single Taser. Cregan had made the bogus call to lure them to their deaths, hitting them mercilessly with a hail of bullets and a hand grenade.

Alex, usually so calm and composed, an ice man in the fire; not now, not when he knew what Cregan had done to those girls. It was a truth too hard to bear. He had to walk away, rage pouring out of every sinew of his body.

The killer lifted his head. He had only one eye, the other replaced by an onyx one. It was black, like a dark hole in his face. I stared into the abyss. There was no sunshine. No chink of light amid the darkness. Just a big hole of empty nothingness. I felt cold. I kept my composure, but it was hard to stem the tide of thoughts sweeping through my mind.

After about ten minutes we put him in a police van to be taken away to custody, escorted by armed cops. That's when it hit me. *How has it come to this? What the fuck has just happened?* I felt outraged. Disgusted. And heartbroken for the girls and their families. My phone wouldn't stop ringing and I couldn't answer it because I was dealing with Cregan. Unbeknown to me, news of the horror had filtered through to the outside world. Eventually I managed to answer my phone. It was my girlfriend. 'Are you alright? Are you alright?' she screamed desperately. 'We got told cops had been shot. I thought it was you.' My missus knew I hadn't come home all night and thought it was me that had been killed. She had been frantically trying to contact me. 'Are you OK?'

'Yes, calm down, it's not me,' was about all I could manage.

Every uniformed cop in Tameside was sent home. Myself, Alex and Rob stayed on, offering to do whatever was needed. My stomach churned. I was in a state of disbelief. The next day it emerged Cregan had been holding a family hostage just a stone's throw away from the drug dealer's house whose door we'd gone through the morning of the police killings. He'd used one of his nobody criminal mates from Hattersley as his gofer to fetch him cocaine, booze and cigars for what appeared to be a farewell party. The terrified barber whose house it was later revealed he was forced to trim Cregan's beard so he would be ready for his police mugshot. And he told how he watched in horror as Cregan placed a grenade on the fireplace and toyed with his Glock semi-automatic pistol in the living room – the gun used to kill the cops.

I went home the night of the murders and was filled with rage. And I think it was this rage that drove me to be back at work at 6am the next morning, raring to go, willing to get back out there and start taking out anyone and everyone who had helped this animal while he was on the run.

That morning the covert side of the operation kicked into overdrive. Using telephone technology we pinged Cregan's gofer to an address in Hattersley. It needed to be hit there and then so we could get him into custody because there was every chance he would flee if we didn't act quickly. The boss rang Rob and said they just didn't have time to get a firearms team together. This was a guy who'd been in the house overnight with Cregan while he was armed with a grenade and a Glock pistol, hours before he murdered two police officers, and there wasn't time to get a firearms team. In many ways it beggared belief.

The boss asked us if we would enter and arrest Cregan's gofer. We knew the risks. We all looked at one another and there was no hesitation on anyone's face. The decision was made. We were going in.

We would take no chances. We were going in hard, fast and aggressive. To dominate everyone there would be the only way. The three of us pulled balaclavas over our heads and crept silently towards the back door of the semi-detached house. In a well-rehearsed drill, the battering ram was lifted then BANG. We smashed through the door and, with a devastating display of force, we moved systematically through the property.

The gofer was the first to confront us. He was unceremoniously subdued, thrown to the floor and arrested. There were six others in the house and three of us. We were outnumbered, so there was no fucking about. We were unapologetically aggressive. We quickly got them under control and effectively crushed any potential threat. Needless to say, the occupants were left in a state of shock. They hadn't met cops like us before. We were about as far away from your friendly local bobby as you get.

The relentless response to the murders continued. The next day, we raided a house in Oldham and I arrested another gangster who'd assisted Cregan. After slaughtering David Short, Cregan called Mohammed Imran Ali to transport him out of Manchester. Within minutes 'Irish Immie', as he was known on the street, turned up in a leased VW Golf and ferried Cregan and two of his men to Leeds, enabling him to evade the manhunt. Then we hit another drug dealer. And another. It was an obliteration, an operation launched to put the fear of God into anyone connected to Cregan or the shootings.

I had no time to think or breathe. I had to stay emotionally detached and not lose my head. But thoughts of 'what if' weighed heavy on my mind. *That could have been us. Those bullets could have been meant for us – and possibly should have been meant for us.* We were the ones kicking in a door just 300 yards from where Cregan was that morning.

I would also carry a great guilt. *Did we cause this? Was it us going through doors, doing what we do, that caused this?* At times the weight of it would be unbearable, and it would take me a long time to reconcile with this guilt.

Cregan was charged with four murders and remanded along with some of his crew at Manchester's Strangeways prison, but there were fears that the gang war would continue to be played out behind bars. Both Cregan and the Shorts had allies and criminal associates in the jail, and the prison security manager and governor were rightly concerned. The last thing they needed was a murder or a second Strangeways riot.

There was also the matter of a major murder trial and the security risks that came with transferring the defendants from Strangeways, or Manchester Prison as it is now called, to Preston Crown Court. The 35-mile trip required a complex armed operation amid concerns the convoy could be ambushed and Cregan sprung. Sound intelligence and meticulous planning were needed.

The investigation into Cregan and his associates didn't stop because he was in jail; if anything, it intensified. The senseless slaughter of two of its officers shook Greater Manchester Police to its core, and the force made it its mission to decimate Cregan's criminal network. The message was clear: if you kill cops, not only you but everyone involved in your criminality will pay a heavy price. The police may not be great at everything they do, but if GMP's serious crime capability decides to shine its light on you, you are going to jail. There are some seriously talented, smart, creative, courageous and utterly ruthless cops that work within these units.

To mitigate the risk of a prison gang war and Cregan being sprung, senior leaders sent Alex and myself into Strangeways. We deployed in the security department on a daily basis and were put on the prisons system as staff and even given keys. Our job was to pinpoint the key players to security managers and advise on where they should be placed to avoid potential clashes.

I spent months in the jail, gruelling 18-hour days. We had to be there before the convoy left in the morning and when it got back at night, ready to feed back any information we gleaned to ensure the safety of the officers deploying in the security escort. My stint in the prison world gave me newfound respect for those that work there. It is a tough, demanding and dangerous job that they do for precious little reward and often under intense pressure. It's not a job I would want. There were some fantastic staff at Strangeways; the ones I met were good people doing a difficult job with good intentions.

The hours I was working in the immediate aftermath of the manhunt were draining, but the horrific murders were motivating me to play my part, just as they did for many other cops across the force. I have to say, the response from officers I worked alongside, their will to take down Cregan's network in the wake of what he did, was the most awe-inspiring piece of police work I would ever be involved in. The girls and boys going out there day after day, taking down this criminal network, were selfless and amazing.

There was no time for me to take stock, to stop and think about the horror, the moments I went face to face with a double police killer. On the day of the funerals I stood with my old mate Christie on Deansgate in the city centre, casually dressed, as members of the public and police in full dress uniform stood side by side in an outpouring of grief. I watched from afar, a face in the crowd, and my mind wandered. *None of these people know what I've done. None of these people know that I hunted him, that I looked him in the eye as he had the blood of those two cops on his hands.* I felt delirious, struggling to compute it all. I thought about my own family. I thought about how the manhunt had been handled by senior cops. I thought about my own part and whether mistakes had been made.

*

On 13 June 2013, Dale Cregan was told he'd spend the rest of his life in jail after admitting to the four murders. He also admitted the attempted murders of John Collins, Michael Belcher and Ryan Pridding during the attack on Mark Short. Passing a whole-life sentence at Preston Crown Court, Mr Justice Holroyde QC said Cregan had had a 'cold-blooded and ruthless determination to end the lives of PCs Bone and Hughes' and 'acted with premeditated savagery' in drawing the officers 'into a calculated trap to kill them'.

Luke Livesey and Damian Gorman were each jailed for 33 years for the murder of Mark Short and the three attempted murders at the Cotton Tree. Anthony Wilkinson and Cregan's getaway driver, Jermaine Ward, were jailed for 35 and 33 years for the murder of David Short. Mohammed Imran Ali, whose house we raided, got seven years for assisting an offender.

Justice had been meted out but the scars still ran deep within the force. After the investigation into the murders of Fiona, Nicola and the Short family revealed a far-reaching web of organised criminality and extreme violence, I helped form Operation Challenger, GMP's multi-agency response now held in high regard as a model to tackle organised crime. It was there that I sadly witnessed at close quarters the deep emotional impact the tragedy had on many officers, particularly those that worked closely with Nicola and Fiona. There would be many more casualties left by Cregan's act of sheer evil that day.

After spending 18 months of my life entrenched in the manhunt and subsequent investigations, I became more and more disillusioned. I saw senior cops, who had far from covered themselves in glory during the operation, getting promotions and plum postings and it sickened me. Then there was the scandal about the force buying the assistant chief constable's house due to a perceived threat from Cregan, only to sell it to a couple without warning them of the danger. It fucking stank. It very much felt like there was one rule for the rank and file and one rule for chief officer ranks at the force. The organisational culture was disgraceful. It seemed to reward sycophantic bag carriers into positions well above their ability, and it would severely damage the morale of many good and decent officers in GMP and ultimately the force as a whole. As I write this, Greater Manchester Police has been plunged into special measures by the Home Office – an unprecedented move and a reflection of its disastrous leadership. I can assure you that the writing was well and truly on the wall many years before. Those in positions of influence were warned. They stood by and did nothing.

There was no debrief or decompression for myself, Alex and Rob following the Cregan operation. No 'What can we learn from this as an organisation?' – or at least if there was, the likes of us on the ground who'd put ourselves at risk certainly weren't invited.

There were nights when I would lie awake, struggling to switch off. I would pace around my bedroom playing events over and over in my mind. Not just Cregan, but Moss Side, Cambridge, all the undercover jobs I'd done. The places, the faces. I'd find it so hard to shut them out. It wouldn't happen every night. It was sporadic, like a slowly dripping tap. But every time, I'd go to work shattered, consumed by a feeling of deep-seated anger at certain senior bosses. I thought the only answer was to escape GMP. So when I saw an advert for a source handler at TITAN, the North West Regional Organised Crime Unit, it appeared a good solution.

Source handlers, or covert human intelligence source (CHIS) handlers, work in secretive units and their job, as the title suggests, is to identify, cultivate, recruit and run informants, or 'grasses'. It's a world just as secret, if not more secret, than the undercover world, and it's fraught with danger and risk. If any role in the police is ever going to get you sacked or jailed then handling grasses is the one. The age-old problem with informants is that many are duplicitous liars that are not to be trusted, and you need a cop with a keen eye and strong enough character to ensure they are the ones firmly in control and the tail is not wagging the dog. Informants can, however, be the difference between life and death in some cases and are a key tactic in the fight against organised crime and terrorism. Some are courageous and do it for all the right reasons.

The Regional Organised Crime Unit is a coveted place to work. They look at top-tier OCGs, often operating internationally. I would be going up against qualified and experienced source handlers from all six police forces across the north-west of England. I was not a qualified source handler, albeit I'd recruited many informants and operated largely in the covert arena. Some colleagues told me I wouldn't get it. 'The job will be sewn up,' they said. 'It's a new team at the regional organised crime unit and all the handlers are going for it. They will know who they want already.' I was wasting my time, they said.

Undeterred, and desperate to get the fuck out of GMP's Serious Crime HQ, I went for it. Surprisingly, I was called for an interview and went before a panel of three senior cops led by Jane, a detective superintendent.

They set about me with questions on the law and quizzed me on various scenarios. Jane led and I immediately liked her. She was no-nonsense and even managed to inject some humour into a formal process. She was my kind of cop. I explained that while I wasn't a qualified source handler, I was experienced in the covert world, and tried to compensate with my other experiences. That afternoon they phoned to say I'd got the job, much to the annoyance of a number of GMP's experienced handlers who had gone for it. I felt relieved to be getting out of GMP. I thought, *This is the fresh start I need.*

On my first day Jane called me into her office.

'I'm going to tell you something in confidence, Shay,' she said.

'Yes, ma'am.'

'I was severely warned off you by your old superintendent at Omega.'

After all these years, those bastards still wanted to sabotage me. I couldn't believe it. Jane's response was brilliant.

'He's a wanker.' I nearly spat my coffee out with laughter.

'In my experience all the best cops have certain personal flaws, Shay. I also spoke to a couple of other people who know you, and they told me if anyone could recruit me some topnotch informants, it would be you. So you're here on merit and for a reason. Go and do what you do.'

So I did. I passed the advanced CHIS handler course, which was a breeze in comparison to the UC course, and I quickly began identifying and cultivating sources of information. I was good at it and was even awarded a citation of merit for recruiting and running an informant who gave me the location of a cache of firearms and ammunition that belonged to one of the most violent organised crime groups in the UK.

Jane promoted me to detective sergeant days after I passed the relevant exams, and I became the regional expert on the use of covert tactics in prisons on major investigations.

Professionally I was thriving. But personally things weren't right. The tap was still dripping. Sleep was poor, my mind would race and I would think worst-case scenario. I found it hard to trust anyone and thought everyone was plotting against me. My hypervigilance started to grow. Now it was becoming fuelled by anxiety I couldn't put my finger on. Then, for reasons I couldn't fathom, my sensitivity to noise heightened. Even someone speaking at a normal level would sound like a train going through my head. It became unbearable at times. I would drive home from work some nights and pull into a motorway service station just to feel at peace and sleep for an hour before I got home.

Did I seek help? Absolutely not. My answer was to throw myself deeper and deeper into work. And it wouldn't be long before the next big job came along. On Sunday, 26 July 2015, I was sat at home when I received a call from Paul, my mate and former DS on the murder squad. He was now detective inspector.

'Paul Massey has just been murdered – shot dead with an automatic weapon. I'm stood at the scene now. Get busy, I want as much information as you can get.'

CHAPTER 14
WAR

Paul Massey was something of an iconic figure in Manchester and Salford. I'd heard his name many times growing up and was aware of his standing as a gangster. Massey wasn't the biggest and most physically imposing man, but he had gained a formidable reputation as someone whose mettle lay in his loyalty and charismatic ability to lead and organise others. He was widely known to be intelligent and capable of serious violence. The security boss who controlled nightclub doors was respected and feared in criminal circles for decades and went on to enjoy legendary underworld status as one of Britain's so-called Mr Bigs.

When I heard he'd been murdered I was somewhat taken aback. On the face of it, he was at an age where he had stepped back from frontline, hands-on criminality and had even stood as a candidate for Mayor of Salford. He had a lot of friends and allies. After taking the call from Paul at the murder squad, I thought, *This is not going to end well.*

Massey had stepped out of his silver 5 Series BMW clutching a carrier bag containing a bottle of Bacardi when a gunman in combat gear and a fisherman-style hat ran from across the road and opened fire with an Uzi sub-machine gun. The bottle smashed across his driveway as Massey, badly wounded, staggered backwards and fell. He then desperately tried to dive for cover behind his bins but couldn't escape his assassin, who shot him again. His killer fired 18 rounds in total, hitting Massey with four – in the shin, through his side, which entered his heart, and in both hands. The blast took fingers off his right hand, but he still managed to call friends and 999 to tell them he'd been shot outside his house in Clifton, on the outskirts of Salford. Two of Massey's pals, Thomas Jeffreys and Lee Taberer, were first on the scene. 'He's fucking dead,' they shouted. 'Get an ambulance.' Within ten minutes paramedics arrived. It was too late. Massey's injuries were 'unsurvivable', the bullet through the heart proving the fatal blow. Taberer, who had comforted his dying friend, had dried blood on his hands. More of Massey's circle arrived at the police tape that marked the boundary of the crime scene along Manchester Road. Among them was Massey's long-time partner and mother of two of his five children, Louise. Also there was 'Scouse' John Kinsella, a notorious Liverpool gangster who Massey had become friends with in prison while serving 14 years for a stabbing.

Massey was 55 and was believed to no longer be taking an active role in crime. He appeared to have become very much a mentor figure to the younger generation of Salford criminals, including the leader of the notorious A Team, Stephen

Britton, who he'd taken under his wing. In the months before Massey's murder, the A Team, a brash and brazen OCG made of lads who'd grown up together in Salford, were fighting a war with a splinter faction who police labelled the anti-A Team. There'd been a spate of extreme violence, but word on the street was that Massey was acting as a mediator, trying to stop the bloodshed rather than giving orders and calling the shots. His execution felt like a significant shift in the Salford criminal landscape: a symbolic targeted assassination, a removal of the old guard. This was the new breed of ruthless gangsters saying, 'We don't give a fuck about reputations, you don't run this show no more. We do.' Many people thought Massey, with his mythical reputation, was untouchable. Clearly, he wasn't.

I was still at the Regional Organised Crime Unit and knew immediately that I would be drawn into it and tasked with gathering intelligence using the covert assets we had available. I knew that this was going to be a major investigation into the Salford underworld; for a cop like me, an operation of this nature couldn't be more interesting. I was still fascinated by the workings of organised crime and the characters that inhabited that world. I knew this wouldn't just be about identifying Massey's killer but also preventing reprisals for his death. Massey had some serious connections and friends who had access to guns with the motivation, determination and capability to bring violent mayhem in the name of revenge.

In the months that preceded Massey's killing, what started out as a petty dispute and punch-up in a cafe a year earlier escalated into full-blown gangland warfare. In January 2015, thugs used a Stihl saw to remove the roof of a Volkswagen Golf on the Duchy estate in Salford – belonging to a former partner of the suspected anti-A Team leader, Michael 'Cazza' Carroll. When they spotted the terrified woman looking out of an upstairs window, they threatened to cut her head off. It sparked a series of assaults on the A Team. In February, leading member Abdul Rahman Khan was blasted by a masked man with a 12-bore shotgun after a tracking device was fitted to his Mercedes. A month later, Aaron Williams almost had his jugular severed in a ferocious machete attack. Then a grenade was thrown at the family home of A Team associate Ryan Coward. Within hours, the A Team hit back, shooting suspected anti-A Team member Jamie Rothwell three times at a car wash in Wigan – he survived, but it was another signal of a war being fought with lethal intent.

Members of the two groups had all been friends at one point. Now they were trying to maim and kill one another. This wasn't a running street gang fight involving youths arguing over a ten-pound bag with rusty 9mm handguns. These were committed, organised criminals. These were men with high-grade weapons, money and serious underworld connections both at home and abroad. The Salford boys are an old-school family network of professional villains, many coming from generations who've involved themselves in serious crime. They are renowned, not only in the UK but also internationally, for being some of the most dangerous organised criminals around and were once described as the country's armed robbers par excellence. Their main asset is that they rarely go outside their own peer group and are extremely savvy when it comes to police techniques. That makes them incredibly difficult to infiltrate.

Before the fallout, the A Team was tight. Formed in around 2012 from a group of 50 or so game Salford criminals, the gang is believed to have controlled significant amounts of the cocaine and cannabis coming into Manchester and built up a fearsome reputation for being adept at armed robberies. The Warmington twins, said to be high-ranking members of the gang, were charming and charismatic playboys who partied with celebrities and were suspected, but never convicted, of being professional gem thieves. When the A Team weren't grafting, they'd be a familiar sight in Manchester's trendy bars and restaurants, where leading members would turn up dressed all in white. They'd jet to Puerto Banús on Spain's Costa del Sol to splash their ill-gotten gains on clubbing and cocktails. But behind the pearly-white smiles was real venom. When a young woman threw a drink in a nightclub, lads who had grown up together became sworn enemies overnight. Leading the breakaway group was Carroll, a shrewd and elusive operator who would later be dubbed by police 'the Scarlet Pimpernel'.

It was Pete Jackson, head of the murder squad at the time, who threw a blanket over the attacks, linking them as a series, and launched an investigation into a spiralling gang war showing no sign of slowing down. It was named Operation Leopard and would develop into one of the UK's biggest-ever probes into serious organised crime. Identifying suspects for Massey's murder would be a painstaking task requiring the senior investigating officers (SIOs) to keep an open mind. Massey had been involved in crime from his juvenile days right through to his adult life. As many friends as Salford's 'Mr Big' may have had, he had also accrued his fair share of enemies. Police couldn't immediately rule out that this wasn't a blast from his past, someone who had sat on a grudge for years and decided to strike. Detectives on the murder squad therefore had to trawl through Massey's extensive criminal history to identify anyone with a potential motive to kill him.

Back at Regional Organised Crime Unit HQ I was able to access ultra-sensitive '5-rated' intelligence from every regional police force in the north-west. One name kept coming up: Mark Fellows. He was someone who wasn't particularly high profile and flashy like some of the Salford boys. He had been an active criminal all his life and was connected to Carroll but was low-key in the way he went about his business. Two weeks after Massey's murder, Fellows was shot in the backside outside his nan's house. He managed to get through the front door just in time – one of the rounds entered the house and whistled past his grandmother's head as she watched TV in the living room, millimetres away from killing her. It wouldn't be the last time the A Team would show reckless abandon when targeting a gangland rival.

Fellows was the first to be shot after Massey. This was the street talking to us. I felt it was a strong indicator the A Team had a good idea who was behind Massey's murder. Fellows was recalled to prison by his probation team on an unfinished sentence, and that is how he fell under my spotlight in my role at the Regional Organised Crime Unit. I began to research him and get a feel for who he was. He had taken a familiar criminal path: petty crime as a juvenile leading to cash van robberies – any good Salford criminal's stock in trade – then on to dealing drugs. He had a colostomy bag and was said to be fastidious about hygiene to the point of OCD. He didn't drink, ate healthily and would run for miles. Fellows appeared to be someone who was disciplined and kept routines. Then there were his nicknames: in some circles he was known as the 'Iceman'; others in the Salford underworld mocked him as 'Mongy Mark'. Did he have the profile of someone who could carry out a gangland execution of this nature? In my mind, absolutely. I tried to put myself in his shoes. I imagined him planning the execution. It would take someone with a level of calculating discipline and patience to sit and wait in undergrowth, and someone with a knowledge of police tactics to avoid leaving a trail to or from the crime scene (the killer had left virtually no trace). It was an execution that bore the hallmarks of a professionally premeditated hit, and in my mind he fitted the bill as the trigger puller – but not the instigator.

Armed with the knowledge I had on him, I set about obtaining more information, using the covert capabilities at my disposal, and was able to gain intelligence to corroborate the theory that he could be the killer. But intelligence is just one piece of the jigsaw. While it can help SIOs make the decision to appropriately shift their resources and attention onto an individual, it's not enough just on its own. What police need is hard evidence.

I fed back the intelligence to Paul, my former murder squad boss who had been appointed deputy senior investigating officer on the Massey murder hunt. He called me into GMP's Serious Crime HQ – my old place of work – to brief Detective Superintendent Pete Jackson about my findings. Though I'd never worked for Pete before, I knew him by reputation. He was a seasoned senior detective – one of the most experienced murder case SIOs in the country – and a man of unshakable principles. Pete had been briefed on my background as a UC and role in the Cregan operations. We shared a similar working-class Manchester lad DNA and hit it off immediately. He was intelligent and down to earth, with a great sense of humour. I briefed him on the information I'd gathered. He listened to my ideas for covert tactics and was open to innovative and bold methodology in tackling the case. Shortly after the meeting, Paul rang me and asked me to consider coming back to GMP from the Regional Organised Crime Unit. Pete had been impressed with what I'd delivered in the meeting and wanted me dedicated to Operation Leopard.

As with the Cregan hunt, detectives were struggling to break down the wall of silence in Salford. They needed someone who could engage with criminals and get a feel for what was going on. Salford is a tight and tough community known for being notoriously difficult to crack. When 37-year-old Lee Erdmann was shot dead in the packed Wellington pub in the Ordsall area in September 2011 – in clear view of punters – not one person would come forward, such was the fear of the gunman. But let me be clear here: there are lots of good community-spirited people in Salford who want rid of this kind of violence and terror gripping their streets. It's not necessarily an 'I won't talk to police' attitude that stops them from revealing information; it's the fear of comebacks, that if they talk they'll be in the sights of some of the most dangerous criminals in the UK. And who can blame them? But the real intelligence you need doesn't sit with the decent families going about their lives; it sits with those immersed in the criminal underworld. That is the pool you have to be prepared to swim in, and some cops are more adept at it than others.

Less than 18 months earlier I'd been desperate to escape GMP after Cregan due to my personal misgivings and mental struggle, but I was still hopelessly addicted to the world of big criminals. The bigger the challenge, the more I still wanted in. And the truth was, the chance to have a crack at Salford reignited the spark in me. I put aside the fact my sleep pattern was all over the place and that at times my hypervigilance and sensitivity to noise played havoc with me. The lure of the big job was pulling me back in. *I've got to be on this job. This is what I do.*

Pete had me transferred back to GMP and straight onto Operation Leopard. My role was twofold: to work with him and advise on covert strategy and to get on the ground, build rapport and obtain information from the big hitters. But I couldn't do it alone. If you're going to hit the ground in Salford, you need someone who will have your back.

The Major Incident Team at the time was full of fantastic analytical detectives skilled at dealing with offenders and witnesses – in fact, much better at a lot of police work than I am. But a lot of them didn't really get how to handle major organised criminals, or how to build relationships, coax information from them and find their Achilles heel. They'd come to work power-dressed in pristine shirts and ties or pencil skirts and blouses – but that's not going to get you very far on the streets of Salford. There was one man who could back me up, however – someone with the same drive and chat: Alex.

He'd moved from Operation Challenger to a detective post in the city and wasn't really being put to best use, so after I briefed Pete, he pulled some strings and Alex was back with me as my oppo on Operation Leopard. We got out on the streets as we had done throughout our careers and started making waves. The reputation of the villain didn't matter one bit to us; if we got tasked to speak to them then we would track them down. If it meant executing a warrant and going through the door then we would go through the door. The operation to hunt Massey's killer and hinder the Salford gangs from operating paid many dividends: we found kilos of cocaine and large quantities of cash, ammunition and stolen cars.

We even met with many of Paul Massey's family, who I have to say were dignified in their dealings with the police. Whatever else Massey may have been, he was still a father, a partner, a dad and a grandad, and the family rightly wanted justice. There was a rumour that certain sections of GMP marked his death with a cheer. I can say I never saw or heard anything of the sort, and there was certainly none of that on the Operation Leopard team. This was a serious investigation, and officers treated it with the same dedication as any other murder hunt. We had all seen the impact of murder on a family many times before and that it always left more than one victim.

I was charged with seeing all the big players in what we call a trace and interview action, or trace, interview and eliminate (TIE). These guys were serious criminals, and while the expectation they would actually give us anything useful was virtually nil, what we also didn't want to do was give them any information; the more serious the villain, in my experience, the more adept and manipulative they are at inadvertently getting info out of the cops they speak to. It was a dance I'd done many times with many a serious villain, and I was every bit as calculating as them when required.

I spoke with Peter 'Snaggle' Williamson, a Salford businessman with allegiances to Carroll. He said nothing. Snaggle would later be gunned down and killed outside his Spanish villa.

I visited Stephen Lydiate, Massey's brother-in-law and a veteran gangster. He was on licence from a jail stretch he was handed in 2000 for masterminding a brutal kidnapping and torture spree after a failed hit on him as he watched Manchester United play Leeds at the Ship pub in Pendleton. There was talk that he and Massey didn't get on, and he'd just been badly assaulted and attacked with acid at Massey's funeral. He was measured and quietly spoken but, as expected, gave nothing away.

One of those believed to have called a halt on the attack on Lydiate was 53-year-old John Kinsella, Massey's pallbearer and a notorious mob fixer from Liverpool, who was at the scene the night Massey was murdered. A martial arts expert and an influential figure in the Merseyside underworld, Kinsella hit the headlines after he was named as the man who stepped in to end gangland threats against football star Steven Gerrard. After I'd tried in vain for weeks to get hold of Kinsella, he agreed to meet me at a motorway services and I went along with Alex.

It was his choice to meet us in a public place, not in the back of a car or somewhere that could have been seen as clandestine. I could see he was someone who thought two steps ahead. Kinsella had a full head of grey hair that didn't match his dark eyebrows, and he was well built and smartly dressed. He refused the offer of a coffee but was polite and well mannered. Minutes into the meeting, it was apparent he had a high level of intellect and carried himself as someone confident in their own abilities. He had a bit about him and I could see he was a wily and shrewd criminal. Later on in the gang war, it would become clear just how much of a threat rivals viewed him as.

Kinsella told us he went to comfort Massey's family after Taberer rang him, but he stuck to the criminal code and gave us nothing of use. He knew we wouldn't go away and he had the wherewithal to speak to us in a transparent setting, which couldn't leave him open to claims he was being a grass. I wouldn't be surprised if he had someone watching the meeting just to show it was above board. It was something I found throughout my career: the higher up the hierarchy the criminal, the more adept they were at dealing with the police. To the top-tier gangsters, we were just a hazard of the trade.

Just before we parted I couldn't resist asking him about the Gerrard fixer saga. He just laughed and brushed it off.

'More was made of it than what it was,' he said. After that I got told to stay away. It turned out source handlers had tried to recruit Kinsella without success and noses were put out of joint that I'd managed to sit down with him. If it hadn't been for the drama, I'd have tried to recruit him myself, but then again I tried to recruit everybody who could be of use. That was my job and I enjoyed the challenge: the bigger the villain's reputation, the more I'd try to recruit them.

This wasn't the all-guns-blazing approach used to hunt Cregan and dismantle his crew; it was much slower, more methodical. We knew taking on Salford would be a painstaking task. But it was one that was absolutely necessary, because the tit-for-tat attacks were not letting up. The feud plumbed new depths of savagery in October 2015.

Seven-year-old Christian Hickey ran into the hall of his house in Eccles when he heard a knock at the door. Peering through the glass into the darkness, he told his mother, 'Mum, Mum, there's a postman stood at the end of the drive.' Christian's mother, Jayne, opened the door and a man wearing a cap leaning casually against her VW Golf asked if her husband was in. 'One sec,' she said, turning to call her partner. In that instant, a second man emerged, with a Heckler & Koch P7 semi-automatic pistol, and fired at least three shots, blasting the mother of two in the legs. One bullet passed through both her legs before hitting little Christian in his left leg. The gunman fled as the mother and son lay bloodied in the hallway. Neither were the intended target, it's believed – the gunmen had been sent there to get Christian's father, Christian senior. He was believed to be close to Michael Carroll. This was seen as a clear attempt to avenge Massey's murder. And it didn't stop there.

In February 2016, a hit squad travelled to Spain, where Carroll had fled a month after Massey's killing. But any assassination plot was foiled following a raid on an apartment in Marbella, when Policía Nacional officers, alongside GMP detectives, found a haul of weapons including knives and a loaded pistol. Detectives believed the hit squad intended to capture, torture and murder Carroll before dumping his body in the Mediterranean – a weighted body vest was among the items seized. A Team leader and Massey protégé Stephen Britton was remanded in Spain over the firearm. However, the gang were never pursued for conspiracy to kill Carroll.

The war was still raging but the pursuit of Fellows was going cold due to a lack of evidence. Internal politics were also threatening to derail the investigation. Pete, the dyed-in-the-wool detective who was leading the murder squad, was shafted by top brass, forcing him to leave the post, and Alex was taken away to another department. Management was changing, the pace was slowing and the job was becoming laborious. The new management didn't see the same need for the covert strategies I'd help put in place with Pete, and they weren't a fan of cops like Alex and me being on the ground, developing relationships and getting information.

The fact is, I'd grabbed everyone I could grab, spoken to everyone I could speak to. It was now about painstaking detective and analytical work, and there were much better detectives for that than me.

When I wasn't diverting my brain with work, those feelings of dread that consumed me after the Cregan job remained. The headaches, the sleepless nights, were getting more frequent. The tap was still dripping. My relationship was suffering at home. I was always on edge. I couldn't handle crowded places. I remember going into town to watch the Chinese New Year parade and have a bite to eat with my missus. I couldn't stand it: the noise, the sheer volume of people. I suggested we go to a bar, but that was also crowded and the feeling of being swamped persisted. I looked around and saw faces from my past. I thought everyone wanted to come at me. Everything was worst-case scenario. I told her I wanted to go. 'Why?' she asked. 'We've just got here.'

I could feel myself getting more wound up. But I couldn't tell her why – I couldn't even explain it to myself – instead launching into a burst of anger. 'I'm fuckin' going. I'm fuckin' going. Makin' me stand through this shit.' She didn't get it, and why would she?

Shortly after Pete's departure from the operation, my old boss from the Regional Organised Crime Unit contacted me. He had transferred into West Yorkshire Police on promotion and was in charge of the organised crime unit covering Huddersfield. They were having big problems. In

January 2017 armed police had shot dead suspected drug dealer Yassar Yaqub after they'd stopped the car he was in near the M62, so tensions were high with the local Asian community. They were already battling an explosion of drug-fuelled gun and knife violence on the streets. My old boss told me of the problems they were having and that the plan was to launch an undercover operation, which he wanted me to run while overseeing the organised crime unit. It sounded like my kind of gig, so I started the transfer application and was successful. But my work in Manchester wasn't quite done yet.

On 22 May 2017, Manchester was rocked by one of the most barbaric acts the city had ever seen. Thousands of families were leaving the Manchester Arena at the end of the Ariana Grande concert when Salman Abedi, a 22-year-old of Libyan ancestry, walked towards the crowds and, in what I can only describe as an act of sheer evil, detonated a home-made bomb in his rucksack, killing 22 people, including an eight-year-old girl, and injuring hundreds more.

It was an atrocity that tore apart families and devastated Manchester as a city. Everyone in GMP's Serious Crime department was immediately made available to the North West Counter Terrorism Unit. As a detective sergeant, I was tasked with leading a small team identifying CCTV of the terrorist's approach to the arena, and I found myself back in my old stomping ground, Moss Side, leading an armed raid on an address where two individuals connected to Abedi were residing.

In a moving tribute, thousands of well-wishers laid a sea of flowers and lit candles as they turned St Ann's Square into a public shrine for those who'd lost their lives. There were obvious concerns that a mass gathering could be vulnerable to another attack given that the terrorist alert state was at critical. On many occasions, I covertly mingled with the crowd, looking to identify anyone or anything out of the ordinary to help keep people safe. After around a month of consistent 12-to-16-hour shifts, I was cleared to see out my remaining days as a GMP detective ahead of my move to West Yorkshire.

I was still trying to outrun my own deteriorating mental health issues, again thinking a change was exactly what I needed. I felt the busier in work I was, the better I could function. I hid my issues from everyone, buried myself in work and only really engaged with people I knew. My home life was slowly paying the price for my refusal to acknowledge my inner struggles. *A move – that's what I need, then everything will work out fine,* I'd tell myself.

In my final week at GMP, it was my turn on the force rota to work nights as a detective sergeant covering the force, advising each divisional night detective constable on any serious crimes or suspicious deaths. I was mainly office-based but that just wasn't my style, so I'd get out on the ground and go to the most serious scenes.

My last ever night in GMP is one I'll never forget. I attended a suspected suicide with the night DC and walked into a 13-year-old boy's bedroom to find him hanged from a chain designed to hold a punchbag from a ceiling joist. We took him from the chain, and I took his weight and laid his lifeless body on his bed. I knew he was gone before the paramedics declared, 'Life extinct.'

As I drove my car away from the scene of the tragedy, it was the middle of the night and I heard on the police radio reports of a doorman stabbed in the neck at a warehouse rave in Salford. I was only a few minutes away so decided to get there to ensure the scene was preserved properly and identify any investigative opportunities. There was every chance it would end up fatal and turn into a murder investigation, so scrutiny on the first or 'golden-hour' actions, as they are known, would fall on me.

As I arrived, the booming beat of house music pounding my ears, I could see the bouncer was bleeding out from his neck in the back of a Range Rover outside of the venue, with his mate applying pressure to the wound. There were no paramedics in sight and no ETA. I made a judgement call. I knew Salford's Hope Hospital was just a mile away and that, given the time, the streets would be deserted. Two uniformed cops were standing near him. 'Get your lights and siren on and escort them to hospital, right now,' I told them. I turned to his mate and told him to sit in the back of the Range Rover with the victim and keep pressure on the wound, then told another of his pals to drive behind the police car and follow it to the hospital. It was a decision some would have frowned on; it was also the decision that saved his life.

A uniformed cop showed me where the stabbing had happened, pointing to a shoe, a broken bottle and blood spatter all over the road. They had put a bit of scene tape up on an adjacent fence. It had been a long night and I barked at them.

'Get this fucking road shut and get it taped off properly now, then you stand there and you stand there,' I said, pointing to the spots where I wanted the cordon. 'No one comes through. Is that clear?'

'Yes, Sarge.'

I shouted up on the radio to get more uniform resources to the scene when another young uniformed cop said to me, 'We're gonna get them all cleared out of the warehouse, Sarge.'

'I'll decide when they come out,' I snapped. 'Do not kick anyone out of that building to walk through my crime scene. This could be a murder. Is that clear?'

Another doorman, seeing that I was in charge, approached me and pointed out three lads standing nearby. 'They're the three that did it,' he said. I turned to the young uniformed cop and told him to come with me, before racing over and arresting the three of them for attempted murder.

I finished duty late that morning, ensuring statements were complete, and drove home with the stench of death clinging to my clothes. And as I drove, the weight of the night hit me.

What drives a 13-year-old boy to want to end his life? How can a little boy arrive at such a state of despair for him to place his head through a chain and hang himself? What torture? What trauma took him there? It made me think of my dad. *My poor dad. What was going through his mind? What depth of despair? I wish I'd helped him. But I didn't understand back then. I was too young. Too selfish. Too immature.* Guilt consumed me.

Maybe I was just imagining the smell. Maybe it was all in my slowly twisting mind. But when I got home, I stripped in the kitchen and put the shirt and pants I'd been wearing into a black plastic bag and then double-bagged it to go in the bin. I couldn't escape the stench. I stepped into the shower and scrubbed myself down until my skin was almost red raw. I needed to sleep, but I lay there thinking over the night's events and about my dad. *It will be OK soon – just keep running. I start at the organised crime unit in Huddersfield next week. That's all you need, Shay – a new challenge. Just keep running.*

CHAPTER 15
A FISH OUT OF WATER

Huddersfield on the face of it is a sleepy market town nestled within the Pennine Hills of West Yorkshire between Manchester and Leeds. Terraced houses and old textile mills line the streets, and there's an abundance of ethnically diverse communities. But there's an ugly side to the town that seems disproportionate to its size – a dark underbelly of guns, gangs and drugs.

There were about 200 firearms incidents in and around Huddersfield in the four years prior to my arrival, which coincided with a sharp rise in drugs lines serving up crack and heroin. Terrifying gang battles exploded. In one particularly violent clash, mothers and children screamed in horror as two mobs armed with machetes rampaged through the shopping centre on a busy Saturday afternoon.

The criminality was happening on several levels. Organised crime groups connected to big-hitting city suppliers in places like Bradford, Leeds, Manchester and Liverpool were bringing drugs into the town by the kilo. Street gangs were fighting feuds with machetes, knives and guns. Ruthless dealers exploited the vulnerable, spreading misery with drugs line after drugs line and feeding an almost insatiable appetite for class As. County lines gangs were sending couriers, often young teenagers, to transport and sell drugs to places like Blackpool and Hull. And to top it all off, there was significant friction between police and certain sections of the local community after suspected local supplier Yassar Yaqub was gunned down by armed cops. Police were battling hard to try and stem the surging crime wave, and it was clear I would have my hands full when I arrived in November that year.

My job was to run a small team of around 12 cops in the Organised Crime Unit and coordinate the proactive and covert response to the county lines gangs, the local drug dealing and the gun crime. One of the tactics to take out the drugs lines was to deploy an undercover operation. It would be a Level 2 test-purchasing job that would involve buying small amounts of crack cocaine and heroin from low-level street dealers. There'd be an operative on the ground and a team in the background identifying and gathering intelligence on upstream suppliers.

In a way policing drugs at that level is futile. As soon as you shut down a line, it will be back open within the hour. Knock out one runner and there's another waiting in the wings. There's a hierarchy to these criminal operations, and the low-level dealers are expendable. What it does do, however, is give the police an opportunity to disrupt the market and gather intelligence on those at the top of the chain. It can also help stamp out the inevitable violence that goes with drug dealing – not just among rivals but also against the vulnerable. I understand the view that the UK police response to drugs supply needs overhaul and reform, but there are many innocent victims drawn into the trade through no fault of their own, and I for one had no qualms using current legislation and tactics to take out anyone preying on the vulnerable. One victim I came across was a war veteran whose flat had been forcefully taken over and turned into a base where the gang could store and peddle class As – or 'cuckoo'd', as it's now known. We simply couldn't just stand by and allow that kind of exploitation.

Planning for the undercover op began several months before I got there. My old boss at the Regional Organised Crime Unit had the idea that he would bring me in to run it as well as the Organised Crime Unit. But the goalposts were moved when I arrived – he'd been poached back to GMP after another promotion. It meant my top cover was gone, and I wouldn't have his backing to run the unit and the undercover operation as I would have truly liked. You need someone in the background with the rank supporting what you do and how you do things to get the job done.

The DS who had run the Organised Crime Unit before me had now moved on to run the test-purchase undercover unit. He had a little experience of that world, but he hadn't been an operative. The DI above him was also new in post, with little if any exposure to undercover policing. For whatever reason, it was clear that they didn't want me involved. Rather than welcoming my experience, they pushed away from it. Maybe it was because I'd transferred into the force and they didn't see me as one of them, maybe they didn't like me personally, or maybe they felt professionally threatened. I would never know and quite frankly I didn't care. I wasn't looking for new friends. I was fetched in to do a job; it was as simple as that in my eyes.

I was made deputy senior investigating officer of the op, but in reality I was in charge. The SIO was there as a figurehead only and would change a number of times. I was the one who would be making the decisions on the ground. Four cops from my unit were selected as the operational behind-the-scenes team to support the undercover, and they worked out of a secret location away from the rest of the Organised Crime Unit. On day one of the undercover deployment, I could see there was going to be trouble ahead. The DS who used to run the unit I had taken over started meddling with the team I'd chosen, bypassing me and tasking them like they were still his staff. It caused friction. It's not the way the police operates. There is a chain of command for a reason, with people allocated different areas of responsibility. It's to ensure nothing is missed and every action is accounted for. I kind of wore it at first; I was still involved in managing the other side of the unit, who were busy with surveillance, conducting warrants and making arrests. Plus it was early days on the op, and it can take time for an undercover to bed in. I kept my distance, maintained a watchful eye and was making the lads debrief me every day.

But it soon became apparent that I would have no choice but to step in and get hands-on involved. The UC was gaining traction and had made some buys from drugs lines operating near the town centre, which was good progress and, on the face of it, a job well done by all concerned.

During one of the debriefs, I asked the lads to talk me through the buy that day – exactly what had happened and how. They explained that the operative had approached a street beggar, asking for an introduction to his dealer. In exchange they said he'd split a bag of heroin with the beggar.

'How many times has he done that?' I asked, not liking what I was hearing.

'That's what he does all the time,' one of my guys replied.

'You do understand that's a criminal offence, don't you?'

'What?'

'Supplying class A drugs – which is what he's effectively doing by splitting the bag with the beggar – it's a criminal offence.'

It was basics. I thought to myself, *For fuck's sake, I should have been on this from minute one, not stood back.* I briefed my new boss, who had been appointed the SIO, but they had no understanding of the undercover world. I said the evidence obtained so far was tainted and worthless. The undercover unit wouldn't have it. They thought they knew better. In the end, it took a senior Crown Prosecution Service manager to tell them that the evidence was unusable. The operation up to that point had to be scrapped and the UC had to go.

I thought I could sit back and observe, keeping an eye on the job while running other operations. I gave the undercover unit the rope, and they hanged themselves. Enough was enough. I had no choice but to step in, even if that meant butting heads with the DS and DI.

I gathered the four staff from my unit and told them, 'This operation will run how I say now, and nothing will happen without my say-so.'

The unit chose a replacement UC, who through no real fault of his own was quickly compromised, so it was back to the drawing board. Management then made the inspired suggestion of putting a female UC in a secret shelter for women who'd been domestically abused to use it as a honey pot to attract drug dealers. I couldn't believe what I was hearing. They wanted to attract drug dealers to a sanctuary for vulnerable women and have a female undercover live among them. That's when I realised they didn't have a clue what they were doing and it had gone beyond inexperience: this was a suggestion of utter stupidity. I sent round an email addressing in the strongest terms possible why this could not happen, stopping short of writing on the subject line, 'ARE YOU COMPLETELY FUCKING STUPID'.

My challenging of the tainted evidence and the proposed tactic did little to ingratiate me with the UC unit management. They really did not want me involving myself at all, and their attitude towards me was pretty dire; we could barely stand to be in the same room. They didn't have the humility to say, 'Do you know what, Shay? Clean slate. You obviously fetch a lot of expertise and experience here. Let's sit down and work together to make this the best operation we can.' Instead, they saw me as a threat. That's when we started to fall out. I told the DS he wouldn't task my staff directly and any instructions would now come through me. It almost led to a breakdown on the whole job. I had no choice in the end but to go to my superiors and say I just couldn't work with the UC unit management. 'I don't want the mess on my hands of what this job is going to be,' I told them while explaining everything. To be fair, they listened, and a few days later they did the unexpected and promoted me to acting detective inspector. It was a promotion in the field, an unprecedented move. I wasn't even qualified as an inspector; I'd not even sat the initial exam. But the promotion came with a proviso: 'Get a grip of this operation.'

So I did. A new UC came in who was a fantastic lad. I really liked him and he had huge potential to go on to become a Level 1 operative. He did an excellent job and the staff at the UC unit were really good people, really professional, and I developed a good working relationship with them. The fact I now had a bit of rank seemed to take the sting out of my relationship with the UC unit management. But the damage was done. The relationship was soured. They would slate me behind my back and think I wasn't aware of what was being said. I just avoided meetings with them, basically dictating how things would go, and in the end, after a number of false starts, the operation started to gather momentum.

There was a great bunch of young cops in the Organised Crime Unit. They were keen, wanted to learn and took to my unconventional management style. I encouraged them to be creative in how we tackled operations and didn't need to play the rank card. I quickly won their trust and respect.

On the face of it, I had come into a new police force not knowing anyone, been promoted in the field, got a grip of a covert operation and started making inroads against other organised criminals in the area. Secretly, however, I was struggling to hold it together. Inside, I was continuing to crack. I hadn't been welcomed in West Yorkshire, and rather than embrace my skills and know-how, they saw me as competition. I felt like a fish out of water. It was a gruelling job fighting fire after fire against the UC unit management, and it didn't help my already fragile mental state. It was wearing me down.

I wasn't dealing well with the confrontations. I might have got the operation over the line, but beneath the solid exterior, I was embattled and embittered. I just didn't have the same inclination or energy to do the job. I remember being just about to go through a villain's door early one morning and thinking, *I don't want to do this, I don't want to be here.* This was part of the job I used to relish. The adrenaline would be pumping and I'd be waiting for that moment to strike – then BANG – and I'd always be the first man in, ready and prepared to deal with whoever or whatever came my way. The bigger the gangster reputation, the better; the harder the villain, the harder I'd go in. I'd almost be disappointed if they didn't kick off at times, and when they did fight, I didn't give a fuck. I'd deal with them.

But not here, not this morning. Here I was a pale shadow of that man. I felt like I didn't have the stomach for it. I was flat and I didn't feel strong in myself. Riddled with anxiety, I was thinking about everything and anything but going through that door and dealing with the job in hand.

The change in scenery, the new job, the running away – none of it was helping. In fact, I was getting worse. I was running, but it felt like I was running in quicksand. Back in Manchester, there was a major breakthrough in the Massey murder hunt. The man I'd gone to see, John Kinsella, was shot dead while out walking his dogs with his pregnant partner when a cyclist opened fire with a revolver near his Merseyside home. A Garmin fitness watch seized by detectives in a raid had a GPS function which put the wearer to a field opposite Paul Massey's home three years earlier. That watch belonged to Mark Fellows. The anti-A Team hitman would later be sentenced to a whole-life term for both murders. Fellows's childhood friend and criminal associate Steven Boyle was also convicted of John Kinsella's murder.

When I heard Fellows had been found guilty for both killings, I couldn't help but think GMP wouldn't have got the murder of Massey home if he hadn't killed Kinsella, but in the end GMP and Merseyside Police had taken a very dangerous man off the streets in what was a complex, painstaking investigation into the highest levels of organised crime. I'd played a big part in the early stages of that operation and should have been raising a quiet glass in celebration. Instead, I was mired in my own turmoil.

I'd lie awake at night struggling to wipe away the images of my past: the black hole in Cregan's face, the 13-year-old boy hanging, my dad. Noises battered my ears. I was plagued with anxieties, overthinking every little scenario. There was now no respite. Normally, I'd be able to shut the dark feelings out while I was at work, use the job to distract and consume me. Not this time. Now they were following me into the office – like a huge shadow I couldn't step out of. Dull aches pounded my head for hours on end. I'd have to attend meetings, and the voices would blend into one and I wouldn't be able to make out who was speaking. My clarity of thought was leaving me. There were times when I had to escape the unit and go outside and just be on my own so I could clear my mind of the office chatter, which felt like a pneumatic drill in my head. *Just give me a break, please.*

My home life continued to suffer. I struggled to get a grip of my anger, my rage. My torment. Aggressive thoughts swirled in my head. I was paranoid, thinking everyone was against me, but at the time it felt real to me – like I was under siege. My patience threshold deteriorated. If someone walked past my living room, glanced in my window and caught my eye, I'd think they were looking into my house, looking for me, and I'd fly into a rage, shouting, *What the fuck are you looking at?* My hypervigilance took over, but instead of being the tool that kept me safe, it was working against me. My fight-or-flight response was completely out; I could no longer decipher between what was a real threat and what wasn't. Everything was a threat. Everyone was out to get me. One afternoon two young scally-looking blokes were sitting in a car near my house, occasionally looking at it. I'd been watching from the bedroom window for half an hour. It was slowly winding me right up. *Why are they just sitting there on a quiet street like this? They're here looking for me, aren't they? What are they doing? What do they want from me?* I couldn't take it anymore. I felt like I was going to explode. I stormed outside and fronted them up.

'What the fuck are you doing sat on my street? What the fuck do you want? Fucking looking for me, are you? Well, I'm here. C'mon, let's fucking go – the fucking pair of you, now.'

At the time I was nearly 16 stone solid; weight training and Thai boxing were the only hobbies I had. Their eyes widened in disbelief as they frantically locked the car doors. There was no way either of them was getting out. A neighbour of mine who'd watched the confrontation ran out, asking me to go inside while he spoke to the two men. It turned out they were charity collectors taking a break from knocking on doors. I explained to my neighbour what I thought was going on and he apologised to the two guys, who were understanding. My neighbour's wife told my girlfriend that they thought I wasn't right, and she begged me to seek help.

'There's nothing wrong with me,' I said, dismissing what I saw as insulting accusations. 'I need help. Me? As if. Shove your fucking help.'

I was still convinced the two guys in the car were lying and even sat up most of the night, waiting and ready for their return. It wasn't like I could sleep anyway. They didn't come back. But in my twisted mind they posed a threat. Everyone walking down the street was gunning for me. I was rapidly losing control of my senses. Rage rushed through me like an avalanche. I didn't trust myself not to react aggressively, possibly even violently.

Having a set of balls and being programmed to back down to no one had been my biggest advantage when portraying and taking on gangsters. Now it was proving destructive.

There was no flight in my fight-or-flight response. I was tackling any perceived threats head-on, no fucks given. My thoughts were getting darker and darker, reality was slipping away from me. The tap was no longer dripping; it was pouring.

I drove back to Manchester after work in Huddersfield one day gripped by anxiety and fighting hard to get a grip on reality. For reasons I'm still at pains to try and explain, I ended up in Moss Side. I remember parking up on Claremont Road and walking down the street, thinking, *I want someone to recognise me as Mikey. I want the confrontation. I want them to know I'm around. If it's gonna happen I'll get it over with now.* I wanted someone to spot me and say, 'You're that undercover cop that put me away.' No one did, but it was like I was playing out some kind of death wish. I walked up and down, looking at the derelict building that used to be the Nest pub, and I thought about the near misses. *What the fucking hell was I doing here? Why did they let me do this job? What was in their heads? What was in my head?* It wasn't the only time I inexplicably returned to Moss Side.

The undercover job in West Yorkshire was highly successful: 53 people arrested, numerous drugs lines shut down, and hundreds of thousands of pounds' worth of class A drugs seized and guns and ammunition found. We helped vulnerable victims whose houses had been taken over. We aided the recovery of some of the arrested addicts by getting them into rehab services. We built up untold intelligence into the bigger players that continues to feed into investigations against serious criminals in that community to this day. By the end of the operation, however, I was burnt out. I'd completely isolated myself from colleagues and quietly my mental state had spiralled further out of control. Somehow, I managed to hide my turmoil from people at work – or at least I thought I did. In any case, no one ever said anything. I was using work to try and divert my thoughts, but I wasn't really there. Not in my mind. The darkness was tightening its grip and I couldn't find the light.

I drove my girlfriend away, who had stuck with me through thick and thin. No longer able to cope with my erratic behaviour, she left. Sitting on my own in my house with nothing but my own poisonous thoughts, I became convinced she had left me for someone else. There was no one. Unable to sleep, I started to pace around the empty house I owned at night. I flew into violent rages, kicking doors straight off their hinges. Delusions crept in. My judgements and decisions were becoming more irrational; the threats were real and present in my mind. I was still turning up for work – on an hour's sleep if I was lucky – but I'd isolate myself and do my utmost to avoid colleagues.

Close family and friends were becoming more concerned, phoning me to tell me to go to the doctor's. I didn't think the problem was with me. I felt like everyone was against me. *My own friends and family have turned on me,* I thought. It was the loneliest place I'd ever been. *I've got no one now.*

My mum turned up at my home and pleaded with me. 'You desperately need help, son,' she said.

'You're one of them,' I told her. 'You're against me as well.'

It got to the point where, other than for work, I wouldn't leave my house. I wasn't sure I'd be capable of controlling my destructive impulses if I did. *I don't care if I'm alive or dead anymore. I'm gonna get everyone who's crossed me. Everyone's out to get me and I'm gonna get them first.* I thought the police would sack me if I went off sick. I became convinced villains I'd taken on would be seeking vengeance. I'd lie awake thinking they were coming through my door. I even barricaded the front door and hid weapons around my house: knives in bookcases, a hammer under the settee cushion. I was wracked with paranoia but I couldn't see it.

All that time in Moss Side – even going through the doors on the Cregan job – I'd been protected by the persona I'd created. Mikey O'Brien was dangerous, aggressive – didn't give a fuck about confrontation. Throughout my career, I tapped into Mikey and the traits he possessed. He kept me safe. He was my alter ego, my shadow. Now he was back and for all the wrong reasons – he had well and truly taken over.

Three weeks after my partner left I was on the brink. Shattered and exhausted, I'd not slept a wink and I was in dire straits. At night it would all come alive. The ghosts of my past circled in my head like a horrifying merry-go-round. Those two poor cops, Cregan, the bloodied hands, the hanging boy, the baby crawling in the crack den stinking of shitty nappies. The murder victims, the gangsters I'd put away, the cops who'd used me. There they were, in glorious technicolour, going round and round and round. I slammed my head against the door. Once. Then again and again. *Stop! Stop! Stop!* I had nothing left. Everything I was good at had left me. All my strengths.

My mum pleaded again and I agreed to go to the doctor to get sleeping tablets. Not because I believed I was on the point of insanity, but because I wanted sleep. *Twelve hours will do. That's all I need, a good run of sleep and I'll be able to get myself back on track.* Get past this, I thought, and I could look for the next big job and start smashing it again.

Dishevelled and unshaven, wearing a tracksuit I'd been wearing all weekend, I walked into the GP's surgery one Monday morning and was met by Dr M, a GP around my age. I'd never met her before. In fact I'd rarely been to the doctor's other than for minor ailments.

'I just need some sleeping tablets. Just give me some sleeping tablets, would you,' I said abruptly. I could see that she was looking at me intently.

I couldn't speak. 'Please just give me some sleeping tablets, will you. I can't go to sleep.'

'I don't just dish sleeping tablets out. That's not the way it works.'

I stayed silent and stony-faced before pleading again. 'I just need some sleep.'

She pulled her chair directly in front of mine and her voice softened as she looked me in the eye.

'You don't look well, Shay. Tell me what's going on. What's the matter?'

I held my head in my hands. I couldn't hold it in anymore and broke down uncontrollably, pouring it all out. I told her everything.

She looked gobsmacked and I wondered for a moment if she believed my story. But she was absolutely amazing and went above and beyond to help me. She could see the level of trauma I'd encountered and ruled me unfit to work.

'You can't go out on the streets as a police officer,' she said. 'In your current state, you're a danger to yourself and the public. You're seriously unwell, we need to get you help.'

A stark realisation sank in. I'd spent my life being the protector; now I was the one who needed protecting. Not just for my sake, but the sake of others.

I was sent to hospital for a mental health assessment. They considered sectioning me but decided against it after Dr M rang my mum to seek assurances I would have her support. I was prescribed with diazepam to help me relax and sleep while numbing the anxiety and racing thoughts. Dr M rang me every day and would make me come in to see her so she could check on me. I was told to attend the mental health unit twice a week, where I'd remain under assessment.

I was in good hands, but that didn't mean my problems were over. Far from it. I could now no longer go to work, something I struggled to comprehend. *It's what I do. I get up, I put on my professional mask and plan operations to take down drug-dealing, gun-toting gangsters. I'm fucking shit at everything else.*

The time off work sent my mind into overdrive. The diazepam didn't touch the sides. I still couldn't sleep. And I still couldn't break down the barrage of dark thoughts. Now in my mind I'd lost my job. *They're gonna sack me. They're gonna look for something to sack me.* Everything I'd worked so hard for. My career was in tatters. Just because I'd broken down didn't mean the turmoil had stopped. I'd merely put a plaster on a septic wound. I stopped eating, showering, washing. Conspiracy theories streamed through my head. The merry-go-round returned. The frightening flashbacks. The panic attacks that left me struggling to breathe. *I can't take this much longer. I can't make it stop.*

Then, in the middle of a sleepless spring night in April 2019, as the ghosts flashed across my mind like a broken film reel, I just did it without thinking. I tied a ligature to the bannister in the hallway and placed a chair underneath.

CHAPTER 16
SHADOWS

*T*his is my option if I want to take it, I thought. *This is my way out. If it gets no better, this is my way out.* Rather than feeling distressed about the prospect of taking my own life, for some reason it gave me a feeling of relief. I felt as though I'd made peace with the fact that if I wanted to end things then I could.

This final act would be my choice. *My relationship has gone – not my choice. People are coming for me – not my choice. I can't go to work – not my choice. The noises in my head won't stop – not my choice.* This would be *my* choice. I felt everything else had been taken from me, and this decision represented the only power I had left over my life.

The illness had tightened its grip on me, but there were moments of clarity when I thought ending things seemed the most rational and sensible choice I would ever make – not just for me but for others in my life. And there was a sense of calm in the feeling of taking back control, that ultimately the decision to end my life was mine and mine alone.

I started to understand how someone can get to the point of wanting to end their own life. I stood in the shoes of my dad, and I thought how he must have felt like I did now. How maybe he was at peace with his decision too. Like my dad, there would be no cry for help from me. There'd be no phone calls, no note. *If I want to do it, I can – and no one can stop me.* I'd always had an exit strategy during operations and was always thinking two steps ahead. This was the final plan. *This is how I turn the tap off.*

The chair stood in the same position for days. The ligature didn't move. Letters piled up unopened at the front door. From solicitors, from police. I was officially signed off with stress but it was pretty clear the police thought I was taking the piss. There were threats to drop my pay if I wasn't back in work by a certain date. Banks demanded money. Financial pressures mounted. Officers from my force even contacted my ex-partner, asking if there had ever been any violence in our relationship and if she wanted to make statements against me. Nothing of the sort was ever reported, or indeed ever took place. I was disgusted. I may be a lot of things but a violent abuser of women is not one of them. It felt like I was now the subject of a police witch-hunt to demonise, arrest and sack me – make it all my fault. I was standing on a cliff getting closer and closer to the edge.

Following a particularly bad night of no sleep and incessant haunting from the demons of my past, I hit the self-destruct button. Consumed by an uncontrollable and deadly rage, I destroyed my kitchen. Cupboard doors were sent flying off their hinges, plates and glasses smashed to pieces. The demolition must have gone on for half an hour before I put my fist straight through a double-glazed window with a brutal right hand to bring an end to the rampage. With blood spurting out of the wound in my wrist, I walked into the hallway and climbed onto the chair, then put my head in the noose and kicked the chair from under me. It was all done in a frenzied instant. No hesitation.

There'd be no time for contemplation as my feet swung hopelessly in the air. I felt the noose tighten immediately. I could hear the bannister creak as it took my weight. I was choking. Panic set in. I didn't want to die. Not really. *How can I get out? I need to get out! I don't want to die!* I pulled my legs up with all my might and wedged my back against the staircase, then managed to grip my feet onto the wall in the hall. Somehow, I pulled my head out of the noose and fell to the floor in a heap, breathless but alive.

I sat for a while, despairing, slumped against the wall with my head in my hands, when I saw someone banging at my door. I wasn't sure if I was imagining it at first. It was my old mate Alex, the cop who I had been through so much with. *What the fuck is Alex doing here?* Unbeknown to me, neighbours had heard me smashing up the kitchen and called the police. Alex and another cop, a good and decent man I had known for years, had heard my name and address over the police radio and, despite being detectives that didn't respond to 999 calls, they sped to my house.

Alex saw the noose hovering above me, the red ring around my neck and my blood-soaked arm. He took me straight to hospital to get my wrist looked at and contacted the mental health unit I was under to get me assessed and into a place of safety. The only reason they didn't section me was because Alex and his wife offered to take me in to stay at their house in an act of kindness I can never repay and will never forget. They say you only find out who your friends are when things are going wrong; if that's the case, I'm a lucky man – I know who mine are.

For his act of compassion and friendship, Alex was heavily criticised by a DI for not arresting me at the scene for criminal damage of property that I owned outright. When I digested this, it confirmed my view that there are some police officers who are not equipped for leadership. What hope do the vulnerable and unwell have when officers in positions of influence elect to criminalise rather than help those in a mental health crisis?

I was placed on an intensive therapy programme and had my medication reviewed. Dr M, who had gone above and beyond, remained in the background, checking in with me regularly. I can't thank her enough. I truly believe that without her wherewithal to see something more serious was going on the day I first sat in front of her and her willingness to go the extra mile to help me, I possibly wouldn't be here today.

The police used a box-ticking HR process to deal with me, sending no real offers of help or support. Any trust I had for the police was gone. There was no genuine interest for my welfare. I truly believed they were looking to arrest and sack me, which I've no doubt would have been the most convenient solution for them. I just don't think the police, as an organisation, are properly equipped to identify and deal with officers caught up in a mental health crisis. They stick to unfit-for-purpose, outdated HR processes like shit to a blanket. Emotional intelligence, empathy, welfare and support go out of the window through a lack of knowledge riding alongside a desire to cover their own arses.

My old friend and mentor Christie, now retired from the police, was – unbeknown to me – desperately contacting senior officers at both my old and current forces to try to get me help. He hit brick walls at every turn. No one wanted to know; I was seen as a liability.

As part of the process, they sent me to a private consultant for an independent assessment. After hearing my story, the psychiatrist drafted a lengthy report. This is a summary of her diagnosis:

'Mr Doyle is suffering with post-traumatic stress disorder, specifically complex PTSD. This is evidenced by the presence of significant and multiple traumatic incidents during his undercover and police work, which satisfy the exposure to stressful situations or even situations of exceptionally threatening or catastrophic nature criterion.'

The police were not equipped to deal with the kind of cumulative trauma I'd suffered. I don't believe there was complete malice in their lack of intervention over the years. They just don't fully understand the impact of the high-risk, high-stress work many officers are asked to undertake. The trauma doesn't end just because it's the end of a shift or deployment.

In 2020, after 17 years' service in the police, my career was over. I was medically discharged with complex PTSD. On my last day, there was no senior boss ringing me, wishing me luck, or thanking me with a handshake. Instead, I met a supervisor in a pub car park and handed over my warrant card. It almost felt like one of my undercover drugs deals. It wasn't the way I'd have expected to have parted company with the service I'd given so much to, but in a way it felt apt.

I'd tried my best during my police service. I went in every day with the mindset to do good and protect people, to put myself in harm's way so that others could be safe. I hope somewhere along the journey I achieved that. In the end I was undone by my consistent immersion into high-risk environments and operations.

While there was a sense of relief that my time in the police was over, there was uncertainty surrounding my future. I'd spent my life at the sharp end, chasing gangsters, taking down OCGs. Feeling the adrenaline of going through the door, the rush of a big arrest. All that was gone. *What does someone like me do now?* I asked myself. *Where do I go from here?*

Above all else, I needed to get well. As I continued my path to recovery, I started to take stock. I thought about how I could somehow use my experience for the greater good. I realised that my story was as much about mental health and the frailties of the human condition as being an undercover cop and chasing the bad guys. My dad's suicide was a catalyst for me to do something with my life, to be someone. Yet I almost ended up suffering a similar fate. I'd been brought up to show no fear, I was completely driven and single-minded. To show fear was weakness, to show vulnerability was to display a chink in my armour. That's how I'd lived my life. Yet ultimately, these were the very traits that almost undid me. *Men like me don't seek help,* I'd think. I see now that seeking help isn't weakness. It's strength.

I was ill and was the last to know or accept I needed help. If my story can encourage one person going through the kind of mental turmoil that I went through to get help, then this is a book that's been worth writing.

I have developed a passion for helping others, and the feeling of reward is as strong as that which I gained from my undercover work. My drive now is to work with organisations to try to break the stigmas around mental health, particularly in frontline emergency services.

I also feel it is my duty to help underprivileged kids, youngsters from estates like I grew up on, to show them there is an alternative to going down the wrong path and steer them clear of gangs, guns and crime.

I know my battle with mental health will be lifelong, and I have to put strategies in place daily to stop dark thoughts consuming me. I am rebuilding myself and if that takes as long as I am on this earth, then so be it. I still have therapy and I still take anti-psychotic drugs. But I've got myself to a place where I am coping. I'm starting to understand who I am, what I am and what I've been through.

At the same time, I'm acutely aware that if I'm not mindful, things can go wrong once again. Every morning I look at myself in the bathroom mirror, determined to start my day with a positive mindset. I ask myself, *How can I make progress today? How can I help someone else?* Every now and then, I look at my reflection and I see him staring at me over my shoulder, his snarling face contorted with rage and menace. It's Mikey, my shadow. He wants to get out. But he no longer has control of me. He's just there to remind me of how far I've come and that I don't need him anymore. I swill my face with cold water and I say to myself, *Not today, Mikey. You're not having me. Not today.*